The Blood
of His
Servants

BOOKS BY THE AUTHOR

Protégé
The Lucifer Key
The Blood of His Servants

THE BLOOD OF HIS SERVANTS

by

Malcolm C. MacPherson

Times
BOOKS

Published by TIMES BOOKS,
The New York Times Book Co., Inc.
Three Park Avenue, New York, N. Y. 10016

Published simultaneously in Canada by
Fitzhenry & Whiteside, Ltd., Toronto

Library of Congress Cataloging in Publication Data

MacPherson, Malcolm.
  The blood of his servants.

  1. Jews—Ukraine—Podgorodtsy—Persecutions.
2. Holocaust, Jewish (1939-1945)—Ukraine—Podgorodtsy.
3. Kanaan, Haviv.   4. Menten, Pieter Nicolaas, 1899-
5. War criminals—Netherlands—Biography.
6. Podgorodtsy (Ukraine)—Ethnic relations.   I. Title.
DS135.R93P5945   1984   940.53′15′03924   83-40089
ISBN 0-8129-1098-2

Designed by Doris Borowsky

Manufactured in the United States of America

84 85 86 87 88 5 4 3 2 1

DEDICATED to Haviv Kanaan.*
Without his courage, tenacity,
and devotion to the memory of
his family, this story could
not be told.

*Haviv Kanaan changed his name in 1948 from Lieber ("Bibi") Krumholz to acknowledge his citizenship in the new, independent nation of Israel.

"...'tis writ in the Law of Moses, the man of
God: Ye nations, cause his people to rejoice,
for the blood of his servants will he avenge;
yea, he will wreak retribution on his foes, and
cause his land and his people to be atoned for."

Memorial Service/Yiskor

"I lived on this earth in an age
when man fell so low
he killed willingly, for pleasure, without orders;
mad obsessions threaded his life,
he believed in false gods.
Deluded, he foamed at the mouth."

**From "Fragment"
by Miklos Radnoti,
killed May 19, 1944,
written on the wall of
Block 18
Auschwitz**

"There is no such thing as concealment.
Commit a crime, and the earth is made of
glass. . . . You cannot recall the spoken word,
you cannot wipe out the foottrack, you cannot
draw up the ladder, so as to leave no inlet
or clew. Always some damning circumstance
transpires."

**From "Compensation"
by Ralph Waldo Emerson**

The Blood
of His
Servants

PROLOGUE
✍
"... the Knight of Pentacles."

BIBI KRUMHOLZ LAUGHED later at what the gypsy had said, and while he laughed, a few grains of sand fell through the glass, against the time when the gods would drown his laughter in their tears. Just now, in the summer of 1935, Bibi was spending his last vacation in Podhorodse, a village in the mountains of eastern Poland, on the estate of the Pistiners, his closest relations, whom an intense evil would follow for reasons that the gypsy alone could explain with her soiled cards.

Alone among them, Bibi's uncle had seemed to understand. The family patriarch, Isaac Pistiner had neither laughed nor uttered any sound at all. He had been the family member to first turn to the gypsy's art—the tarot, astrology, and palmistry—as an atheist is drawn desperately to prayer when all else fails. And all else had failed for Isaac. Secularization had not materialized in Poland, as Isaac had fervently hoped; bankruptcy had brought him and his family hardship and personal embarrassment, and for now the economic shambles of Poland made a business recovery improbable. He was fighting a rearguard legal battle for possession of his beloved country estate and all it symbolized. Isaac did not rest much weight on the scales of Polish justice; anti-Semitism was on the rise, with new and more brutal pogroms in the cities; and more ominous, Nazism, that perversion of the German spirit, was threatening the peace of Europe.

Isaac's wife, Frieda, and their eight children had not just been humoring Isaac when they showed interest in spiritualism. They had thrilled at its parlor-game aspects. The children, along with their cousin Bibi, the bright, budding journalist, had watched the library shelves fill with books on the subject, and they had eavesdropped in silent wonder as Isaac and his lawyer friend, Dr. Sigmund Gelmann, had traveled their mystical voyages. Sometimes, the whole family had sat around telling fortunes, but a few months before, Isaac had turned serious, and no longer begging from mystical gods a return of wealth, health, and happiness, he would not permit their parlor blasphemies as mere distraction. As if he were discovering a path to some purer extract, he demanded one response to one question in which *all* answers lay buried: "How long will I live?"

He had not yet asked the gypsy.

Bibi did not know where Isaac had found this old woman. She evoked in each of them a different response. The Pistiner girls remarked on her smell—earthy and pungent, like a forest animal—and her shiny, obsidian eyes and the gleam of her jet-black hair. She represented human wildness, a feral determination and immutability. Bibi thought she was a crazy old coot, but he knew to respect an intelligence identified by her fluency in Polish and Ukrainian and, he imagined, in Romany, too. Alone among the Pistiners that summer, Frieda, Isaac's wife, was upset by her appearance. She feared that the old woman, who draped hooked carpets over her frame in a makeshift *sarafan,* would excite Isaac needlessly. A stern, imposing, humorless woman, Frieda thought never more so than now that Isaac needed rest and quiet. He tired easily, and the dark pouches under his eyes haunted her. He was thin, and no amount of her delicious cooking filled the wattle on his neck.

Just before sunset that evening the children, Isaac, and Frieda were listening on the new Elektrit Patria Z to the singing of Jan Kiepura beamed from the city of Lwów, fifty miles away. The balky gas generator thumped behind the house, which was far and away the largest in the village. Not quite a "villa," though Isaac proudly insisted on calling it an "estate," it was constructed of sturdy timber beams, rising two floors from the earth, with stables, barns, and smokehouses behind and a front garden that blazed in summer with the blossoms of bright red roses. Their fragrance perfumed the wide, mowed lawns that sloped to the forest. In the distance, the grandeur of the Carpathian Mountains almost transformed this place and, by extension, the village and the region beyond the Stryj River into the stuff of Isaac's imagination. Every summer since the Great War, the village had welcomed them, so that now it had become a natural part of their lives' rhythm.

That evening the children were worn out from climbing the boulders by the banks of the river. They had eaten supper, and now they read, played chess, daydreamed, and talked in the fading light. Bibi, a handsome young man with bright blue eyes, ginger hair, and a sensitive mouth, straddled the "rocking stag" on the porch. The large forest animal had been shot when Prince Lubomirski owned the estate. Probably taxidermied as a plaything for *his* children, the stag had stood on the porch winter and summer for two generations. Bibi was looking through the stag's regal horns toward the gravel road that led down to the center of Podhorodse, when he saw the old woman as she emerged from the lengthening shadows cast on the lawn by the fluted, towering poplars.

She was not expected, but her appearance surprised them no more than a wild pet that comes from the forest for scraps from the table. She was alert and poised, timid, and when she reached the porch, just where the rose garden began, she stopped, watching, as if the family were actors in a tragic play that she alone could see. She made no demands; she never did. Unless someone had motioned for her to climb the steps, as Isaac did with a swing of his arm, she would have vanished into the forest as quietly as she had appeared. When she reached their level on the porch, Isaac pointed her to a bamboo chair at the table. The family came around. She put her arm under the woolen *sarafan* and drew out a packet of cards. The others knew this evening would be special.

As she spread the cards on the table, she said, "Now I will tell you a profound secret—what awaits you." She spoke boldly and in a low voice. She stared momentarily at the palms of her hands, as if she were cross-checking the direction of their fate in those spidery lines.

An oil lamp was brought out. A match touched its wick. From

the seventy-eight-card deck the gypsy, her face bathed in yellow light, chose six of the shuffled cards and made a cabalistic count for the Essence. She chose twelve cards and spread them counterclockwise in one fluid motion on the wooden table. Her eyes moved that way, too, as she read the alignment of the cards—Past, Present, Future, and Karma.

Isaac did not seem to notice the relationship of one card to the other, but he must have known what they indicated, even before the gypsy explained. In the quadrant of Past she had laid the Ace of Swords ("You are thinking, but you are not feeling; you are immobilized"), the Eight of Swords ("You do not know how to escape your present predicament"), the Three of Swords ("Great sadness"), then to Karma. She had laid the Eleven of Swords ("You are uncertain"), the Knight of Swords ("You are thinking in chaos"), the Five of Staffs ("There is strife, but you are not acting in the correct manner; you are going about things wrong"). In the Present she had chosen and put down the Five of Pentacles ("Deprivation"), the inverted Six of Staffs ("There exists a choice between two paths, and between them there is indecision"), the Seven of Pentacles ("You are not strong enough to combat the forces against you"). And for the Future she had produced from the deck the inverted Eight of Cups ("Strife will remain at the center of your lives"), the Nine of Swords ("Despair"), and finally, the Ten of Swords ("Decline and fall").

She looked up, and her eyes fell on each face in the circle until she came upon Bibi, to whom she said, "Child, you will go away."

The girls giggled because everybody knew that Bibi planned to leave for Palestine that fall, and the gypsy probably had heard the village gossip, too. He nodded at her.

"And you will go away, too," she said, resting her eyes on Mara, the closest in age to Bibi; naturally she wanted to be counted among the *Halutzim,* but that had to wait for now.

Mara said, "You mean to Palestine?"

"No, child, to the east, to Kazakhstan."

But what would I want to do there? Mara thought. Kazakhstan was in the middle of Russia, an inhospitable place from which she could only imagine fleeing.

The gypsy concentrated on the cards. She said, "Now I will tell you where and when you will die."

When she had finished, Isaac broke the embarrassed silence by asking her for a more specific interpretation of the cards, as she had promised. Such was her sudden expression, as if she were surprised, that they listened with care at first, and then with growing concern, as she told Isaac how she saw graves and even pointed to the rose garden over the porch rail. Before she finished her recitation, Isaac had the answer that no other "medium" had ever supplied. But now he wanted more, to go beyond imagination. And he asked, "Who will it be?"

The gypsy spread the shuffled cards as she had done before. In a negative succession to the right of the Essence card (the inverted Pope), she laid the Castle, inverted Death, and the Knight of Pentacles. She said, "It will be someone who is out of control of himself, who, like an animal, satisfies his own feelings. . . . It will be someone who *was* your friend."

BOOK I

CHAPTER I

❈

"The Feast of Kupalo"

THAT SUNDAY MORNING, July 7, 1941, in the village of Podhorodse, Samuel Schiff, the sawmill owner, felt death would be a
blessing. All the good things in his life—a rich wife, a beautiful
daughter, a big house with a view of the river, a successful business—were overshadowed by sharp, painful stomach cramps
from something he had eaten the night before. A fat man for
whom any intestinal upset was a major disorder, Schiff had tried
to put mind over matter first at the synagogue with prayer and
then with the power of sheer concentration at the *tartak,* his sawmill. But matter would not cooperate, and the one solution left, he
had thought, was maybe a bicarbonate from the widow Halpern's
general store. He had told his partner in the business, Moshe Altmann, that he would return when he felt better. As he walked he
sniffed the mountain air on that magnificent summer day, and,
unusual for such a positive person, he worried. Schiff's stomach
churned again, and he thought that maybe he should not make
more of a rotten stomach than what it was.

The Podhorodse that Schiff walked through that morning was
as old as anyone could remember. The older local people said that
the village had been settled first as a ford. A precarious raft, a
simple floating platform of seven logs lashed together, could still
be poled across to Podhorodse's "sister" village, Sopot, more than
a mile downstream on the opposite side of the Stryj River. For
generations the villagers had worked for titled landowners, like
the Prince Lubomirski who had sold his vast estate before the

Great War to a Rumanian, who in turn had sold it to Isaac Pistiner. Since the war the woods had become valuable. The rasping sounds of the sawmills and the rich smell of sawdust attested to that, as did the narrow railroad on the Sopot side, built in 1917–18 by Italian prisoners of war, that hauled timber from the village to the rail junction at Synowodzko Wyzne. For a long time, people had thought that the earth beneath the village held oil, a conjecture fueled by the discovery of rich deposits only about two miles away in Urych and beyond. Until oil was found to make the 2,158 Podhorodse villagers rich, they would continue to till small, insignificant plots of earth, raising chickens and, if they saved, a milch cow, to supplement such meager incomes. Life was hard, but nobody starved or needed shelter, and until recently, anyway, everyone had shared a unique and precious intangible: Podhorodse was snuggled deep in the Stryj Valley, surrounded by the majestic foothills of the Carpathians. For this geographic reason, the villagers felt safe, as their ancestors had felt since the fourteenth century when Podhorodse fell in the shadow of the Tustan Fort (the name of the village literally means "under the protection of the fort"). Now, so far distant from the new cities and accessible only with a sharp eye on a good map, Podhorodse continued to stay out of harm's way—which is why Samuel Schiff's worry that morning was singular and odd.

Maria and Philip Wecker came down the gravel road from Isaac Pistiner's villa on the hill, past the big house with the glass windows and around the corner of the small, modest house of the village's second richest Jew, finally to stop at the widow Halpern's general store. As everyone remarked, Maria, Isaac Pistiner's eldest daughter, was a rare beauty—certainly the most beautiful woman in the village. But Maria was not happy, and that could be seen in her dark, lifeless eyes and her stooped bearing. A handsome Austrian Army officer from Vienna had once made Maria's eyes sparkle. But the romance had ended unhappily, and they had not married. Philip Wecker, ten years older than Maria, had proposed marriage. For want of other offers, out of desperation and a gothic sensibility, Maria had accepted. Philip was short; she was tall and willowy. Maria danced like a fairy princess; Philip did not. She dreamed of the city and cafés and fun; as *kluchnik,* the manager of

Pistiner's estate, Philip needed the country with its soft and predictable rhythms. He loved Maria, but she could not reciprocate. For her, Philip was a convenience and barely a companion with whom she felt obliged to share the chores on her father's estate and some of the burden of concern that weighed on them in these times, as it did on every Jew in the village. Now, the two of them entered Halpern's general store to trade on rumor and what shreds of fact they knew with the widow, Schiff, and Shabtai Katz, who was stocking up on canned goods because of what his nephew had told him about Boryslaw.

The village of Podhorodse—in fact all of eastern Poland including the capital city of Lwów—had been under Russian domination for almost two years, since September 1939, with the partition of Poland at the outbreak of World War II. The Russian occupation had been hard, especially on urban Jews, who had been transported en masse to Siberia. But at least there had been no pogroms. Two weeks before on June 22, the situation had started to change when the Nazis broke their non-aggression pact by invading Russia. Now, after sixteen days of fighting, the 360th German Infantry Regiment had rolled past the village. The 9th Company of the 360th had reached Drohobycz and the 10th Company had taken Boryslaw. By some miracle, not one German soldier had entered Podhorodse during this massive military sweep, although at night the villagers had watched the distant sky glow orange and had heard the far-off rumble of German and Russian artillery. Indeed, the only concrete disruption caused so far by Barbarossa, the German invasion, was the suspension of the once-daily mail service. However, other less definable changes created more anxieties among the villagers once the real dangers had passed.

The people of Podhorodse had grown up side by side, worked the same fields and forests, swam the same rapid-running river, and walked the same dusty streets. In times of stability people shared and cooperated. Ukrainian, Jew, Pole, and Volksdeutsch were neighbors who were all dependent on the land, likened in song, fable, and tradition to a woman, always mischievous, moody, and predictably unpredictable, but always alluring. Like a woman, too, the land aroused passions—love and hate, anger and

13

jealousy. No one had bestowed Utopian blessings on these simple people, but they had always managed to get along. It was always outsiders who had caused the real troubles, like the Soviets nineteen months before, when they had occupied the region and redistributed the land, confiscating from traditional landowners and giving to disenfranchised Poles; and now the Germans, under whom authority was changing hands once again. Since the invasion in June, the Volksdeutsch were in control of the village civil administration. Philip Müller, the Volksdeutsch German who was born in Podhorodse, just days earlier had proclaimed himself the new chief of police and village *wojt,* or "mayor." Almost overnight—or so it seemed to some of the Jews who laughed at him behind their hands, Müller had been transformed by the Nazi victories into a strutting, strident fool. Expecting the imminent declaration by the Nazis of a Ukrainian Free State, Müller had organized a Ukrainian volunteer militia, a rabble of farmers and foresters who most probably would do nothing more combative than wear swastikas and shower Wehrmacht stragglers with flowers.

In response to such changes, the villagers now noticed their differences, mentally segregating themselves almost by way of defense. Unresolved, long-festering prejudices and hatreds floated to the surface. Because of the strangers, an essential element of self-control was snapped inside many of them. As they might have in normal times, people did not feel so entirely responsible to fellow villagers for their actions. Strangers gave them license to abandon elemental decency, and soon in the village every petty, mean, and ignorant impulse started to surface under the unaccustomed pressures of uncertainty, rapid change, and the approach of outsiders whose actions and motives they could not predict. Never before in the village's memory had the villagers talked so much rumor.

In widow Halpern's store, Katz now repeated the suspicious tale that his nephew had carried from Boryslaw, a city only twelve miles away that the Nazis had captured the week before. Dr. Terlecki, the Ukrainian Nationalist leader there, had asked the Nazis for special permission to liquidate all the Jews—he promised to finish the job in twenty-four hours. With the fear of death at his heels, Katz's nephew had run through forests to Podhorodse with the news. Now in widow Halpern's store they asked, would the same happen here? The overwhelming consensus, of course, was no. Boryslaw was an impersonal *city*, after all, in which neighbors did not share the same histories as they did in the villages. And what did Katz's nephew, a foolish and impressionable young man of eighteen years, know, anyway?

A bit later, around one in the afternoon, Schiff, the pain in his stomach suddenly forgotten, was standing in the middle of the living room of his house, not daring to move, as if a step in any direction might alter his destiny for the worst. The sound outside confused and frightened him. Of course the church bell had rung earlier in the morning to call the Catholics to Mass. That happened every Sunday. But the bell was ringing again—loudly and insistently.

Our luck has run out, Schiff was thinking. His wife and daughter were in the back room, on the bed. All he wanted was for the ringing to stop. Suddenly Schiff was startled by a knocking on his door. Reluctantly he went to the door, and Katz rushed inside. "Schmoel, have you seen?" Katz asked. "Something unusual is happening." Before Katz could explain, they heard voices coming through the window of the Ukrainian's house next door. A child's voice asked, "Mama, why don't you wear the dress with the flowers?"

A woman's voice answered the child, "You can come. Father is nearly ready."

Schiff and Katz looked at each other uncomprehendingly. The bell stopped ringing, but they were not relieved. Katz looked at Schiff, then went to the window and saw six of the ragtag Ukrainian militiamen coming up the street. They wore armbands and carried rifles—Manlicher 1895s. Katz turned away and said to Schiff, "I don't think there is any danger."

Ukrainians walked toward the gravel road leading to Pistiner's estate on the hill. They wore suits and dresses, and their children had on their best clothes; but it was too late in the day for church services. By their expressions they were in a festive mood; the Ukrainian militiamen actually joked with their neighbors as they went from house to house, knocking on the doors of Jews. Schiff thought, maybe Katz is right.

A short time later Moshe Altmann joined his business partner, Schiff, and Katz with the question, "What can it be?" They looked at him and he said, "I stood at the window and I saw a car, Schmoel, a *German* car. The man in the back had his hand on a machine gun."

Again the church bell rang, but this time, Schiff thought, it tolled assembly, a warning, a moment of change. He moved the curtains back, and he said, "It's like they are going to a picnic." The Ukrainian and Polish families were walking toward the Pistiner estate, dressed for a celebration.

While the church bell was still ringing, there was another knock at Schiff's door, and this time he jumped in fright. Katz and Altmann stood in the center of the room, their faces chalky. Schiff opened the door, and in the frame he saw his neighbor, a Ukrainian, in a suit that Schiff had not seen him wear for as long as he could remember. The neighbor was deeply upset. "Schmoel, quickly." Then he saw Katz and Altmann, and his expression and tone changed. *"Panne,* Mister Müller has ordered all Jews to come over to the Village Hall. Wives and children, too."

Katz began to cry, "In the name of God, what is happening? Why are they telling us to come? *Why?"*

"Stul mordu," the Ukrainian replied, "shut up."

Schiff could barely speak, such was his terror. He did not fear his neighbor. They were good neighbors and friends; their fathers had been good neighbors and friends before them. They had grown up together, more or less. He was a Jew; his neighbor a Ukrainian Uniate Catholic. But what did that mean? Very little separated them except religion. Schiff had to believe that this man would protect him and his family if they were threatened by the strangers in the German military car. But what was his neighbor saying to Katz? *"The Bolsheviks won't defend you anymore?" "Dirty Jew?"* He said to Schiff, "Why are you standing there?" It was not a question. Katz and Altmann walked toward the Village Hall, at the far end of the street, near the church. What else could they do?

Schiff joined his wife and daughter in the back bedroom. "Don't cry," he told the little girl. And to his wife, "I don't understand what is happening to the Ukrainians. On a simple day like this, they enter our house. In such a way to enter our house by

16

force. To behave in such a way! The war teaches people to become *animals."* He told her to calm their daughter. Before they went out the door, he told his wife, "Take some money with you."

The Village Hall, a one-story wooden structure funded many years ago by the Sejm, the lower house of parliament of the Free Polish State as a symbol of "progress" and Warsaw's "authority," had been used as a meeting place during the Soviet occupation for the Komsomol and for Ukrainian organizations, the Ridna Shkila and Prosvita. On Saturdays in the spring and summer Poles and Ukrainians socialized there, always in front on chairs when the weather was warm and dry. In the evening air the men played cards, talked, and smoked pipes and cigarettes they rolled themselves; the young people danced and sang *domkas* into the dark nights. More than one romance had blossomed on Saturday nights in front of that hall, from which young couples drifted into the shadows of the moon near the riverbank a few yards away. Once the sun had set, candles were brought out; their flickering light signified the end of the day, and people would soon start for home and bed. Jews had their synagogue with one Torah, a small former house that was notoriously cold in winter, and as a rule they did not join the Saturday night social at the hall, although no religious law forbade it. No, Saturday, when almost everybody else was at the hall, they were at home with their families. For them the next day, Sunday, meant work.

They did not know why they had been called to the hall. The longer uncertainty reigned, the more intense their fear became. They—121 in all—had been ordered to stand quietly facing the walls. Mrs. Schiff, certain that something bad was about to happen, told her husband she thought her heart would stop beating. Although she could not imagine how, she felt this day would not end well. "Why are they keeping us?" she asked Samuel, who was standing at her side. No one questioned them, as they had thought, and no one demanded ransom money for their release, as they had expected. This sudden, unexpected isolation in a village so small made no sense to anyone.

Almost without exception, the children in the hall cried, not because of anything that had been said or done to them, but because they saw such fear contorting the adults' faces. As children they were mostly unaware of anti-Semitism in Poland. The term "pogrom" meant little by personal experience. But the children saw more clearly than their parents, who were losing control of their emotions. The parents were scared, but the children were told not to be afraid. "Do not show you are afraid" was their admonition, while their eyes and the delicate muscles of their mouths betrayed their real feelings. To many of the Jews, Philip Müller represented a responsible authority with whom they were familiar, if only briefly. So what if he was foolish with his boastful talk about Hitler? They knew—or guessed—that Müller was now taking his orders from the outsiders who had arrived in the German military car. And Müller transmitted those orders to his Ukrainian militia. All the same—despite all the evidence—Müller, whom the Jews knew, would act responsibly as a police chief should. The fact that he had proclaimed himself chief of police and village *wojt* still meant something. Yet they were being held captive in the hall, and to be singled out as unique never ended well for Jews.

Near the front of the hall people were raising their voices. The village schoolteacher, Romanowicz, appeared among their gesturing arms and turned heads. A circle immediately formed around him. People asked in a babble of questions ("When will we be released?" "Why are we here?" "Where is Philip Müller?" "What do they want?") one paramount question: *"Are we going to be safe?"* Romanowicz, an older man with a goatee, had their respect and trust as a man of learning. He swore he had no idea. "I heard only that our Dutchman is here with the Germans. He has gone to Pistiner's," he told them. "He is looking for Isaac."

"Isaac went to Lwów," said one, at the same time another one said, trying to be helpful, as well, "He's not here."

So palpable was their relief in the Dutchman's presence that they exhaled the tension, some chattering to disguise their embarrassment for their fear. Some felt like laughing. If the Dutchman had accompanied the Germans to the village, then everything would turn out all right. Not that there had not been sharp disagreements, but the Dutchman had ties to the village that made him different and somehow more reliable in their minds than the other strangers, the Germans. Nearly two years had passed since anyone in Podhorodse had seen the Dutchman, who had fled to Lwów and then, they had heard, to Cracow and the German administration. But two years did not change a man so much, and in their minds above all he was "the owner of beautiful horses," a friend to their children, the husband of a charming and cultivated woman, "an embodiment of much that was enlightened in Western culture," many of them had said. Maybe there had been conflicts and nastiness, and maybe they actually knew very little about him, but he had lived among them for several weeks out of every year for seventeen years, and that counted for something real and substantial. They could not imagine anything different. With him present as a witness, everyone—including the Germans in the car, the Volksdeutsch, and the Ukrainians—would act responsibly toward them, especially now that they were being ordered to leave the Village Hall as a group and march up the hill to Pistiner's estate.

At a leisurely, summertime, hand-in-hand stroll, the walk from the hall to the estate took a quarter hour. Today the journey was quicker. A few hundred yards after the turn off the street, chimney-like poplars provided welcome shade. At the end of the gravel road, an expanse of dark-green lawn beckoned. Out in the back, near where the gas generator for power coughed and rattled, there were swings, a seesaw, and stands for straw-filled archery targets. Between the road and the children's play area, the rose garden was overgrown with weeds, and the bushes were not trimmed back as mercilessly as Isaac would have insisted if this were a summer unvisited by strangers. The one constant, the stuffed stag, alert as ever, maintained its sightless vigil on the porch, its glass eyes peering from the split-rail banister across the lawn. Except for minor details, nothing at the estate had changed since the Pistiners had last stayed there as a complete, happy clan.

But on this warm Sunday, the German military car rested on the lawn's gravel-road edge, near the porch. For almost a full hour now, Ukrainians with shovels had been digging a pit in the lawn near the rose garden, and now they were nearly finished. Cut in a rectangle, the pit measured 16 by 11 feet, and 10.8 feet deep. The Germans lazily supervised the excavations from the shade of the porch, which the Ukrainians had strewn with fragrant and color-ful cut flowers, some even tied with ribbons in bouquets. The men in uniforms—the Germans—sipped an amber liquid (rum? co-gnac?) from small glasses. On the round table on the porch was an open bottle. Beside the bottle a Bergmann model 18/1 lay loaded with a full clip of 9mm ammunition. A German with blond hair and a dull, stupefied expression handled the machine pistol every now and then, as a talisman. Holz Apfel of the Rabka Police School for the instruction of mass murder wore on the sleeve of his tunic the flash of the runic double-S, the symbol of the Schutzstaffel. The silver button of the Death's Head on his cap was a reminder of *Kadavergehorsam,* "the obedience of a corpse," the mark of Cain. A black-bordered swastika armband circled his right bicep. *Meine Ehre heisst Treue* ("Loyalty is my honor") was inscribed on his silver belt buckle.

Holz Apfel carried the rank of *Hauptsturmführer*-SS, or captain, of the Sicherheitsdienst RFSS, the elite corps. If rank were any gauge, Apfel should have commanded the detachment, but he did not. The man with the light-brown hair, the Dutchman, held sway despite his rank of *Hauptscharführer*-SS of the SD (Sicher-heitsdienst, the security police of the Gestapo) equivalent to a war-rant officer. Perhaps age was a consideration of command that day—two months ago the Dutchman had turned forty-two. On the Dutchman's black uniform, insignia of the SS and SD had been stripped from the sleeves, as had the Death's Head from the hat. He wore a belt from which hung the holster for a 9mm Para-bellum model 08. The tops of his gleaming black boots were just below his knees. While he supervised the work in Pistiner's gar-den, he combed back his straight, oiled hair again and again, tak-ing exaggerated care that it looked correct, then replaced his hat in a gesture of preparation and vanity suggesting an actor in the wings of a theater about to enter onto the stage.

A few people thought the Dutchman possessed the good looks of a matinee idol, but their judgment was influenced, at least in part, by the trappings of expensive, tailored clothes that he often wore, and by his aura. Women found him irresistible, but they too might have been deceived by his impulsive generosity and brazen-ness. Except for his eyes, his face was cruel; he had a large nose, ears that stuck close to his head, thin lips, and a high forehead. Heavy lids drooped over his eyes, which were a light, milky blue, a cold color that gave off nothing. He had a barrel chest, broad, powerful shoulders, and a stomach that was strong but turning soft. He carried himself like a large man; he tilted forward and seemed all force and determination and swagger, despite his 5-feet 8-inch height. He might have been handsome, the matinee idol of the villagers' description, if his nose had not been of such a proportion. An irregular and fleshy protuberance, it overshadowed the neighboring terrain. If his eyes had been softer and his lips thicker, he would have worn the expression of a pugnacious bum or a drunk. As they were, his eyes and lips suggested a potential for cunning violence; in concert with that nose, they made him appear a man to fear for the most frightening of all reasons, that he might welcome violence purely for its exhilaration.

The militia commander, Philip Müller, leaned on the table to bend close to the Dutchman's ear. He asked for further instructions, now that the pit was complete, with a wall of loose black earth twenty-eight to thirty-one inches thick around its four sides. Müller straightened up and, speaking in Ukrainian, instructed his militiamen to lay a wood plank eight inches wide across the center of the pit. They secured the plank by tamping its ends in the loose dirt with their boot heels.

About this time, the Jews from the Village Hall, bunched and jostling one another past the sentinel poplars, neared the top of the curve. Still, even now, if they had a premonition, they showed no sign as they marched on, toward the back of the big house. Seeing only the barest glimpse of the German car, one of them said, "Gestapo." Otherwise not a sound was heard until Müller shattered the silence. "Altmann and Schiff, return with your families to your houses, and stay there." His voice alerted every person there, but in the confusion neither Schiff nor Altmann understood the order and continued to walk forward. The Dutchman, on the porch near the stag, shaded his eyes with his hand. Spotting Schiff and Altmann, he said in a loud voice, "Didn't you hear? Schiff and Altmann, get out of here, go home, immediately." This time they understood. Grabbing the hands of their wives and their children, they ran back down the gravel road.

Herded inside Pistiner's house, the remaining Jews were again told to face the walls; now every adult knew, if not exactly how and when, he knew. At first weak, then louder and louder, there arose a keening. Women, beside themselves with fear, struck their heads against the walls. Some held up their hands to God and asked, "Why?" Others repeated the words, *Shema Yisroael,* "Hear, O Israel: the Lord our God, the Lord is One."

Over the sounds, a voice demanded silence. *"Panne* has something to tell you," Müller told them, using the Polish term of respect. Again hope entered the room. *Panne* was the Dutchman, and he would not let this happen. But by now, they did not know what to believe or what to hope. The Dutchman came to the door. When they saw him, there was an audible groan of a person who has been punched. He said, "Every woman must return home with her children. Only husbands will remain. Only men." The militiamen pushed the women toward the door. Some of them ran down the hill, crying, lost to panic and shock. One of the freed women veered off toward the Catholic Uniate Church for the priest.

The Jewish men would soon be brought out. But first, the Dutchman had other accounts to settle. For days now, ever since the German invasion had begun, Alexander Nowicki, Albert Stephan, Vladimir Pistolak, and Petro Starzinsky had worried. The vast majority of villagers—Ukrainians especially—had the most to gain and the least to fear from a German victory. This Sunday, for example, they had sat at their open windows and stared into the street. The more ambitious of them had tended their front-yard flower and vegetable gardens, or to avoid the heat, they had waded in the river. Unconcerned, the majority had only to wait for their German "saviors," who had promised them independence, to give them what the Soviets had taken away: religious freedom and private ownership of the land. Now that the Germans had invaded and conquered, so much that they had waited so long to achieve would be fulfilled, and the reclamation would be all the sweeter for the prejudice that they had perceived to have suffered at the hands of the Jews and Poles.

Pistolak, Nowicki, Stephan, and Starzinsky worried because they had rebelled against the majority in Podhorodse, throwing their support to the Bolsheviks after the September 1939 occupation of the region. Now they found themselves as the sworn enemies of the German "saviors." An idealistic nineteen-year-old Ukrainian, Pistolak had formed a local Komsomol, or young Communists' Club, which he had disbanded hastily, burning its membership records, after the Soviet retreat. Nowicki, a teenage Pole with a pretty wife of one year, had joined the club, too, ridiculing Hitler, as he had done openly for many years, but also believing with the Soviets that the forests should belong to all the people and not just rich landowners like Pistiner and the Dutchman. Stephan and Starzinsky shared this view. The brother-in-law of Nowicki, Stephan had been won over to Bolshevism by experience with the "evils" of capitalism. Hadn't the Dutchman "forgotten" to pay his wages? And as employees of the Dutchman, hadn't they witnessed excesses and inequalities?

But their differences with the Dutchman had not been of a seriousness to warrant special treatment. With Stephan there had been nothing but a few harsh words, a minor wage dispute. Nowicki had only whispered his suspicions of the Dutchman to the Russian civil administrators. Yet, however minor they perceived those differences to be, the Dutchman now ordered Müller to bring out Nowicki. To everyone's surprise, Nowicki's wife, Bronislawa, had stayed with her husband. Together, they were led down the steps to the edge of the pit. The corners of Bronislawa's colorful red-and-green *babouska* fluttered in the light breeze. The Dutchman, his 9mm Parabellum drawn from its holster, walked behind them, followed by Holz Apfel, by now dizzy with drink, with the machine pistol slung beneath his arm. Apfel ordered Nowicki to stand on the plank, near to the middle. Before he reached a point that satisfied Apfel, Bronislawa started to scream, "If you kill him, kill me . . . if you kill him, kill me!"

The Dutchman raised his pistol. "Do you still think Hitler is a snotnose?" he asked. Before Nowicki opened his mouth to reply, the Parabellum exploded in the Dutchman's hand. Alexander Nowicki fell into the pit, dead. Bronislawa Nowicki screamed, "Philip, Philip, help us!" But Müller only pushed Bronislawa to the end of the plank. Her brother, Stephan, was placed beside her, and they were prodded by Apfel toward the center. The Dutchman

23

said, "So, *Panne* Stephan, you always complained that I didn't pay you what you were owed. Today I will pay." He motioned with a branch he had picked from the ground, and the Bergmann went off in Apfel's hands. Stephan fell dead into the pit. Two bullets hit Bronislawa, but she remained on the plank. As if she constituted an affront to his vanity, the same as he might have felt toward a stain, the Dutchman reached out and pushed her, just enough to unsettle her precarious balance on the plank, as on life. She fell heavily on the corpses of her husband and brother, but she continued to struggle, still alive.

Next, Pistolak was prodded onto the plank and shot. Then Starzinsky went with a fatalism embodied in his silence. As the Bergmann worked, he fell from the plank for his membership in a club. Only wounded, he waited on the bodies for the Germans to finish. Surely then a Ukrainian or a Pole would help him to safety.

While the Dutchman waited for the Jews, the priest from the Uniate Church suddenly came running up the gravel road, his surplice askew. Even if he had not heard the sharp reports from the German weapons (an impossibility given the proximity), the priest would at once have taken in the horror on the hill. As he crossed the lawn, the priest saw one of his parishioners, Dimitri Sawulac, being forced to the plank. Sawulac had worked for the Dutchman and they had been friendly, but as a Bolshevik and Komsomol member, he too had to die. Mrs. Sawulac ran to the priest, begging him to save her husband. The Dutchman then listened to what the priest said and made a bizarre counteroffer, perhaps recalling that he was the godfather to the Sawulacs' daughter, Slavka. Sawulac would be spared if the priest chose six other Ukrainians to die. Sawulac said, "I will work for you for the rest of my life for nothing if you do not do this." But the priest refused to make the choice, and Sawulac's offer received no reply from the Dutchman, who was distracted by the appearance on the porch of the first Jewish victims.

Like three monkeys, the Selner sisters covered their eyes as they stood on the bed of pine needles under a tree about a hundred feet from the pit. They would have muffled their ears to block out the sounds if they could. All around them more than 200 Poles, Ukrainians, and Volksdeutsch, men, women, and children, gawked at the uniformed killers near the pit, perhaps trying to imagine that this was unreal, a fiction or a joke. Ivan the Terrible, the old raftsman with the red beard, was there, as was Paolo Klepasz, the devilish ex-gamekeeper with the bullet lodged in his neck, Paolo the Cripple, the gamekeeper Stash Brenicz, and scores more. Earlier, they had even permitted their children to play on Pistiner's swing and seesaw and to climb the branches of the trees—for a better view of the "festivities." The Jews' isolation was their problem, their fate was their own.

Some Jews were friends. Sabina Selner had recognized Samuel Schiff, whom she knew was a rich man. Eleven-year-old Sabina attended class with Schiff's daughter. Friends or not, however, the Jews on Pistiner's hill were a group, distinguishable for their Jewishness; but with the execution of three Poles and one Ukrainian, nobody was certain now. Suddenly, the killings were real; the victims were *Christians*. Earlier they had laughed at what they saw to make this seem a joke, but once the people in the pit remained inert, the gaiety curdled. The Selner girls blocked their eyes, as if searching for illusion to transport them from here.

Only two hours before, the Selner girls had sat cross-legged on the floor of their father's house on Drohobycz Road, wrapping twine to make wreaths for the Feast of Kupalo, when they heard the motorcar. Carolina Selner had stepped to the window. To the astonishment of her sisters, she had turned and knelt, right there on the floor. What emotion had overcome Carolina, or what she had imagined, she did not know, but she crossed herself and started the prayer, "Hail Mary full of Grace, the Lord is with Thee. . . ." Her sisters did not understand such seriousness—or such sacrilege. After all, this was a day in which, as frivolous girls, the Selners—Sabina, Paulina, and Carolina—were expected to rejoice in the delicious fear of *rusalky* and *mazky,* vampires and witches, and *opyri,* the unclean dead, who, Ukrainian myth said, wandered the village sucking the blood from anyone who dared to sleep on this day. The girls knew that the local priest at the Uniate Church disapproved of Kupalo's pagan rites, stressing that this was St. John's calendar day. Old Church records described the rites of Kupalo as "hideous," "possessed of an evil spirit," and "unseemly." But the priest had long ago stopped sermonizing

25

against the excesses—the tearing to pieces of scarecrows, the burning of maple saplings, the placing of stinging nettles in barns and on windowsills. When they heard the motorcar, the girls had already collected wild flowers, burdock, gentian, wormwood, and lovage herbs with which to fashion their wreaths, which they would soon take into the forest to this year's chosen *kaubailo*, the most beautiful girl their age, around whom they would dance while she lay with arms across her breasts at the bottom of a pit. Many of the wreaths and flowers prepared for the feast now lay strewn on Pistiner's porch and around the perimeter of another pit, the burial pit on the hill.

As the first of the Jews were brought out, the words "Hear, O Israel: the Lord our God, the Lord is One" were on all their lips, a sound of sobbing more than prayer. Benzion Neuman approached the plank. Only an hour before, he had been wielding a wooden mallet, hammering in place the joints of a chair he was crafting in his furniture shop. Facing his blond executioner, he murmured the words of the ancient Hebrew prayer. A motion of the twig in the Dutchman's hand and a burst from the machine pistol ended his life. Next came Josel Nass, the *melamed,* who taught the Jewish children to read Hebrew. He had waded across the Stryj earlier to find out from the "regulars" at Zeeman's Inn if anyone in Podhorodse had heard any news. He slumped as a shot rang out, and he fell into the pit. Moshe Halpern, the retired postman from Sopot, who knew all the villagers by name and always had a cheerful word, raised his head to the sky, and he too died with a bullet in his chest. Uzik, the son-in-law of the innkeeper, Zeeman, followed. Earlier that day Uzik had opened his "office." An amateur dentist, Uzik pulled out rotten and painful teeth with more persistence than skill—with the ancient "tools" of a string and a doorknob. Shabtai Katz ("I don't think there is any danger") came forth trembling, and he did not look into the pit. He stood straight, like a small boy, with his hands at his side, his stomach out, perhaps hoping to please. Alfred Favel, who had earlier been copying a love letter from a book of poetry to send to his girlfriend in Lwów, stepped on the plank and died seconds later, the unfinished letter in his pocket. The village butcher, the father of the overworked and irritable principal of the *hedder* ("day school") for Jewish children, Mendel Yeckel had spent most of the morning, as he had done for the last months, worrying about finding his daughter a nice husband. Now he went forward on the plank, dying as he turned. Mordechai Londner, Voit Heller, Pinchas Bernstein, Mr. Greenberg, Geiwel Hellman, Haim Jakov, Schlossberg and Schleiffer and Zuckerman, when they reached the plank, they looked toward the Dutchman—certainly not for mercy. They watched his hand signal for the blond German to fire the Bergmann. Bodies fell one after another into the pit—between nineteen and twenty-four Jews shot dead in less than five minutes—more than sufficient time to destroy the soul of a village, never to be resurrected.

Maria Wecker, the beautiful daughter of Isaac Pistiner, had had special feelings for the Dutchman. They had danced on summer nights in each other's arms, she remembered, and so too must he. Was this now the man about whom she had dreamed? She could have asked, "Remember how the gramophone was brought out in the evenings and you would *reign?*" But now she realized how thoroughly her imagination (her dreams) had seized control of her feelings toward him. Looking at him now in this Nazi costume, she could not claim to know him any better than anyone else in the village. She had been so wrong. He had been ruthless, ambitious and greedy, and all the rest, just as some villagers had said.

Maria was crying, her hands by her side, her shoulders stooped. She stood on the porch, her husband, Philip, beside her. Through her tears she demanded of the Dutchman, "What are you doing?" And although Jewish villagers had already fallen into the pit, she screamed in their defense, "Let them live."

The Dutchman looked back, then mounted the steps and stood near Maria on the porch, his expression giving nothing away. Maria sank to her knees to hug the bright black leather of his boots. Whether his intent was to injure or to push her back in surprise and embarrassment, he kicked her. She screamed, "He must not die."

Over her protests, Philip was led to the plank. Perhaps in the belief that he was dying to save Maria, the woman he loved so unhappily, Philip did not complain. He stood straight, looking toward Apfel, who shot him an instant later.

27

On the porch, the Dutchman turned to look down at Maria. He said to her for all to hear, "Get out or I will kill you, too. I will kill your whole family. Tell Isaac. Tell your father. He can't hide from me. Tell him, wherever he is. Tell him I will find him, and when I do I'll kill him."

When all was done, the spectators from the village cast down their eyes until the Germans and the Dutchman had departed in the car. Then they approached the pit. Their belief in evil now fortified beyond any doubt, the Ukrainians paid homage to *Zemlianyieid'ko*, the Devil of the Earth and the guardian of enchanted treasures beneath the soil. So that the victims could buy space from *Zemlianyieid'ko* to settle for all eternity, they tossed kreutzers and kopeks on the bodies in the pit. Then they wandered off.

CHAPTER II

❈

"I'll miss you."

THAT SAME SUNDAY, July 7, 1941, more than 2,000 miles away from Poland in Palestine, Sergeant Lieber ("Bibi") Krumholz, now of the British Mandatory Government's Palestine Police Force, viewed the slaughter with barely half an eye. He dreaded the sight of the assembly line of death around him. Along with ten other policemen, he patrolled the Ramallah Road abattoir, where blood ran in gutters, and hunks of flesh littered the floor. Three rows of fifteen severed goat heads—their bright brown eyes open, their pink tongues slipped from their mouths, their ears pinned back as though in rapid flight—were stacked against the right-hand wall near the stand from which Bibi watched over the proceedings. Near the door the Jewish and Moslem butchers were bent at the waist, side by side. One of the butchers' apprentices, thin and hardworking young men, had tied the hind legs of a calf with a short rope. Another apprentice stretched the animal's head toward the ceiling, as the first apprentice kicked the legs from underneath. Without an ounce of wasted effort the chief Arab butcher, his trousers rolled to the knees, flicked the knife over the animal's outstretched neck, severing the jugular. He jumped back, his arms raised like a picador. The arterial blood from the animal arched in the air, then lessened, and lessened some more, with the dying spasms of the animal's heart.

Duty required Bibi to watch for fear that an Arab would give the knife to a Jew, or a Jew to an Arab. Somebody in this stifling atmosphere was always at somebody's throat, especially this sum-

29

mer, when the air was charged with emotion as the German armies advanced to the Caucasus and the future of Cairo as an Allied stronghold dimmed. Jerusalem came next after Cairo was defeated, and the Palestinian Arab leader Mufti Haj el-Husseini anticipated a swift victory for his Nazi allies; his followers, down to the butchers, had grown emboldened.

But in moments when Sergeant Krumholz turned his eye, he opened a book that a friend had recommended as a guide to muckraking journalism at its finest, and he read, "It was so very businesslike that one watched it fascinated. It was porkmaking by machinery, porkmaking by applied mathematics. And yet somehow the most matter-of-fact person could not help thinking of the hogs; they were so innocent, they came so very trustingly; and they were so very human in their protests—and so perfectly within their rights! They had done nothing to deserve it; and it was adding insult to injury as the thing was done here, swinging them up in this coldblooded, impersonal way, without a pretense of apology, without the homage of a tear."

Bibi adored this blunt prose. Upton Sinclair's writing showed him how a collection of facts was woven to enthrall, inform, and finally change a reader's mind; journalism had no need to bore. Every day for months hundreds of animals had been "processed" in the abattoir, but more than to help him see what he had missed, Sinclair showed him how to feel. He read: "And how was one to believe that there was nowhere a god of hogs, to whom this hog personally was precious, to whom these hog squeals and agonies had a meaning?"

Perhaps the abattoir experience, as Bibi's wife, Mala, said, reinforced his increasingly morbid thoughts, helped by the passages from *The Jungle*. But the reason for his deepening gloom had more to do with a cumulative effect. He had not heard from his family since May, nearly two months before, when his father, David, had written a spare description of life under the Russians: food was scarce and times were very hard. Families had been expelled from their houses, and the Soviet occupation forces demanded that everybody share the space. David said that he longed for the day when the Soviets would allow them to emigrate to Palestine. But two weeks ago, something had happened, Bibi knew in his heart, that had destroyed that hope, at least for the foreseeable future. On June 22, 1941, Operation Barbarossa had commenced, with the Nazis now rolling through Lwów toward Moscow. The treaty destroyed, the Russians were now the Germans' sworn enemy. Bibi remembered what his father had written earlier, and he reread the words often. "Please pray God that the Germans do not invade Lwów. If they do, they will kill all the Jews." When he read those lines, he felt overpowering guilt.

Although Bibi believed in the wisdom of his decision to emigrate to Palestine, he felt that he could have rescued his family by going to Poland. He had failed them, he thought, and he feared every waking moment now that his failure would result in their deaths, so that, according to his tortured reasoning, he would be responsible in some small but important way. Now, he totally abandoned his earlier rationalizations that they were safe because they were *his* family, that they were the exceptions, that they were hiding in a bunker somewhere, their safety guarded by friendly Poles and Ukrainians. No, he said to himself, none of that is true. But the agony of his uncertainty continued, placing his life in limbo in which he found the expression of any emotion—either love or hate—difficult. He would wait and wait without daring to plan for three more nearly intolerable years. The single reality on which he relied for hope was memory.

Bibi's earliest memory was of fleeing across the frozen wastes of Eastern Europe swaddled in the protective arms of his mother, Malvina. Fourteen months after Bibi was born in 1912 in the Rumanian frontier town of Kuty on the Czeremonsz River, Archduke Ferdinand's assassination at Sarajevo unleashed vast armies that crushed the Jews in the Pale of Settlement, as Russian forces wrested segments of Austrian Galicia and Bucovina from the Hapsburgs' control. In mortal terror of czarist domination—and the cossack spearheads—Galician Jews fled westward. But the Army had requisitioned the trains, and there were no cars. Moreover, the government of Austria admitted no conceivable reason for Jews in the Pale to want to flee their protection. With David among the first to be drafted into the Austro-Hungarian infantry of the Central Powers, Malvina was forced to rely on her own devices to reach the relative safety of Hungary. One night among many, no village appeared on their route as the sun went down, and with no food, Malvina had no choice but to feed Bibi snow. After many days, nearly starved and exhausted, they reached the two-room flat on Jokai Utca Street in Maramarosh-Sziget, Hungary, that an aunt of David's and two of his cousins had rented.

An inventive woman, Malvina supplemented David's army pay by working at a pedal sewing machine and in partnership with her sister-in-law as a waitress in a coffee "house" in the apartment. One morning, while Malvina served coffee and Bibi played on a black hearse that the Catholic undertaker parked in the backyard, the postman arrived. Even as a small boy Bibi understood news as a harbinger of unwanted, and mostly unpleasant, change, and he tried to intercept the postman, who asked, "Why do you look at me like a dog?" Malvina took the letter in trembling hands. There was no cause for Bibi's downcast expression. It was *not* from the Army. To their delight, Isaac had written that the war would soon end and that Kuty, where Malvina planned to return, was no place to raise and educate a child. He had purchased two estates in the neighboring villages of Podhorodse and Sopot, in Polish Galicia, on opposite banks of the Stryj River. Isaac wanted David to manage the estates until the fortunes of the young family improved. Even before she consulted with David, Malvina sat down to write a reply.

Once David was discharged, they traveled by train, a great luxury, to the rail junction at Synowodzko Wyzne in Poland. Wilk, a Pole with a red mustache, drove them in a carriage to the ford near Zeeman's Inn in Podhorodse. David wondered if they should stay the night at Isaac's big house or cross the river for the "hunting lodge" in Sopot, the rough-hewn cabin where they planned to live. Ivan, a tall Ukrainian raftsman with a shirt that hung down to his knees, decided for him. The raftsman threw their suitcases on the raft, showing Malvina, with a chivalrous sweep of his arm, the fragile wood bench in the stern.

If Malvina had not pointed out the imperfections of the hunting lodge, David would not have noticed. In the Army he had known far worse, and besides, each morning he was up early, shaved and dressed and in the saddle of a horse, tackling with energy, if not expertise, the management of the estates. On the Sabbath the family attended the synagogue off Main Street, across the river in Podhorodse, and afterward they socialized with the village's more prominent Jews—the Katzes, Schiffs, Zeemans, Halperns, Lasts. Bibi attended Polish school, but Malvina, fretting as usual, hired a tutor from Lwów, Sala Rendelstein. On Saturdays Bibi listened while Sala read romances to illiterate Ukrainian girls, who wept at the broken hearts and lost loves. In those days Bibi, like thousands of other boys the world over, saw himself as Jim in Stevenson's *Treasure Island,* with Long John Silver as the imperfect hero he worshiped, at a time when heroes for Jewish boys were much in demand. Josel Nass, the *melamed* from Sopot, taught Bibi the Hebrew alphabet, and Paolo Klepasz, a thin, grizzled war veteran, told wild stories of hunting the forest's legendary white bear. Klepasz even allowed Bibi to touch the bullet lodged under the skin of his neck when they hiked with Wonder, the family pet Alsatian, to the twelfth-century monks' grottoes in the mountains around the village. For Bibi, Podhorodse and Sopot were paradise.

One evening David galloped his lathered horse toward the Sopot cabin. Earlier, on his rounds of the estate, a group of Ukrainian guerrillas had rushed out of the forest. "The war is over," they told him. "Jews are with Poles, and we don't want you here. If you stay, we will kill you." Hurriedly, David brought his family from Sopot across the river to Isaac's large house on the hill overlooking Podhorodse. That night, David stood guard until dawn, but the experience changed their lives. They never returned to live in Sopot, and they learned to fear the Ukrainians. Malvina, always a proud woman (some called her a snob because she read Heine and Schiller and Tolstoy, and insisted on wearing a mink coat to synagogue), forbade Bibi to associate with Ukrainian children. David, because of his position as *kluchnik* ("manager"), did not want Bibi playing with the workers' children either. Bibi was six, and he was lonely.

Soon after the Austro-Hungarian armies had surrendered at the Armistice, the Bolsheviks prepared to re-annex the Ukraine, but they were resisted by near-suicidal bands of Ukrainian nationalists, who did not want to live under Soviet domination. As

33

much as they detested Communists, the Ukrainians hated Jews more for their imagined support of the Reds, and in 1919 the followers of Ukrainian Nationalist leader Simon Petlura shot up Jewish neighborhoods and hunted from house to house for "hooked-nosed commissars," as they called the Jews. In just one year, nearly 500 pogroms killed 70,000 Jews. White Russian armies, which also moved against the Bolsheviks, similarly identified Jewry with the Russian Revolution. A third force, the new Polish Army, battled what *it* thought was the Bolshevik menace, the Ukrainians. For nearly three years, the Ukrainians fought the Poles, with Jews in the middle. In all, during those bloody years immediately after World War I, a quarter of a million Jews died.

One day, Ukrainian fighters bivouacked on the lawn of the Podhorodse estate where the Krumholzes lived. Bedraggled and hungry, they ransacked the house for what they could find. In their search they discovered three rifle cartridges deep in a desk drawer, and automatically believing the occupants of the house to be Bolsheviks, the Ukrainians threatened to execute David, Malvina, Bibi, and baby Marek, only one month old. The next morning just after the sun rose, Malvina summoned the courage to tell several officers working for the Ukrainians how their men had behaved. "Don't be afraid," they told her, and rode off to raise the Ukrainian national flag of gold and blue on the church steeple. Two days later, the Ukrainians retreated before an advancing Polish army, which entered and set out *their* flag on the church steeple. "Don't be afraid," they too said. But by now, Malvina was sick of being told not to be afraid, when she was more than just afraid and knew how the same fear was stunting little Bibi. The time had come to find a place where a Jew did not feel constant fear.

She chose the Polish city of Lwów because Isaac spent the winters there. Lwów in the 1920s was a boom town, and like all boom towns, besides being an establishment of businessmen, professionals, and shopkeepers, it attracted profiteers of one plumage or another—adventurers, ruffians, hucksters, swindlers, cardsharps, whores, black marketeers, art dealers and art fakers, loan sharks, soldiers of fortune, contract killers, magicians, acrobats, actors, and men with dancing bears. They called the city Lwów (in Pol-

ish) or Lvov (in Russian) or Lemberg (in German) or "the Paris of
the East" (in all languages), the capital city of East Galicia, the
Laredo in the Wild West of Eastern Europe. The third largest city
in Free Poland (population 300,000), Lwów had a new commercial center along Akademicka Street, a *corso* where the ladies displayed their finery from the salons of Vienna and Paris, a bronze
statue of Adam Mitzkewitch the poet, and electric trolleys and
cobble (but not yet asphalt) streets. In the Old Market the lan-
guage was Yiddish spiced with Lwowian curses, and a real bargain
was rare. Actors played in the City Theater, two Polish theaters,
the Ukrainian theater, and the Gimpel Family's Yiddish theater,
where Abraham Goldfaden had tried his luck at the start of the
century. The matinee idol Yadwiga Smosarska was seen on the
screens of sixteen movie houses. There were forty-five synagogues for 100,000 Jews, a three-story Jewish hospital that Maurice Lazarus had built in 1903, a Jewish Community Building for
weddings, and an Artisans' Club for Jewish trade unions (and Zionist and Bund groups). Lwów also had twelve high schools and a
great university with the most respected medical staff in Poland.
For food it had Dorfman's and Backo's restaurants, where at the
twilight hour Polish nobles and Catholic priests went to eat gefilte
fish. Near Sloneczna Street the day came alive with the cries of
traders in currencies, gold and silver, diamonds, and jewelry.
There were stalls, stores, workshops, lodging houses, and rooms
for the prostitutes, who carried yellow licenses issued by the
health department. Lwów had crooked courts, cops, and politicians, and no time for pity. Charity was dispensed as an after-
thought, once the violence was exhausted, like an apology after an
insult. At night the toughs sang, "Will you be to me like a lamp?
First hang, then burn, go out at night and then in the morning
may the flies stick to you."

David and Malvina rented an apartment at Chodorowskiego
Street #10, near the army barracks, in the poor neighborhood of
Polish Catholics and Ukrainian laborers. Malvina brightened the
rooms with paint and imagination. Gentle and delicate—her
blond hair and smile turned men's heads—she soon wondered
what they had done by moving here. She had grown to dread
Podhorodse, she admitted freely, but they had traded a village for

a city that somehow was insidious. The dangers lurked in the shadows here: men in tailored suits beamed friendliness while guarding wickedness in their hearts; few things were as they seemed; deception was survival; simplicity and honesty were the virtues of fools; it was a topsy-turvy world, and Malvina felt sickened, as if she were spinning too fast on a carnival ride. Malvina was a religious woman who kept a kosher home, but when she attended synagogue, she heard too much talk of Zionism, which she understood only as a concept. She knew how Zionism seduced young people, and she wanted to protect Bibi from its temptations. Her anxiety, and she laughed at herself, was premature. How could Zionism attract Bibi when religion did not interest him? Bibi lighted candles for the dead, but he never lingered. At his bar mitzvah the rabbi said, "I hope you will be as happy as your parents have been to have you as their son." Bibi uttered words in Hebrew to prove that he had studied, and David looked solemn by his side, but neither father nor son was at all a religious Jew.

By any reckoning, in his first teenage year Bibi possessed few gifts for academics in Dr. Rozia Mamberowna's Zydowskie Gymnasium Classic for men. Handsome and tall at thirteen, his heart beat for experience beyond the confining walls, the charts, and the math formulas. The Jewish national soccer team, Hasmonea, the constant underdog to Pogon, the Polish national side, stirred his early passion. He saw the movies of Charlie Chaplin, Buster Keaton, and Jackie Coogan and found adventure on the army barracks' parade field, where he learned for the first time the feel of a rifle. "What are you doing there?" Malvina yelled at him from the kitchen window. "You'll be killed. A rifle in your hand?"

Bibi yelled back, "Mama, it's the life. Everybody goes into the Army."

"Stay away from there," she warned.

And he disobeyed, his first disobedience, although he was not yet old enough to break free. One day on their way to meet David after work, Bibi and his mother entered a bookshop, and as he browsed through the shelves a strange woman tapped Bibi's shoulder. "Yes?" he asked politely. "Boy, would you like to come fuck me?" she asked, smiling. Frightened, he fled into his mother's arms. "Why are you so white?" Malvina asked. He told her. "Don't be afraid," she said, comforting him. "You refused, and she won't bother you." Again, Malvina must have wondered. . . .

If the serenity of Podhorodse beckoned—and the village *did* look better from the perspective of Lwów, as people, towns, and years past and unrecoverable often do—the course of their lives was set. No longer a simple *kluchnik* (Isaac had replaced him with his son-in-law, Philip Wecker), as an entrepreneur David barely had time for the family anymore. On the Sabbath he worked at home, and often in the evenings he conferred with associates on strategy for making his small clothing manufacturing company grow.

Malvina often thanked God for her brother. A man of wealth and status, Isaac owned a ten-room apartment on the second floor at Slowackiego #3, near the main post office. Even more impressive, his country estate in Podhorodse symbolized a certain permanence and reliability. In so many ways she depended on him to get things done, to provide for her family and, privately, as an ultimate refuge from which she and her two sons would not be turned away, no matter what.

Like Malvina, Bibi enjoyed the closeness between the Pistiner and Krumholz families. Sharp laughter, intense conversation, and secret whispers filled the Slowackiego apartment, a house renowned for its love, warmth, and friendship. Much to Malvina's constant concern for propriety, Bibi spent a great deal of his time there because he saw himself in the Pistiner family as no mere cousin. His best friend was Isaac's son Dzionek, a year younger but smarter in mathematics. They shared the attraction of opposites: Dzionek was thin, short, and fastidious, a better student who often helped Bibi just to get him through. As much as boys could differ, Bibi was mercurial and quixotic, and Dzionek steady and controlled, diplomatic and mannered. Bibi peered at the world over the margin of the page, and Dzionek found a complete universe in the written word. They competed in nearly everything, as Dzionek was doing in a sly manner on the day at the Gymnasium when he whispered to Bibi, "Yesterday we had a visitor. We were all sitting with our mouths open when he was talking. What country do you suppose he comes from?"

"You're asking *me?*" Bibi replied, impatient with the game.

"Holland!" exclaimed Dzionek, as if the word itself contained magic.

The newcomer was the first Dutchman in Lwów that the Pistiners and Krumholzes knew about, and his arrival matched that of a circus or a whirlwind as a unique event. That day after class, Bibi and Dzionek asked Isaac's daughters what they knew about the visitor. The Dutchman came from an aristocratic family "in Amsterdam," Mara Pistiner said, feeling accomplished for such fresh and important information. "His father died, and his mother remarried a *university* professor." A brother of this Dutchman was a famous athlete, and the Dutchman himself was a wealthy businessman who was opening an Eastern European field headquarters in Lwów of the family-owned export firm. The stranger was "handsome and elegant," "full of life and fun," and not "just a businessman," either, but an art collector with a new house at Piaskowa Street #15. They had spoken German, the lingua franca of Eastern Europe, to communicate, the girls reported to Bibi, but the Dutchman was learning Polish, which he spoke with an endearing accent. He smoked Egyptian cigarettes, carried a silver-topped walking stick, and his wife, a former fashion model, possessed the beauty of a movie star, in Mara's estimation. Bibi listened with growing suspicion that the Pistiner children had banded together to play an elaborate joke. Nobody of such wonder could exist.

Bibi soon forgot about the phantasmagorical Dutchman for soccer. Naturally impetuous, he could not wait to learn the score when Hasmonea played out of town. From the window of *Chwila,* the Polish-language Jewish daily in Lwów, the returning sports reporter would yell, "We won!" or more often, "We got fucked!"

Newspapers—news!

David subscribed to *Chwila* and *Nowy Dziennik,* the Cracow daily, and two other Polish dailies, and now and then he bought *Neue Freie Presse* of Vienna (once edited by Theodor Herzl, the father of modern Zionism). But *Chwila* really showed Bibi how newspapers brought vital information, if only soccer scores, from afar, and he decided then to become a professional journalist when he grew up. He started now by writing a simple, explanatory letter to Dr. Berkelhammer, the editor of *Nowy Dziennik* in Cracow, asking what stories interested their readers. Before the editor replied, a subject—*the* dominant subject for Polish Jews—literally struck Bibi dumb with fear.

The date was June 13, 1929, a Sunday, and Catholics celebrated the Feast Day of Corpus Christi by marching behind colorful satin-fringed church banners, as students at the Jewish High School watched the endless street procession from the windows. A young Jewish girl screamed when the chair on which she was standing shook under her. Outside in the street, the Poles turned angrily toward the sound. A cry went up that Jews had thrown garbage in the street (an orange peel, the student hooligans would later admit), ridiculing sacred Catholic ritual. Amazingly, a full week of anti-Semitic rioting ensued with Bibi's Jewish High School the focus of Catholic rage. University and polytechnic students rampaged through Lwów, wrecking buildings and attacking Jews, some with sticks inlaid with razor blades. For the first time Bibi was threatened directly—without his parents to protect him —by anti-Semitic hatred.

On that Sunday he ran terrified, as fast as his legs would carry him, to the editorial offices of *Chwila,* where he breathlessly demanded to speak with Henry Hescheles, the editor, to whom he gave an eyewitness account. Hescheles said, "Our correspondent has not telephoned. How come you have the story already?"

Bibi replied, "I was in the crowd."

Hescheles told him to write a longhand account of what had happened. Less than thirty minutes later, to Hescheles's surprise, Bibi handed him the finished story. "So you want to be a journalist? You are still young, but stay in touch," he advised. (During the night Polish Catholics, led by Macielinski, a notorious anti-Semite, shattered *Chwila*'s presses. The next day the usual sixteen-page issue was printed as a two-page broadsheet on borrowed presses. Bibi's article never appeared.)

As he walked home, taking care to use the back streets, Bibi felt the joy of a first "scoop." Even that word, he thought, was a pleasure to roll off his tongue. It sounded tough and professional. There was nothing now that he could see to separate him from a journalism career: Hescheles had accepted him, almost, as an equal; anyway, he had encouraged his interest. . . . Suddenly, hearing shouting behind him, Bibi turned and he nearly went cold with fear, as thoughts of a career gave way to survival. A group of Polish students had rounded the corner, and when they spotted him, they ran toward him, waving clubs over their heads. His dominant thought was that he had done nothing; a journalist, he should be immune. He knew that the beating should not have surprised him. The clubs rained down on his head, and he fell, curling in a ball to protect himself. The Poles left him there, soon in search of fresh victims.

Near unconsciousness and bleeding badly, he staggered away. The incident had split his skull, but it had opened his eyes as well to the hatred and injury that lay in the future of any young Jew who remained in Poland. This time the riot ended with cuts and bruises, but what about the next time, or the time after that? With the fires of anti-Semitism so hot and near the surface, every Jew had to leave this cursed country, Bibi now knew beyond a doubt. Every Jew had to abandon the Pale of Settlement, or every Jew would soon die. In that moment when the Polish club drew blood, Bibi changed forever. He resolved first to start a career that he could practice anywhere, even outside Free Poland, and he came to espouse the revolutionary concepts of the militant Zionist leader Vladimir ("Zev") Jabotinsky, the *Wunderkind* of Russian Zionism, the war correspondent, the warrior at Gallipoli, the Revisionist romantic and adventurer, a man with daring and vision. Bibi agreed with Jabotinsky that anti-Semitism was endemic in Europe and East European Jewry was *doomed;* that a Jewish *army,* however small, was necessary for self-defense; and that there must be a gradual "transformation of Palestine into a self-governing commonwealth under the auspices of an established Jewish majority." The Balfour Declaration and the Mandate had called for a Jewish national *home,* but Jabotinsky dared to speak of a national *state*—"There are two kinds of nationalism," he said one night in a speech that Bibi heard. "The one aggressive, out for territorial conquest; the other the natural defense effort of a people which has

40

no homeland and is faced with the threat of extinction: If this is militarism, we are to be *proud* of it!"

Later, Bibi joined the movement for young people led by Jabotinsky himself. Most young Jewish men joined one or another of the Zionist youth groups, like the socialist Hashomer Hatzair, to which Bibi had been preordained. But Revisionism offered a concept so different from the socialists, it was revolutionary. Unabashedly militaristic, it drilled members in the manly virtues called *Hadar,* then missing in Jewish life—ideals of respect, self-esteem, politeness, and loyalty. The hero of *Simson,* Jabotinsky's famous novel, told his people that all great civilizing states are founded by the sword. "There is nothing more valuable in the world than iron," Simson preached. Bibi soon began to practice *Hadar* unconsciously and without effort. In his immediate family, to be sure, the men had only so much to teach. He loved his Uncle Isaac and of course his father. But they were not educated men, and their travels to Western Europe rarely took them outside the Jewish communities in Vienna and Berlin. They appreciated culture, but they had no real experience with it. They had suffered too much indignity in silence and breathed too deeply the pollutant of fear. The constant friction of anti-Semitism had rounded their characters as it stooped their shoulders. As relatives, Bibi judged them by more demanding standards. A Revisionist, a follower of *Hadar,* and a devotee of Zev Jabotinsky, Bibi sought different heroes to imitate.

One Saturday in that same year, 1929, David called for Bibi to deliver a letter across town to a new business associate. In those days, Piaskowa Street had not been laid with cobblestones, no sidewalks had been built, and winter boots, wagon wheels, and the pounding of horses' hoofs made the street a mire through which Bibi trudged to the address on the envelope. As he knocked he heard the yapping of dogs, white poodles, he saw, when the master of the house, the Dutchman, opened the door and invited him inside, refusing to accept the envelope without offering refreshment. Bibi looked around him and was dazzled: the furnishings—he only guessed their value—were more beautiful than he had believed possible. The Dutchman placed an arm on the boy's shoulder and showed him to the den. Bibi struggled to speak, as he was only then learning German at school. When he confessed his problems with German, the Dutchman volunteered to tutor him, an offer that Bibi accepted readily, less for the chance to improve his fluency than for the regular opportunity to know this unusual man. In exchange, Bibi offered to help the Dutchman with Polish.

Bibi was too young and much too dazzled to wonder why a rich entrepreneur, an accomplished art collector with a beautiful wife, a man from an important family in Holland, would want anything to do with the Krumholzes and Pistiners, struggling Jews. Or why he had settled in Lwów, "Jewish Poland," worlds even from Warsaw in *Catholic* Poland, which was cosmopolitan and modern with night clubs, croon and tango bands, symphonies, pretty women, suave, intelligent men, restaurants, *boîtes* for the café society. Lódz ranked after Warsaw, *then* Lwów. Foreigners rarely even *visited* Lwów, and they never settled, not unless they were on the run or out for no good. The answer apparently was that the Dutchman had been sent to Eastern Europe on orders from his father, when their firm had resumed trade with a Free Poland after World War I. The Dutchman, capitalizing on Holland's colonial power, said he hoped to sell merchandise from the Dutch East Indies (tea, spices, cocoa, coffee, tin, and rice) in exchange for Polish commodities like timber. He boasted of his previous, pre-Lwów success ("I am the Tea King of Warsaw," he told anyone who would listen), his contacts, his acumen, his "empire," his acceptance by the new elites in Free Poland and the old aristocracy. There might have been something worrying in his exaggerated need for acceptance: a great man doesn't explain his greatness. But Bibi, indeed, all the Pistiners and Krumholzes, had no basis for judgment, just as they had no easy way to verify certain rumors—a *szmarciarze* ("ragpicker"), a pushcart, a swindle, troubles with the police in Danzig? Who was this exotic Dutchman and why had he entered their lives? The Pistiners and Krumholzes did not want to ask. The Dutchman satisfied their deepest fantasies about themselves as modern, secularized Jews with important Gentile friends whose acquaintance gave substance to their vision of the future.

The young people especially seemed drawn to the Dutchman's

childish, simple manner; he sometimes made himself look silly for their benefit, as if he sought *their* approval. He entertained Bibi, especially, without patronizing him, treating him almost as an equal. He seemed more relaxed, more *natural* around younger people, as if the need for constant watchfulness over something secret and hidden diminished in their company.

At first, Bibi and the Dutchman shared a mutual passion for soccer; the Dutchman said he personally knew Albin Garbien, the superstar of Pogon, the Polish national team. Bibi often asked about Holland, and once, he asked why the Dutchman never returned to Amsterdam. The older man was silent until finally he said, "Look, Holland is a monarchy. After the last war, there is no place for a king or a queen. They belong to the old times. If I return there, I will become a victim of political crimes by monarchists." Bibi pondered this for weeks, and he understood it only vaguely as the highest expression of *Hadar*. The Dutchman was a bright, spectacular light that quickly flooded every corner of Bibi's world—an idol with whom, unlike Zev Jabotinsky, he could actually talk, to whom he listened, and from whom he learned. Bibi finally had found a real hero.

That next summer the rose garden of the estate in Podhorodse paid bountiful dividends for the pruning of the previous fall; the trees around the house had been doctored by "surgeons" from Lwów. The house strained to accommodate twenty guests, mostly Bibi's friends from school. Each day the young people followed the same drill: After breakfast everybody headed down the gravel road through the village to the Stryj. Downstream, between the ford and the Sopot landing, smooth, water-sculpted boulders formed sheltered pools that hid them from the prying eyes of the Ukrainian teenagers from the village who stared at "half-naked" girls in black bathing costumes. The posing and posturing of courtship demanded what energy remained after they had swum and bathed in the sun. Bibi often fished, hurling a line into the center of a still pool. At noon, when the sun peaked, they returned to the house for lunch, then read or rested on the lawn, played chess, practiced archery, or talked quietly on the porch. Sometimes in the afternoons, they rode horseback through the forests. On very festive days they piled aboard hay wagons. And finally on warm evenings when fireflies twinkled over the lawn, the gramophone was brought out on the porch and they danced.

That summer the Dutchman made the first visit to the Pistiner estate. He brought light and laughter to the house, and if for nothing else, the Krumholzes and Pistiners admired him for being simply "a civilized man from the West." The children tried to imitate his easygoing manner, his bold, confident stride, to talk with the same voice, to dance with the same fluid, gliding grace; they even copied his stance—a slouch with hands on his hips. The girls saw how the boys imitated him, and while they laughed, they hoped a little of the Dutchman's polish would rub off.

David returned that summer from a business trip abroad with a present for Bibi—a lightweight, single-shot .22-caliber rifle with a carved stock. More than anything, the weapon symbolized a rite of passage. Now he could hunt, too. Once, after Bibi and the Dutchman had been unsuccessfully stalking boar in the woods, they passed on foot through a small village. The Dutchman accosted a pretty local girl. She walked with them into the woods, and after a time he touched her breast and she laughed. Emboldened, he put his hand under her dress. When they finally continued on their hunt, Bibi had yet another "manly attribute" to imitate.

That summer David bought a carriage, and, exhilarated by speed, he raced the team from Podhorodse to the nearby towns of Skole and Stryj. One day, the horses panicked and overturned the carriage at the rare sound of an automobile. David ended up in the hospital with a concussion. The automobile was a shiny, yellow V-8 Talbot sports car owned by the Dutchman's brother, who lived in Amsterdam and according to rumor had swum for the Dutch team in the 1928 Olympic Games. He had not won a medal, but he was an "Olympian" whom Bibi summoned the courage to "interview." Afterward he invited Bibi for a spin to Stryj in the Talbot. In Stryj they ate ice cream in cones.

After his brother returned to Amsterdam, the Dutchman set about to photograph everything in sight (though he himself did not like to be photographed), making no secret of his hobby. The villagers were flattered and posed for his camera willingly. One day in the summer of 1932, Bibi noticed on a hunt that the

Dutchman was not tracking boar after all, but pushing ahead through the forest to the other side, where he scanned the horizon, as if in search of something very specific. Bibi held his rifle as he climbed a tree, then watched as the Dutchman took photographs from between the branches. The following morning, retracing the route, Bibi saw from a perch in the same tree a railroad track for hauling out timber, and he wondered why this of all things was of such special photographic interest. Soon he forgot, realizing that the Dutchman was photographing *everything*—people, places, houses, buildings, factories, forests, bridges, rivers—not just scenery.

Bibi tagged after him, fetching, doing favors, carrying, listening; they even went into the villagers' houses, where the Dutchman sat and drank their beer. An oddity, the Dutchman went around the village carrying a silver-topped walking stick and wearing plus fours, a broad-brimmed hat, and wide-lapelled, double-breasted suits with padded shoulders and turned-up cuffs on pleated pants. The Egyptian cigarettes hung from the corner of his mouth. At a puff of wind he ran a comb through his oiled hair. He even preened at the table.

In the fall of 1932, Bibi had been admitted to the prestigious High School of Journalism in Warsaw. The Dutchman had kept up with Bibi's progress, often asking during summer breaks how Bibi was doing in school. And now the acceptance of his protégé pleased him even more than when *Chwila*, earlier that same year, had published Bibi's story about a charitable organization for the deaf. "Have you seen it?" the Dutchman had asked David on the telephone. "Bibi's name appeared in the paper."

"One day you will become a great journalist," he told Bibi. "I know because I have talked with Polish editors. They know your work already."

Soon after, Bibi traveled in second class to Warsaw with Mundek Mehr, a former Gymnasium classmate. As he walked from the Central Station toward the Jewish Quarter, he noticed that the people he passed in the wide streets seemed richer and poorer than Lwowians. There was more of everything—trams, cars, carriages, elegant shops, movie houses, night clubs, and cafés. The city's variety, elegance, and sophistication overwhelmed him from the start. He boarded in the home of a devout Jew with a daughter, whom Bibi eyed with interest. She had remarkable dimpled cheeks, and after some weeks Bibi made his first date. Hoping that he looked just a little like the Dutchman, he dressed in a dark suit and waited outside in the street, not far from the house, because her father forbade her to date. They had coffee where nobody would see them, and she told him that she had to read the modern Polish writers and go to the movies surreptitiously, in defiance of her strict father. Bibi basked in her beauty, but he had little time for socializing.

Ironically, Bibi published so many articles in Lwów and Warsaw newspapers that his grades at the High School of Journalism suffered. He often wrote about the rampant anti-Semitism in Warsaw. By his second year, provosts at the university had made Jews sit apart on "Jew benches"; later they were ordered to stand in the lecture halls. Later still, they were banned from classes altogether. Bibi told anybody who would listen, "Leave Poland. Go to Palestine!"

"Why?" they sometimes asked. "The Arabs are more dangerous than the Poles."

A few Poles felt ashamed of their countrymen, but by now anti-Semitism was ubiquitous—in the courts, among the police, in public institutions. The government's official "anti-anti-Semitism" policies had no impact on the vast majority of Poles and Ukrainians, and not just in Warsaw. The underlying causes—that the long-promised economic reform never happened, financial stability cost the Poles high unemployment, social services struggled to keep pace with a soaring birthrate, foreign investment dried up, and confidence eroded—forced Bibi to abandon hope. About the only effective sector was education, and newly literate young Poles favored discontent over tolerance. Bibi listened and the more he heard the more urgently he wanted to emigrate to Palestine. *Anywhere* offered more opportunity, more freedom and safety from the constant presence in Poland of fear, ugliness, and mindless hatred.

Nobody knew that feeling of fear better than Malvina, who had been running from it all her life, too. Still, she did not want her son to emigrate to Palestine. She worried for his safety: Arabs were shooting Jews there, and Palestine was so very far away. Emigration was for the children of *other* parents. Malvina did not argue with her eldest son, but she made her feelings known. She wanted her family to stay together, if not literally, then within the same close geographical region. When Bibi asked her permission, she flatly refused, bucking the decision to David, who stuck to his rationale for Bibi's remaining in Poland—that what was good enough for father was good enough for son.

Bibi did not know what to do. He was a good son, always cooperative and, above all, obedient. He tried to please them, God knew. His father had shown an interest in newspapers, and Bibi had taken that interest one large step further, planning to make a career of it. His father had never shown an interest in religion, and neither did Bibi, although he had tried for his mother's sake. She had worried about this indifference toward his faith. But it was Palestine, *Eretz Israel,* Bibi wanted, not ritual. He wanted to remain a good son to David and Malvina, but the time came when he had to defy them openly.

In defying them he grew up. He knew the British had set harsh, if not cruel, quotas on Palestinian emigration. However, the Jewish Agency in Warsaw told him that students were exempted. He applied surreptitiously to the Faculty of Humanities at Hebrew University in Jerusalem and to the Technical Institute in Haifa. Soon, letters of acceptance arrived. He booked passage by train to Constanța, the Black Sea port in Rumania, and from there by steamer to Haifa. Everything was set for the inevitable confrontation with his mother, and yet none of the enrollments and reservations, virtually a *fait accompli* because they were difficult to change, made a difference. Telling his parents was painful. Strangely, David had known all along and did not seem surprised. He made Bibi promise to return in one year, but David was merely trying to make the emigration seem temporary and therefore less a defiance, less a loss. Malvina simply refused to speak to her son. When he talked to her, trying to make her understand, she pretended not to hear.

The summer before he departed, the summer of 1935 when the gypsy with her cards made the voyage seem as fate, he visited Podhorodse alone for the last time. Soon after, in the excitement

47

of his departure, Bibi forgot the gloomy predictions of the gypsy. And when he returned to Lwów from Podhorodse that last time, he had many friends to whom he wanted to say goodbye, because some small voice inside was telling him that he might never return here. Four days before the train was scheduled to depart, he started to make the rounds. On the last night he went to the house of the Dutchman, who greeted Bibi with a firm handshake and asked him inside. As he entered, Bibi thought how close he felt to this man, who could have been an older brother.

When they reached the den, the Dutchman asked, "How about something strong to drink, now that you're about to become a man of the world?"

"Thanks," Bibi replied, off balance. Nobody had ever offered him a drink before. He shook his head.

The Dutchman laughed. "I won't tell your father, if that's what worries you."

Bibi replied, "No thanks. I just prefer not to."

"How about a cigarette then?" And he raised a silver box from the table.

"Those neither," Bibi said, feeling prudish.

The Dutchman put down the box. "So, you're off to Palestine. Tell me, what on earth are you going to do there?"

Bibi found himself replying, "Study Hebrew, I guess. If I get a job, I'd like to work as a journalist." But he thought otherwise. He wanted an education all right, but not one from books at Hebrew University. He dreamed of soaking up sights and sounds—adventures. He hoped to visit bedouin Arabs about whom he had read, to explore the desert. . . .

"But you'll be coming back?" the Dutchman asked.

"In a year," Bibi answered, but he knew, if everything went as planned, in one year he would send for his brother, Marek. Together, they would earn the money for their parents' passage.

"Don't you think you are . . . well, making a bad decision? You should go to Asia. Asia's the place for a young man. Or stay here. You've got a start here in journalism. Why go where nobody knows you?"

Malvina had asked the same question.

His soft reply now was, "It doesn't matter." Then, "I'll miss you."

The Dutchman said, "It's a desert."

He does not understand, Bibi thought. The Dutchman had ventured so far from Holland; Bibi wanted him to know that his example had helped to shape him. Bibi was going far away to make his fortune in a world that was every bit as strange to him as Poland had been at first to the Dutchman. Among the many reasons Bibi had for leaving was the desire to acquire some of the polish and sophistication—the culture—of the Dutchman. He wanted the older man's blessing, and without asking, he wanted his advice. But the Dutchman did not seem to understand.

"Your parents are going to miss you," he said.

And Bibi thought, Of course they will, but he wanted to hear the Dutchman say that *he* would miss him.

"When I left my parents I was about your age; that's the way of things. I'm sure you'll come back, and we'll meet again," the Dutchman added.

Bibi rose from the chair to go. He wanted to say things that he did not dare; they were of his feelings for this man acquired over several years of watching, imitating, admiring. But he could not form the words.

The Dutchman said, "One thing I wish *my* father had told me when I was like you are now. I'll tell it to you. Always listen and obey the voice inside you, because," and he laughed, "if you don't and if you go against it, you'll go wrong."

Bibi did not think much then of what he said. Once more he told the Dutchman, "I'll miss you." He thought he would never see him again.

"Send me a postcard," he said, "from the Holy Land." And with that they parted.

The next morning, October 24, 1935, the Krumholzes and Pistiners drove by automobile to the beautiful, soaring glass structure of the Lwów railroad station. Bibi's train, bound for Rumania, puffed steam as the minutes before departure shortened. *Halutzim*—young pioneers—sang Hebrew songs, the "ghetto look" suddenly gone from their faces. Older *Halutzim* who were breaking with their pasts, leaving professions, status, and money for a new life of manual labor, were more businesslike and subdued.

Uncle Isaac, with tears in his eyes, hugged Bibi and said, "I hope to come one day for a visit. We will meet again, in Palestine." Isaac gave Bibi a box of *bonboniera* chocolates and a bottle of 4711 *eau de toilette* for use against seasickness and the third-class accommodations. Bibi shouldered his suitcase and quickly found his cabin and seat number. He lowered the window and hung out, overlooking the platform, as a long and summoning blast came from the engine, and the conductor at the rear of the train blew a whistle. The train moved off slowly. David, Malvina, and Marek stood frozen on the platform, as if posing for a memory. Malvina was very quiet; she did not wave. Her eyes were dry, and her face expressed neither anger nor love—only a cold acceptance. David wiped his eyes with a large white handkerchief brought along for the purpose, and Marek raced down the platform after the departing train, while the other Krumholzes and Pistiners watched until the last car was out of sight. Bibi looked back the length of the train and felt no sadness for leaving this place. If what lay ahead was unknown, *Eretz Israel* was better surely than what was known in Poland. He no longer had to run, *ever*.

To Bibi, the *Polonia* combined the majesty of the *Queen Mary* with the grandeur of the *Lusitania*. At his first sight of her, she was rocking against the dock in the swells of the Black Sea port of Constanţa. In reality a miserable hulk, the *Polonia* would have been retired but for the upsurge in demand for the transport of émigrés to Palestine, and she seemed almost to protest by noisily slapping the pier to which she was chained. Aboard and under way, ship and passengers settled, at first uneasily, into a relationship of necessity. The *Polonia* had three passenger classes, each with different "kosher commissioners" and menus. Third class was totally kosher; first and second class offered a wider choice of foods. Most of the 800 passengers on the four-day journey, like Bibi, traveled third, packed four to six to a cabin, content to be aboard, if not altogether comfortable. Among the *Halutzim*—but separate from them—were so-called tourists, German Jewish professionals who wanted to explore Palestine as a possible refuge if events should suddenly worsen for the Jews under Hitler. The *Halutzim* called them the "January Zionists"—Jews who had discovered Zionism the month Hitler came to power.

On sighting the wide horseshoe port at Haifa with its smooth white beaches set against the high green hills of Mount Carmel, Bibi felt apprehension. Although his emigration papers were stamped and signed, and all was in perfect order, he was entering a land that did not want him. The British had almost closed their protectorate to Jews by severely prohibiting entry to the moneyless and unskilled; unlike students, other Jews had to show emigration officers £1,000 in British sterling before being allowed to enter. In 1935, Bibi was among only 62,000 Jewish émigrés, and as he approached the customs barrier, he watched as the same roll of bills, tied with a rubber band, was passed back in line again and again to deceive the official into believing that even the poorest passengers had the sum required for entry. Haim Landau stood beside Bibi. A cabinmate during the voyage, Landau had shown Bibi a revolver he planned to smuggle in. Ahead in line an Arab policeman inspected luggage, and Landau nervously asked Bibi what to do. "I already told you that you should have thrown it overboard," Bibi replied, frozen in place. The policemen passed without a glance, and the gun eventually was used for IZL (Irgun Zvai Leumi), the Zionist terrorist organization in which Landau later distinguished himself.

Bibi expected to find opportunity right there in Haifa. Britain was making great strides in developing the port, its "Gateway to India," to accommodate increased traffic between the Persian Gulf and the Mediterranean. The port had massive stone piers to which Shell tankers were tied, and was the last link in the British oil pipeline that originated in the Mosul fields of Iraq. Farther inland, furnace chimneys of cement factories emitted smoke high in the sky to pronounce the health of the construction trades.

Bibi set down his suitcase and dug into his pockets. He counted out four pounds sterling and change, the sum of his assets. He smiled because he had never felt quite this rich before. Here he could have anything if he was willing to work; nobody could tell him no. That itself was real wealth. He smelled the air and

51

thought he detected the unique dry scent of the desert that he had often read about. His imagination started to soar, and for a few moments, he saw himself standing on that same pier awaiting the arrival of his parents and Marek. It would happen, one day, he said to himself.

He took a taxi to a restaurant in Haifa habituated by Lwowians. The restaurant's owner helped him find a vacant bed in a rooming house. The next day Bibi landed a laborer's job, not exactly the work he sought, but with his strapping, twenty-two-year-old physique and such boundless energy, knee-deep in the water of the port he hauled seventy-five-pound concrete blocks with relative ease. Soon he shifted to other construction jobs in Haifa and the hills above the city. The work, six days a week, was hard, exhausting, and in winter, cold.

After a few months and some savings, Bibi wandered on foot first south toward the Sinai, passing through Tel Aviv, the Jewish city par excellence, a new town of immigrants like himself who on the day of his arrival were celebrating Purim, the Jews' deliverance centuries past from the persecutions of the Persian Haman. Walking the streets, he saw people dancing the hora under Purim arches; banners and garlands of flowers festooned shopfronts and streetlights. Everybody was happy, even carefree, completely different from the dour, downcast faces of Jews in Poland.

There was a parade down the wide, tree-lined Allenby Avenue, near the water. Illustrating the theme that year—"Jewry of the World, Past, Present, and Future"—floats represented Zealots as warriors at Masada, the persecution of Jews in Poland, and the assimilation of Jews in France, in which people on that float danced in money underneath a banner that read, "We are not Jews at all." A green, three-headed dragon, its body a welt of swastikas, snaked down Allenby to the steady, insistent beat of drums. The future showed bounty and peace in Palestine, but Bibi, watching from the sidewalk, feared that the Nazi dragon, not Palestinian bounty, represented their future. His mind told him no, it was not true, but his instincts ruled his logic.

On April 19, 1936, six months after he arrived in Haifa, the Arab revolt began. He heard and saw the effect—gunfire and death. At first the cause bewildered him, but then he came to understand that events in Palestine paralleled events in Europe, with nearly the same disastrous effects. The British appeased the Palestinian Arabs to avoid their alliance with the Axis that threatened the Anglo-French position in the Mediterranean. The pro-fascist Mufti Haj Amin el-Husseini had created the Arab Higher Committee in April 1936 to coordinate the campaign of armed attacks on Jewish settlements. Communications lines were cut and crops were burned. But the Jews of Yishuv, the cooperative farms on which most Jewish émigrés worked, did not fight back for fear of upsetting the quixotic British; Jewish leaders adopted a policy of *Havlagah* ("restraint"), denying the British any excuse to further delay the Balfour Declaration.

As long as Jews were the victims, the British did not show undue concern, but when the Arabs stepped up their campaign, attacking the British forces, their attitude changed. Their troops suffered grievous losses against the Arabs' guerrilla tactics, but the War Office in London would not send reinforcements. Confused and frustrated, Whitehall fell back on expediency, handing the defense of Palestine to the Jews, under British supervision of course. From headquarters in Jerusalem, they supplied the Haganah, the once outlawed Jewish Underground military organization. British Captain Orde Wingate, a passionate Zionist, opened a camp to train a supernumerary Jewish police of kibbutzniks and former students from Hebrew University. The minute he heard, Bibi signed up.

Whether or not he knew it then, the police eliminated a potentially serious obstacle to Bibi's happiness in Palestine. He was not equipped for the psychological burdens of the Yishuv, at least at first. Watering date palms, picking citrus, and draining malarial swamps of the Galilee did not suit Bibi's self-image. Journalism called to him, but first he needed to contribute to a homeland and not alone, selfishly, to his own career. He needed to do something actually productive, as Jabotinsky and perhaps even his other hero, the Dutchman, would have wished, not just write about how other Jews risked their lives and in other less perilous ways contributed to Jewish Palestine. He recognized the conflict, that journalism did not *create* enough. The time would come for that, but it was not now.

More than the Galilee of the Yishuv, the city of Jerusalem suited his hunger for romance; exoticism, history, and adventure paved the Old City's narrow cobbled streets. The sounds and smells intoxicated him, but here too Bibi saw a battleground that mirrored the conflict dawning in Europe. The Arabs were no different from their Nazi allies in their hostility toward the Jews; Mufti Haj Amin el-Husseini nurtured the same hatreds as Hitler. A powerful radio transmitter at Bari beamed Nazi propaganda into the Levant day and night: Zionism was charged with being an instrument of British and French imperialism. Red-and-black swastikas and bold, heroic photographs of Hitler and Mussolini appeared everywhere in the German Quarter. By fighting Arab terror with Jewish force in Jerusalem, Bibi hoped to set an example for Jews to follow against the fascism in Poland.

His mind never strayed far from Europe. And he tried to remove his family from the war that he now knew was unavoidable. First he applied to the Jewish Agency, then he wrote to the chief of police in Jerusalem, "Look here, I have a brother nine years younger than me. I want to bring him here. Can you help me in getting him an entry visa?" The plan had not changed from the day he left Lwów. Only its execution was now more urgent. David was not rich, and he could not function in Palestine as a laborer; a shop or small business made the most sense, but where would the money come from? With his brother, Marek, in Palestine, Bibi thought, they could work hard together and in a few years David and Malvina could join them. Time now, as well as money, was the measure. His plan was to remove them from the Nazi threat; the situation in Poland was bad and getting worse. Jews were losing everything, *starting* with their freedom.

Nearly every week Bibi received a letter. He no longer wondered why Malvina did not write. She was recovering from a heart seizure that Bibi had "caused" by leaving Lwów, and she was not yet prepared to forgive him, but David wrote often, mostly about everyday affairs. Marek excelled in mathematics, Bibi learned, and also had an aptitude for engineering. Once, Marek sent Bibi a balsam-wood model airplane. What he wanted, Marek said, was to live in Palestine and fly fighters. One day as Bibi wandered through the Old City, a place that he haunted, he stopped at a tourist stand. He saw a postcard of the Church of the Holy Sepulchre which reminded him of a promise that he now kept. He wrote a few words of greeting; what he really was saying was that he remembered the Dutchman's tales of travels as a younger man, from Amsterdam to Danzig, then to Warsaw and Cracow and Lwów. That had been *nothing* compared with his itinerary, Bibi thought.

Even now, so soon after arriving in Palestine, Bibi reflected a new, powerful self-confidence. Thin and muscular from construction work and the days on the road, his ginger hair had turned blond, and his skin was tanned and freckled from the Jerusalem sun. With a blond mustache and lively blue eyes, Bibi looked more English in most respects than the English. He was all spit-and-polish and toy-soldier rigid in his standard British-issue police uniform, the starched khaki shirt with epaulettes and braid, the pleated shorts, knee socks, and chukka boots. As a non-British policeman, he wore a calpac, a triangular felt cap with a silver crown sewn in the peak. The calpac showed other Jews that he was working *with* and not *for* the British against the Arabs, at a moment in history when a Jew in Palestine had to balance his hatred of Arabs against his hatred of the British. Bibi called his superiors "Mister," and they called him "sixteen oh three," the number of his badge. The British meant well, Bibi supposed, but their policies baffled him. In the Old City Police Station where he worked they had segregated toilets, one for the British and the other for "Palestinians"—Jews and Arabs. Once Bibi had the temerity to use the British lavatory. A Yorkshire sergeant major roared at him, "Why did you use this?"

Bibi answered defiantly, "Because I had to go."

He saved his anger for the Nazis. Mischievously, choosing a detachment of four German Jews, policemen who had once been interned in German concentration camps, he guarded the German Consulate in Jerusalem. Marching in formation down Bethlehem Road to the German Colony and finally the walled consulate, above which swastikas flew, they were met by a stony silence. But news spread that Bibi Krumholz and his Jewish police were *protecting* the German Consulate, a sight many Jews in Jerusalem wanted to see. Bibi rang the consulate bell, and an Arab retainer answered.

55

"I've come to watch the place so Jews won't do something bad," Bibi said.

"Should I open the door?" the Arab asked.

"Of course," Bibi replied. And soon the German consul appeared, wearing a bathrobe. Bibi said, "Good evening," then explained his orders.

"Do you want to enter our private apartments?" the consul asked. Bibi told him no, he could go to bed and sleep safely.

The consul took his hands out of his bathrobe pockets. "Do me a favor," he said, "go away, please. I don't need a guard. Thank your commander, but I don't need anybody, really. I will get this straightened out tomorrow."

Orders were orders, Bibi told him.

The detachment stood guard by the front gate as hundreds of Jews, who had gathered together by now, applauded. The laughter rebounded off the walls of the consulate like stones. Later, Bibi's superior officer said to him, "You have made the consul crazy. He just telephoned the High Commissioner. It is just like Mayor La Guardia." (Months before, New York Mayor Fiorello La Guardia had sent a detachment of Jewish police to guard the rooms of visiting Nazis who had ordered the Waldorf-Astoria Hotel to fly the swastika over Park Avenue. When he heard what La Guardia had done, Hitler in reprisal posted black Nazis outside the American Embassy in Berlin.)

After that, the British officers called Bibi "sixteen oh three" with a new respect, and from then on his popularity was never in doubt. Everyone, even Arabs, found him easy to know and easier to like, including the Jerusalem girls. But they were warned: Bibi had no intention of marrying until his dream of a journalistic career was fulfilled and his family was safely settled with him. But Bibi did not know how love often confounds the most careful plans, as it did one day to him in the Rehavia Garden.

The German Colony police station patrolled Rehavia, too, the most elegant quarter of Jerusalem. The gardens there were a relief to Bibi from the Nazism of the German Colony, and he went often, thinking that this was where he wanted to live some day, among university professors and successful Jewish merchants. One Saturday his partner and friend, Sallah Mohammed Sallah,

Badge Number 231, an older Palestinian from whom Bibi learned Arabic, joined him on a park bench there. Bibi took off the calpac and Sam Browne belt and holster and as they were watching the girls go by, Bibi noticed a tall, pretty one with a full face and tortoise-shell glasses pushing a child in a carriage. But she did not look at him or at Sallah. And maybe because of that she intrigued Bibi, who hoped to see the girl again. One night soon after, Bibi saw her seated in a coffee house along a banquette with other students. Bibi tried to make himself obvious by standing nearby and taking off his new bright blue jacket. She did not look at him. That caused his interest to wax, with frustration strengthening his resolve. He contrived to befriend students through whom to make contact with this maddening girl. Weeks passed and he had nearly forgotten her when he met her at a party; this time she *looked* at him—with some interest he thought. Later that night he asked to walk her home. Mala Majzlic agreed.

It was a spring evening, neither too cold nor too warm, and on that walk, Bibi had never felt so happy. Mala, he learned, had emigrated from a small town near Warsaw in 1934 to study at Hebrew University. She had no intention of returning to her family in Poland. Her future was in Palestine, she said with a fervor that impressed Bibi. She knew what she wanted, and she was sensible in her ambitions. For the first time the thought of settling down crossed his mind. He walked Mala back to her rooming house, and before he said good night, he asked her for a date.

Their courtship continued and their happiness together deepened. Bibi was in love and undecided; Mala was just in love. She introduced Bibi to one of her sisters, who had recently arrived from Poland. Mala told her, "Look here, something has happened between Bibi and me." Before her sister could speak, Mala said, "Don't be upset. Everything has happened, but *nothing* has happened." All the same, Mala's sister immediately suggested marriage, which Bibi was by now ready to accept. Soon after, they married in secret, because of rules against marriage for the Hadassah nurses. When strangers asked why they roomed together, they answered that sharing was an economic necessity between "cousins."

The normal course of their marriage was altered in more serious ways soon after by the Nazi invasion of Poland. They knew no more than what they had heard on the BBC World Service or read in the Palestine *Post:* that the Western Allies in September 1939 had backed Poland with hollow words. Totally abandoned, outgunned, and outmaneuvered, 60,000 Poles died as the Wehrmacht rolled east to demarcation lines along the Bug and San rivers. In keeping with Stalin's "hyena principle" and the secret Russian-German protocol, the Red Army had occupied Lwów, and the two conquerors of Poland—the Nazis in the south and west and the Soviets in the east—started to collect their spoils. David had written in one of his last letters: "Please pray God that the Germans do not invade Lwów. If they do they will kill all the Jews, and we shall be among them."

Immediately, Bibi made the rounds of agencies in Jerusalem, first the Red Cross and then the Vatican. He took as a particularly bad omen the total absence of Jewish refugees from Lwów. He gave the Red Cross the address of his parents and brother in Lwów in the hope that it had heard some news. The British volunteers took down the information and sent it off. Nearly sick with concern, Mala, with seven sisters and parents near Warsaw, told Bibi that she was returning to Poland to rescue her family.

"Is that wise?" Bibi asked.

"What else is there to do?" she replied, and he could see her frustration. The agencies were so slow and awkward, but for all the force of logic, he did not want her going there.

"You can give it a little time, for me," he said.

Mala did not mention the plan to him again, at least not directly. She sometimes referred to "going next year," but the immediacy of the need had disappeared from her words, if not from her thoughts. All of these tensions, however, served to move Bibi to act. If he and Mala could not join their families, he thought, at least he could do something more than continue life as normal. He decided to become one of 35,000 Palestinian Jews who had already joined the British Forces fighting the Nazis. Mala argued against this decision, just as he had argued with her. He was already doing his share for the war effort as a policeman, she said.

"No," Bibi said to her, "because I am not killing Nazis." He decided to fight, and nothing that Mala said would change his mind. But first he had to be released from the police. His commandant, a British captain, wished him well in the Army. "Will you give me something in writing?" Bibi asked him before leaving his office, as he did not want to be charged with desertion.

His commandant waved him off. "It's all right. Say that I gave you permission."

Bibi went to the British Army recruiting station in the King David Hotel. The officer on duty signed him up for a two-month officers' course. "Will you tell the police?" Bibi asked.

"I will take care of it," he assured him.

But Bibi still had nothing in writing, a small thing compared with the war. At the training camp, the quartermaster issued him a rifle, uniform, and bedding. No sooner had he settled in than the officer in charge said to him, "The police are after you for deserting them." Bibi tried to explain, but the officer said, "The Inspector General told us to arrest you." Bibi returned his rifle, uniform, and bedding. An officer drove him to Jerusalem, where he was locked in a cell. His commandant in the police said to him, "Nobody leaves the police. I didn't know that. But nobody leaves the police." Soon Bibi returned to Mala, his calpac, and his small patch of the war, the German Colony.

Eight months later, when he still had heard nothing from their relatives, Bibi decided that if he could not fight in the Army, he could at least see for himself the preparations of the Allies. If they were ready in North Africa, he reasoned, that might indicate how prepared they were to defeat the Germans in Poland. He took leave from his new post at the abattoir and went by bus to Cairo, the Allied military base for operations in North Africa. United Kingdom and Commonwealth soldiers on their last leaves roamed the narrow back streets. Bibi visited the Sphinx, the tombs, the museums, and the Nile, and he returned to Jerusalem with fear: Cairo would fall, he thought, and Jerusalem would become Field Marshal Rommel's next military objective. The Mufti in Berlin already had announced plans to build extermination camps for Jews in the Dotan Valley, Samaria, in Palestine. Lending substance to his fears, the Haganah actually created the Masada Organization for the final defense against the Nazis, with plans for men, women, and children to assemble in the caves of Mount

59

Carmel from which to fight to the death. Irgun planned to capture the Old City of Jerusalem with a couple of thousand Jews, killing the Arabs first, then themselves. The British confirmed already desperate fears with schemes for a hasty evacuation. The High Commissioner offered the Jewish Agency two DC-3s in which to evacuate "whomever they wanted," if Jerusalem were overrun.

Now, every morning when Bibi walked to the Ramallah Road abattoir, he started to dread what lay ahead, but no longer because the sights, sounds, and smells of the place disgusted him. There were, in the atmosphere of the abattoir, strong reminders of the events that he feared were happening in Europe.

CHAPTER III

❈

"... truly, this was greatness."

IN 1911, A HORSEDRAWN phaeton followed the Stadhouderskade
in Amsterdam until the Singelgracht Bridge, where the driver
abruptly reined the two bays right. Once across the road the black
carriage halted in the gravel forecourt of an elegant Renaissance
building. The carriage door opened, and a boy got out alone, saying something, perhaps instructive, to the driver. The boy entered
the high portal of the building's northwest tower, and without a
second's hesitation he climbed the broad stairway. He wore a
dark-blue woolen suit, polished shoes, and a blue woolen cap that
covered a head of light-brown hair. Nobody seemed to notice as
he passed through a large room where guests observed in reverent
silence two great Dutch national treasures displayed on the wall,
"The Night Watch" and "The Staalmeesters" by Rembrandt Har-
mensz van Rijn. Those pictures were "celebrities," but ignoring
these, the boy marched up a ramp into a small side room; he had
studied the Rembrandts along with the other seventeenth-century
Dutch masters, on earlier visits to the Rijksmuseum. Now, he
gazed on the haunting "Young Woman Reading a Letter" by Johannes Vermeer, the object of this visit. After a few minutes with
his arms folded and his eyes straight ahead—an enigma as deep as
the woman in the Vermeer—the boy, Pieter Nicholas, departed
by the same route.

Pieter Nicholas came from the branch of the Menten family that
death and remarriage had shunted aside. However, the relative
difference in affluence and influence mattered only to Menten fam-

61

ily members, most of all to the boy in the Rijksmuseum. "Poor relations," as the direct Menten line called Pieter Menten's branch, had little meaning, such was the shared wealth, starting with the old man of the family, Pieter Franciscus, who had been a cereal merchant from the Catholic south of Holland, near Eurmonk. His business had been "getting by" until one hard winter in the 1840s when the Rotterdam harbor froze solid . . . and stayed frozen for week after week. Just by chance the old man's ships in port were laden with grain. He covered them until one day he sensed a shift in the weather and ordered, "Sell," at that moment when supply was lowest and demand greatest. With that windfall Pieter Franciscus produced margarine, and for a time he was called "The Butter King of Rotterdam." Later he joined with his fellow Dutchman van den Bergh, who merged the company, Margarine Unie, in 1929 with the English Lever brothers to form Unilever, since then the largest food processor on earth.

The death of his wife left Pieter Franciscus a widower in early middle age with one son, Jan Pieter, who in time became the father of the boy Pieter Nicholas Menten. The widower later married a woman who bore him two more sons: Ernest became the Catholic bishop of Maastricht, and Jacob Hubertus, born in 1832 in Roermond, sought his fortune with the Dutch East Indies Company as a prospecting engineer, a fortune that he did not find then. While still in his forties, Jacob Hubertus was retired to Holland on the company principle that one year of tropical service counted toward two years of retirement. Too young for real retirement and homesick for the tropics (he had converted to Buddhism), he returned to Borneo as a private prospector. Again, he went with pick and shovel from island to island of the archipelago until one day in the 1880s in Balik Papua, a region of southern Borneo, he found whole outcrops of coal above the ground that oozed up oil. Soon, Chinese coolies hauled a drilling rig through dense, virgin jungle. The tungsten drill dug down less than a hundred feet to tap a rich reservoir of high-grade oil that soon would light the lamps of Shanghai and Peking and fill Menten's coffers. Jacob called his company Batavian Petroleum, and his story became a Dutch legend, the stuff of schoolboys' dreams. For one very competitive Dutch boy, Pieter Nicholas Menten, the oil strike set a standard of success.

By the 1890s, Jacob really wanted to retire, and he sought out a buyer nearby Balik Papua on the Sumatra archipelago, where other Dutchmen operated an oil company that had warranted a charter, Royal Dutch Petroleum, bequeathed in 1890 by Queen Wilhelmina. Hugo Loudon, a merchant, and Henry Deterding, a bookkeeper, had started Royal Dutch out of Singapore. Jacob offered them Batavian, but Deterding, a maniacal genius, refused. Unruffled, he turned to Deterding's rival in the Pacific, Marcus Samuel, a Jew from London's tough East End. His British company, Shell Transport and Trading, originally a shipper of seashells for macadam, in 1873 had started in oil by hauling Russian crude for a syndicate of the Swedish Nobel brothers and the French Rothschilds. In 1893, after Samuel had helped to break the monopolistic stranglehold of J. D. Rockefeller's Standard Oil through innovations in transport (he designed special tankers to carry Russian and Asian crude through the Suez Canal to European markets economically for the first time), he acquired his own drilling leases. Among the first he bought were Jacob Menten's on Balik Papua for royalties in 1895. Nine years later, Samuel joined Deterding in partnership to form the Anglo-Dutch Royal Dutch Shell, the second largest corporation on earth, with Menten's Balik Papua as its original drilling site.

While Jacob was exploring the far reaches of the Pacific, his older half brother, Jan Pieter, prospered through the trading company Menten & Stark, N.V., back home in Amsterdam at the fashionable address at Keizersgracht #540. The Jewish *szmarciarze* ("ragpickers") of the Jordaan District, along the Willemstraat and Goudsbloemdwarsstraat, had for centuries collected rags and old newspapers house to house and resold them. But cleverly, Jan Pieter had discovered his own "Balik Papua"—an export market in Eastern Europe through the German "port of the future" at Danzig, where buyers were willing to pay more for the rags as components of paper. As Menten & Stark prospered—and it was indeed a success, although nothing to compare to Jacob's oil bonanza—Jan Pieter and his wife, Elizabeth Johanna van Duivenbode, the daughter of a shipowner, seed merchant, and Lloyds broker, raised their two sons as princelings in a "royal" Dutch trading family.

Young Pieter Nicholas Menten, born May 26, 1899, was never, from his earliest days, a stranger to privilege. Yet, despite the riches—the family mansion in *the* Amsterdam suburb of Hilversum, private carriages, special trips to the zoo and the museums— the family frowned on ostentation according to the unbending rule of Dutch social behavior. Young Pieter wore black and dark-blue suits and black shoes, nothing ever of color or plumage or individuality. And the lessons he learned were every bit as severe. He was drilled in a harsh code: money has one purpose, to make more money; neither inheritance nor inheritor ever should lay idle; a Menten is an entrepreneur, an entrepreneur goes where no businessman has gone before, a Menten risks more and reaps more; nothing is permanent; collect beauty but, first, know its value; emotion never stands between a Menten and profit; repay a bad turn before a good turn, never forget. . . .

In those years Pieter occupied a lonesome and difficult half world from which he wanted to escape. Because of the savage belittling by his half cousins—Emile, Otto, and Hubert, the sons of Jacob the oilman—Pieter felt that to be half of something was to be almost nothing. *Real* Mentens, like his half cousins, did not have to prove themselves. Their father "founded" Royal Dutch Shell and their full uncle was a bishop in the Catholic Church. What was his father but a rag merchant? He had made a fortune, but the families never let them forget that the seed capital had come in part from Jacob the oilman. They *were* the poor cousins, no matter how rich.

More and more with each year, Pieter demonstrated the power of his need to fill up that empty half of himself with achievement, but not with just any success. His father exemplified *any* success. Pieter had to compete on terms that the "rich" side of the Menten family revered. In constantly trying to excel he was depressive and uncertain, always standing on his tiptoes to grasp something just out of his reach. Wanting—needing—to transport himself from this reality to almost any other, Pieter paced the floors of the Rijksmuseum, studying the objects on the walls, the Master of

Spes Nostra's "Allegory on the Vanity of Human Life." (The corpse in the painting warned, "If you should pass here, look on and weep. I am what you will be, and what you are I have been.") He wondered at the color in Hendrick Avercamp's "Large Winter Scene" and the life in Franz Hals's "The Merry Toper." He studied Rembrandt's "Jeremiah Lamenting the Destruction of Jerusalem," "The Night Watch," "The Holy Family," "The Staalmeesters," and "The Jewish Bride."

From early in his youth an appreciation and understanding of art had set him apart, but certainly not because of any ambition to paint. He asserted himself through a knowledge of art as his "signature." When he discussed its history, his elders were impressed with his knowledge of so rarefied a subject. And art taught him about religion, geography, history, and commerce. He quickly realized how art represented wealth and status, even culture, in people's minds. Generally, great men owned great collections. *Sir* Henry Deterding, the genius of Royal Dutch Shell, who had started as a lowly accountant in Singapore, had donated Vermeer's "The Little Street" to the Rijksmuseum. Nobody spoke separately of great art and great men. In Holland especially, a trading nation, the great merchants had always endowed artists, who recorded their achievements on canvas. Pieter learned to define greatness in people as wealth and power. Culture per se was less relevant to his thinking. With wealth he could acquire great art, which would convince people of his cultivation as part of his power and his mystique.

First, on his own behalf, he wanted to acquire wealth, and later he would pursue the art. After the Great War, while still a teenager, Pieter went to represent his father's trading company in the newly reconstituted state of Free Poland. He sought a commodity to barter for Menten & Stark's rags. From the moment he arrived in the port at Danzig, where he established himself, he started to warrant his father's trust through his acumen and ruthless trading. Here, he felt free of constraints: he could do anything, be anybody—nobody knew him. And he flourished. Poland's abundant supplies of sulfur, wood, and labor caught his interest. He juggled this combination for a commodity with a dependable market in Holland. By his twenty-first birthday he was a self-made millionaire from ProtoLucifers—wooden matches. And now, he sought to explore newer horizons where more reputable wealth was found. To him "reputable" meant oil, and when he thought of oil, he thought of only one man, who now needed his help.

As the managing partner of Royal Dutch Shell, Sir Henry Deterding's colossal power alone matched his fury in the dying months of 1917. The hated Bolsheviks had ordered the Red Army to seize his oilfields in the Ukraine. Unless he acted, they threatened to flood the world markets with *his* Ukrainian crude, destabilize prices, and break the cartel of Western oil producers among whom he was preeminent. If that happened, Shell would be humiliated, if not ruined. He met power with force, but the Bolsheviks flatly ignored the mounting military and diplomatic threats of the Dutch Foreign Ministry. (Such were the power and wealth of Shell that Dutch politicians believed that what was good for Holland was good for Shell.) When those diplomatic measures failed, Sir Henry employed the Amsterdam banker Fritz Mannheimer of Mendelssohn and Co. to finance a counterrevolution to overthrow the Bolsheviks in the Ukraine and return his oilfields to him. Soon after, Pieter Menten headed toward Lwów with 1.5 million guilders in credit from Mendelssohn and Co.

However, before he reached Lwów, upon the death of his father, Menten sold off the properties owned by Menten & Stark in Danzig to the Danish firm of Langelandskøren, which later called him "a swindler of great allure" when he defrauded them in the sale. En route to Lwów he rented an office in Warsaw at Przyjazd Street #5, an address from which a Polish court ordered him to compensate the Danes with the minor sum of 5,000 zlotys. The experience soured him on Warsaw; besides, the capital city was too large and cosmopolitan for what he had in mind; its people were too wary and in a certain manner too knowledgeable for his charade.

He started off when he reached Lwów by calling himself Pieter *von* Menten, suggesting German royal heritage. The sign "Menten & Stark, purchase and sale of lubricants, metals, colonial products" appeared over the door of new offices at Batorego Street #34. With *objets d'art* brought from Amsterdam, he furnished a newly rented apartment at Piaskowa Street #15, an address with cachet. Young, intelligent, rich, and recently arrived from urbane Amsterdam in this boom town on the edge of nowhere, Menten was soon a beacon who drew a daring variety of people for that stratified society—lawyers, officers in the Polish Army, doctors, politicians, artists, newspaper editors; even the beauty queen Miss Poland, Sophia Batycha, joined his entourage.

With a single-mindedness that often offended, he sought access to people with information. Once, early on, he did not wait for an invitation to visit a powerful Lwów publisher who lived nearby. He saw a light in the salon and simply "popped in," much to the publisher's consternation. He even arrived uninvited at the fourteenth birthday party for that publisher's daughter. When such boldness failed him, he held out the promise of liquor and excellent imported food, and the opportunity to meet women with Miss Poland's allure and beauty. He tried hardest with the intelligentsia, in a society where that class had real importance. Their status derived, as the term implies, from intelligence, which seemed to fail them when Menten called. While pretending to only tolerate his presence, they eagerly accepted invitations, and in return they invited him to their homes, using him as he used them.

In these endeavors, Elizabeth van Haag-Menten helped her husband achieve a certain celebrity. They had married in Amsterdam the year that Menten had made his first fortune in matchsticks and knew that he did not want to live ever again in Holland, where the rules were too rigid. As a former mannequin, she felt the same. With black hair, moist, limpid eyes, and tall, imposing bearing, Elizabeth was at first distant and cool with the new people she met in Lwów through Pieter, as if she thought she were too good for them, or she was too shy. They commented on her mystery.

Elizabeth had been raised with the expectations that solidly middle-class Dutch families had for daughters. After a brief education, they expected her to marry young, raise a large family, and cater to the whims of an industrious husband. But Elizabeth did not follow that pattern. Her exceptional beauty propelled her into a different and very confusing orbit. At seventeen she accepted an offer to model for an Amsterdam couturier; she flaunted herself before the admiring eyes of the carriage trade, which sought out her friendship as if it were a commodity to make them seem more attractive. She understood the limitations, but she wanted acceptance, too. In Pieter Menten she recognized many of her same ambitions. She wanted out of a society in which there was no upward mobility and almost no tolerance. He had rebelled and so had she, and together in Lwów they made people think that they were who they wanted to be.

They had to be honest only with themselves, and while that was an increasingly difficult practice for Pieter, it was an increasingly necessary one for Elizabeth. Dr. Garbien, gynecologist and brother of Albin, the star soccer forward for Pogon, had examined Elizabeth, and there was no doubt that she could not have children—a tragedy beyond words. She described her infertility as an "affliction," an incurable disease.

The concoction of her beauty now had no practical function, if she could not have children. The men in Lwów—particularly the Polish Army officers—flattered her, and she flirted back, as if by proving her attractiveness she could *dis*prove her infertility. Her husband made her desperate with his seductions—often openly—of other women, as if to confirm his own adequacy. She blamed herself, trying to please him by her grace as a hostess. Guests at their house loved her company. Her attentions transported men, lending them a share of the power that attends such beauty. During the day, Elizabeth talked with the other wives about the usual banalities—running a house, cooking, and husbands—but rarely about children. The other women called her a "hausfrau," and they saw how she looked with almost suffocating hatred whenever a child entered the room. The women said that she felt close only to children who were crippled and deformed.

Not long after she had learned of her infertility, Elizabeth began to compete against her husband's philandering with her own extramarital affairs. Her devotion to him was thwarted. Sometimes, to get Pieter's attention, she smashed valuable porcelain art objects on the floor, and she often raged at him without warning. She bought two white poodles on which to lavish her maternal instincts. She dressed flamboyantly in jodhpurs on the *corso* in days when women wore only dresses in public places. A platinum bracelet shaped like a serpent, with its ruby eyes fixed on the bluish veins of her hand, entwined her lower arm. Around her neck she wore a bean-sized chipped pearl. People saw in her eyes how she felt she had failed; they lost more and more of their light each year.

For all their social iconoclasm the Mentens observed strict lines of one caste system in particular. Pieter especially, because he circulated more widely in business, kept Jewish contacts separate and secret no matter what. If not the attitude, the practice was new to him. Despite discrimination against Jews in Holland, Jews and Gentiles had always cooperated there, and a certain harmony prevailed. Menten's family had established profitable ties in business with Jews: his grandfather with van den Bergh of Margarine Unie, his father with the *szmarciarze* in the Jordaan, and Jacob Menten with Sir Marcus Samuel. Indeed, the acquaintance of Jews in Lwów made Menten feel somehow at home. The intelligentsia could be condescending toward him for not having a university education; to them, business was crass. But to the Jews profit inspired respect and admiration. But all that said, Menten reserved one door for the intelligentsia; another for the Ukrainian rebels of the OUN (Organization of Ukrainian Nationalists), whose revolution he was financing; and a third door for Jews, like Isaac Pistiner.

Menten and Pistiner had met over plates of gefilte fish at Backo's. Curiosity had drawn them together. Good and bad, their reputations had preceded them. Pieter Menten especially seemed aware that Isaac wanted to "examine" his credentials—where he had come from, why he was in Lwów, what businesses he owned, how rich he was, what his plans were, how smart he was. Sensing the drift, Menten addressed certain rumors. Yes, he told Isaac, he had sold the Danzig properties of Menten & Stark to a Danish firm, knowing that the League of Nations planned to move the port facilities from Danzig to Gdynia. If the Danes wanted worthless property, he could not stop them, and besides, he had not felt duty-bound to tell prospective buyers what he knew. Isaac understood.

Later, they talked more business in the restaurant of the Krakowski Hotel and the Roma Café. Isaac mentioned the idea to

Menten of a company he wanted to form and call Mazaga. Menten saw an opportunity in the plan and took a share that paid an unexpected dividend of friendship. Soon, Menten visited Isaac's apartment, where they met with Jewish managers, salesmen, and senior German engineers for the new company. Long after the managers and Germans had disappeared, Menten was still there. They were all dancing. And when the music stopped, Pieter and Elizabeth were enjoying ten palmy days at Isaac's summer estate in Podhorodse-Sopot.

In many important ways, Isaac and Menten were similar. In Isaac the drive for acceptance as a person seemed to fuel his ambition as a man, husband, and father. Like Menten, he did not pursue wealth only for its material rewards—the soft fabric of his suits, the fur trim on his coats, the supple leather of his shoes, the luxurious furnishings of his Lwów home, and the vastness of his estates in Podhorodse. He intended these things to earn him a more valuable dividend—acceptance in a world of men who hated him, or worse, ignored him, for being a Jew, an abomination in the eyes of some Poles, a "killer of Christ."

Undeniably, Isaac was a Jew, not a proud Jew, but a Jew who went to synagogue on the Sabbath and wore a yarmulke, a Jew in his humor, his feeling, his attitudes, his soul—but also a Jew who desperately wanted to be known as a "Pole of the Mosaic faith," a Pole by nationality and a Jew by religion. Reasonably, it would have seemed, Isaac asked why Poland could not imitate the successful German experiment in which Jews, spearheading a new secularization, had won wealth, power, Nobel Prizes, and professorships in great centers of learning.

Isaac tried to force attitudes to change. For a while he tried flashy vests and displayed a lavish manner to make the Gentile Poles notice him so that he might become less invisible among them. He sustained this effort also because his children profited, and that much certainly was true. Isaac saw how they enjoyed more freedom of opportunity, movement, thought, education, and profession than in any previous generation of Polish Jews. "You're missing a chance I never had," he yelled at his daughter, Mara, when she brought home report cards with average grades. In the family his wife, Frieda, alone represented tradition. An immutable element for the solid values she expressed, Frieda was a Jew and that was that. Anything else—the notion particularly that a Polish Jew should call himself of the Mosaic faith—was folly. Her pride rubbed against the increasingly exposed nerve of Isaac's desire to disguise what he was. He showed anybody his land in Podhorodse as a sign of his own secular progress: the new laws of Free Poland had upheld the right for Jews to own land. Poland even encouraged Jews to participate equally. Without that, the purchase of such a capital asset made no sense. But even now, a Jew had to suspend belief a bit. Ownership required cooperation with local bureaucrats, peasants, and the neighboring gentry— anti-Semites almost to the man. But Isaac believed too well. He imitated the aristocrats; on his estate and in the village he tried to better them in the way he dressed; he spoke as they did, cursed their curses. But in their eyes he did not pass for anything but what he was, a middle-aged Jew with a small goatee waxed to a Mephistophelean point.

The Podhorodse estate had once been a small parcel of the Lubomirski family's 1,071 holdings that encompassed eighty-nine villages and eight whole *towns*. Lubomirski had sold the acres in Sopot and Podhorodse to a Rumanian speculator, Dr. Adolph Gottlieb. When World War I drove down the price of timber and scattered the labor force, Isaac had taken the opportunity to acquire 2,630 acres in Sopot and 2,300 acres in Podhorodse with all the houses, barns, roads, and rights to minerals and timber, including maple and pine. Isaac needed to make the place pay for itself, but no sooner had he acquired title than the war ended, heralding Polish independence. Within months the whole agricultural economy of Poland started to swing from crisis to crisis, as export markets dwindled and the zloty/Ostmark inflated. Hardship, debt, and foreclosure were widespread, but Isaac struggled to pay his people in Podhorodse even when there was no work. To help make ends meet, he rented out the house on the hill to hunting parties from as far away as Berlin. To make the house more attractive, he modernized the plumbing, installed a toilet, hooked up the balky gas generator, and rigged a hand-cranked telephone. He even stocked what he proudly called a "wine cellar."

If the estate was not the windfall that Isaac had imagined, at least he did not have to sell. He started to view the estate as a long-term investment that he could pay off with profits from Pelis, a brewery, and Mazaga, which manufactured leather boots affordable to everybody in a growing, healthy economy. But the economy was neither healthy nor growing, which was why mutual friends had put him together with Pieter Menten.

After that first visit to Podhorodse, when the Mentens had been guests at Pistiner's house on the hill, the Dutchman began to see a specific opportunity. During the day, usually with Bibi by his side, he explored the territory surrounding the estates. What he saw excited him. When it rained, slicks of incandescence covered the small pools of water in the roads; parents of local peasant children complained of the "tar" that stuck to their feet. One afternoon, Menten drove into Boryslaw, the oil capital of the Ukraine, where he talked with oil engineers, who held the opinion that oil probably existed farther to the west of where they were now drilling. By Menten's reckoning, the eastern boundary of Isaac's Sopot estate lay a mere two miles from fields that had produced 2 million tons of crude a year since 1860. Isaac had owned the land for such a short time, the engineers told Menten, that he had not bothered to sink test wells. But, they emphasized, the land certainly had potential.

Menten kept the information to himself as he formulated a plan to test secretly for oil. In the meantime, knowing that Isaac needed capital, he suggested a partnership. Menten wanted timber from the estate for his ProtoLucifers, which he was now manufacturing near Lwów. He agreed to pay Isaac in rags and used paper from Amsterdam which Isaac then brokered for cash and bartered for raw materials needed to keep Pelis and Mazaga alive. With the lease rights to the timber on the estate in Sopot, Menten felt free to bring a Shell geologist from Berlin, who confirmed the suspicion that an indeterminate quantity of oil lay beneath the surface.

Menten was a good enough judge of men to know that Isaac would not sell the property unless circumstances forced the sale. Despite his cunning, Pieter Menten respected Isaac's experience and acumen. Isaac's one blind spot was the land and what it symbolized. Isaac knew the region and was generous with his knowledge in exchange for what Menten could teach about Western business, technology, and sophistication—about opportunity. The more they talked together of their ambitions, the more Isaac began to value his friendship with this man from Holland. Like the land, Menten represented a small victory in Isaac's battle for secularization. When they spent evenings together on the porch of the Pistiner house, Isaac knew contentment. In Menten's company, he was able to ignore how his dream was dissolving.

Soon after Menten had acquired the timber rights to the land in Sopot, he made his presence known to the villages on both sides of the Stryj. In short order, he befriended nearly every Jew living in Podhorodse. The villagers responded warmly, mostly because they trusted Isaac, who provided Menten with entree. They called him "The Dutchman" and "The Landowner," while to his face he was *"panne,"* a Polish term of respect. Menten wandered the village with the self-assurance of a Polish aristocrat. He looked into the peasants' houses, exchanged greetings with the locals in Ukrainian, and behaved generally in a manner that earned the admiration of even the most suspicious villager.

As part of his popularity, Menten gave something besides friendliness. When they learned he had jobs to offer, the villagers eagerly lined up for employment. First Menten hired Samuel Schechter as the manager of the Sopot holdings. In turn, Schechter hired men to work the forests. Brenicz and Dumbrowski became the forest watchmen, and Paolo Klepasz, the World War I veteran with the bullet in his neck, took over as the gamekeeper and general factotum. Moshe Altmann and Samuel Schiff sawed and finished the timber at their mill, which was soon working exclusively for Menten. A company in Synowodzko Wyzne repaired the narrow-gauge railroad that hauled out the timber. Menten went about the organization with zeal; in the evenings he bought the men beers at Zeeman's, down near the raft dock.

Less adventurous, Elizabeth stayed close to the big house on Pistiner's hill. Occasionally she rode horseback in jodhpurs, her trademark in the village, and she walked with the Pistiner girls. At Pieter's urging, she started to organize the "hunting lodge" in Sopot that Isaac had originally included in the lease "as a kindness." But in the next two years the modest cabin that had once plunged Malvina into gloom for its rusticity underwent an amazing transformation by an architect from Lwów who designed and built an entire estate around the original cabin. When finished, furniture, carpets, and pictures were moved from Lwów, and right away the Mentens invited their own guests, among them politicians, business clients, intelligentsia, and local gentry, who were anxious to meet the new arrivals. Finally the Mentens met the Prince Lubomirskis. An apotheosis of sorts, Menten later talked often of knowing one of Poland's great families.

For all their social ambitions, the Mentens remembered the Pistiners and Krumholzes, who spent the summers in Podhorodse and winters in Lwów. Bibi and Pieter became nearly inseparable on summer days, hunting and fishing, or Bibi just tagging along when Menten went on his appointed rounds. All the Pistiner-Krumholz children thought he was "an angel." Maria, the pretty Pistiner daughter, thought so more than the others.

The first summer she watched Menten, laughed at his antics with the younger children, and saw how much more of a man he seemed than her forlorn husband, Philip. She had tried to fight her feelings, but her sisters saw that she was falling in love; when they were together in the evenings, she brightened and came alive. The first evening that the sisters thought she had fallen in love, they had brought out the gramophone to the porch. Pieter Menten danced with all the girls, and he radiated such an abandoned joy of life that everybody in the house soon got caught up in the fun. Someone played a waltz. And now—he had avoided asking so far—he went over to Maria and, bending low, he bowed to her, reaching out for her hand. She gave it willingly, glancing at her sisters, who watched from a slight distance, jealously. She had felt so weak and wonderful that she did not remember the waltz or the successive dances. But after that, Maria and Pieter spent many nights together, and her life was not the same again. She tried with renewed emphasis to make something of her marriage to Philip, but it was hopeless. And she felt ashamed.

As Menten became an important fixture in the lives of the Pistiners and Krumholzes, through business partnerships and as a neighbor, Isaac's hold on his land became more uncertain, as if by a terrible twist of fate. The first storm clouds had already formed thousands of miles away in New York at the William Street headquarters of Dillon, Read & Co., Inc.

Together with the Chase Bank and a French financial consortium, Dillon, Read had backed its belief in the future of the new Poland by committing $50 million to Bank Polski in a twenty-five-year sinking fund secured by receipts from a Polish sugar tax and gross revenues of the Polish Railroads. A sum of $35 million was actually transferred. Soon after, however, Marshal Josef Pilsudski staged a coup d'etat against the coalition government of Wincenty Witos. The country slid toward chaos under several short-lived governments. In default of its loan, Poland's central bankers appealed for rescheduled terms. Thinking better of its faith in Poland, Dillon, Read abandoned the venture overnight.

Part of the Dillon, Read loan had been earmarked by Bank Polski for Mazaga, which had already received private cash infusions and needed more to stay alive. With Mazaga yet to produce a kopek of profit, the Pilsudski coup frightened off other capital sources besides Bank Polski and Dillon, Read. Isaac was faced with an option that he could not accept in his heart. He now had no choice but to sell the estates in Sopot and Podhorodse, abandoning all they represented to him as a man, for nearly 1 billion Ostmarks, roughly $720,000, to a Rumanian named Mikhail Andjai Jan Bohosiewicz, from whom Isaac then leased back timber rights to maintain his arrangement with Menten. He expected to use the sale's proceeds to put Pelis and Mazaga on their feet and then, if all went well with the economy, he might try to repurchase the estates. But for now, it was as though an important part of himself had been amputated.

Even more unhappily, as the first payment came due from the Rumanian, inflation started to erode the value of the Ostmark, the agreed currency of payment, with which Isaac had planned to buy hard currency. In real terms, he soon discovered, he had sold his precious estates for nearly nothing. Quietly he sued the Rumanian for repossession, arguing before a Polish court that the payment in devalued Ostmarks differed vastly from the price agreed on. The court sympathized but did nothing to redress his grievance.

Now close to desperation, Isaac made a regrettable mistake. He knew that Menten coveted the estates; they had talked about the possibility of Menten's buying, but Isaac did not want to sell to a friend. Whatever thoughts entered his mind he did not say, but he sold the 2,630 acres of Sopot to Menten—land that the Rumanian owned. Menten agreed to pay Isaac a million zlotys over five years with an initial down payment drawn from Menten's account at Mendelssohn and Co.

In need of still more cash, Isaac committed a further fraud. In league with Marek Kulter of the Bank Gospodarstwa and Adolph Kolnik of the Cracow Bank Wzajemnego Kredytu, he exchanged worthless stock certificates for hard U.S. dollars. After a three-year investigation, Felix Mlynarski of the Polish Central Bank exposed the "Mazaga Scandal," and a court sentenced Kulter and Kolnik to one and a half years in prison. Isaac escaped with only his freedom, a share in a clothing business with fifty employees, and the spiritualism in which he now started to seek answers. He had not even the pity of the Jewish community and barely the understanding of his family. Perhaps his desperation spawned the pipe dream to start over in Palestine. His nephew Bibi's enthusiasm had infected him, but the plan never went far. Palestine was not for an old man who had hit bottom.

Menten watched the decline in Isaac's fortunes without helping, even placing as much emotional distance between himself and the Pistiner-Krumholz families as was possible. He read in the papers about the "Mazaga Scandal," the most celebrated fraud of the decade in that part of Poland. Because the Rumanian owner rarely visited his estates in Podhorodse-Sopot, the land fraud went undiscovered. Besides, there was no other way for Menten to find out about it unless Deterding at Shell had wanted to drill for oil. But in the early 1930s, Deterding had other concerns.

Early in 1933, the year that Hitler came to power in Germany, Menten financed the Underground revolutionary newspaper *The Bugle* through the Shell account at the Mendelssohn Bank. With the balance of the money, he paid for sabotage, assassinations, and terrorism by the OUN in the Polish Ukraine. But the Ukrainian counterrevolution failed to catch fire in the Soviet Union because the Ukrainian Nationalists in Poland spent most of their time terrorizing Poles, who replied in kind with internment and assassination. After 1933 the Ukrainian Nationalists sought a refuge from

the collectivism of the Soviet Union on one side and alienation in
Poland on the other. Hitler made them promises and sent oper-
atives in Abwehr, the Intelligence division of the Wehrmacht, to
organize and finance the same counterrevolution that Sir Henry
Deterding of Shell had hired Menten to concoct almost a decade
earlier.

On a trip to Berlin in 1934, Menten met with some of the OUN
leaders, through whom he shared Intelligence with Abwehr. Particularly because he had come recommended by Deterding, with
whom Abwehr was formulating a bizarre scheme for the emigration of Dutchmen to a new federated Ukrainian state after the
Nazi defeat of the Soviet Union, Abwehr showed a keen interest
in what Menten had to contribute. The time approached when
sides would have to be chosen. Deterding's emigration plan, while
feasible, first required that the Wehrmacht conquer the region.
Abwehr confided in Menten that it was formulating contingency
plans in the event of war for the military occupation of the Bory-
slaw-Drohobycz oilfields, just a few miles from his estates in
Sopot and Podhorodse. When he returned to Poland late in August 1934, Menten carried a new Leica, lenses, filters, and a head
filled with Abwehr's instructions about what constituted strategic
installations—bridges, roads, railroads, rivers.

Soon after, as he went through the village recording nearly everything in sight on film, he noticed a dramatic change in attitude
among the villagers. Outwardly, they expressed friendliness, but
privately they withdrew their support of him as a landowner.
They had welcomed him when he offered them jobs, but now he
had deprived them of something more important—a right and
custom that they associated with survival. Isaac—and generations
of landowners before him—had allowed the village peasants to cut
wood for their fireplaces and to graze their cows in the meadows
of his lands. When he "bought" the land, Menten had stopped all
that without explanation. The villagers appealed to Isaac, who
could not help, except to advise them to sue. The Stryj court appointed Alexander Nowicki as its steward. Nowicki, formerly the
postman in Podhorodse, moved into Menten's house in Sopot; his
brother-in-law, Albert Stephan, assisted him to prevent any of the
legal parties from entering the contested forests.

One night soon after, while Alexander and Bronislawa No-wicki slept, fire in the Sopot house spread out of control. Nowicki tried to salvage whatever he could of Menten's furniture and possessions. Once the fire was out and most of the house had been saved from serious damage, Nowicki found files of correspondence between Menten and Abwehr in Berlin, files that proved he was spying for the Germans. The documents, maps, and photographic negatives connected Menten with the Nazis through the outlawed terrorist OUN. Nowicki showed the documents to Bronislawa, who pleaded, "Leave it alone. Don't do anything. It won't end well."

"I am a Pole," Alexander said. He told Mayor Ramel, who gave the evidence to the Second Office, the counterespionage department of the Polish Secret Police. Soon after, Menten was detained in the Stryj jail for interrogation. The Second Office asked about his Polish identity papers and why he lived permanently in Poland. While the Second Office built its case, Menten remained behind bars.

The villagers Moshe Altmann and Samuel Schiff refused to believe the allegations. They were willing to ignore the rumors and the jealousies about Menten because they needed his business, and they remembered how important he had been to them in the past. Their bribes greased the lock of Menten's cell on his tenth day in jail. Once back in the village, Menten acknowledged the act; eventually he would repay their trust with the most valuable gift of all.

Early in 1938, Menten uncovered Isaac's fraud when he started to talk about Deterding's plan to send out oil engineers from The Hague. Word of these plans reached the Rumanian Bohosiewicz, who sent a private army of thugs to seize the Sopot land. In a pitched battle one of the Rumanian's soldiers nailed to the floor of the smokehouse the arms and legs of a former employee of Isaac. In retaliation, thugs hired by Menten shot one of the Rumanian's partisans dead. At that, the Rumanian ordered his army to retreat, but he sued Isaac for damages. Menten also sued, and while the courts deliberated and Isaac's lawyer, Dr. Sigmund Gelmann, appealed every negative decision, Menten suppressed a growing and volcanic anger.

All of this bewildered the Pistiner children with good reason. Bibi especially was confused when his father, David, wrote him in Palestine. The other children did not want to believe the charge made in 1938 that Menten was a German spy. It was clear, Isaac said, that Menten, a Nazi agent, had tried to steal his land and that the Dutchman could take what Isaac owned by using legal tricks and endemic anti-Semitism. In court the accused was an old Jew with a yarmulke, and the plaintiff, a young Catholic, wealthy, powerful, and foreign. The children sided with Isaac, who held from them the truth of his defrauding Menten. To their way of thinking, they were losing the landscape of their childhoods, and that was all that mattered. But by the mid-1930s the climate had turned against Jews, and they believed that this was another example of robbery by the law. What could a Jew do? Isaac asked rhetorically.

CHAPTER IV

∞

". . . a thing with its own ferocious will."

MRS. ELIZABETH MENTEN, Pieter's mother, was angry when she arrived at the Sopot estate from Amsterdam in the summer of 1939 with her son, Dirk, in his speedy V-8 Talbot. A widow of fierce independence, she had invested some of the money her husband had left her with Pieter, who had failed to pay her "dividends." She had traveled all that way over bumpy roads to learn why. But when she finally reached Sopot, unwelcome events greeted her. Pieter had hired "boxers" to protect him from Bohosiewicz's thugs and not incidentally from the local peasants who were angry at him for taking away their grazing and wood rights. Laughing, Pieter told his brother, "I may win the lawsuits, and the only thing they can do then is shoot my head off." From then on, Dirk was seen to carry a revolver.

The rumors of war were by now reaching even Sopot, in greatly exaggerated form. Almost knowingly, the Mentens laughed at the Poles for reciting a view of the war that defied reality. They said, "We can win alone, without England. We'll march alone to Berlin." Pieter laughed loudest of anybody, so pleased was he by the prospect of war. He had no experience with it, but he knew that war's companion was chaos, in which quick profits were to be made. Pieter, so certain of a German invasion, had even moved his valuables from the Lwów apartment to the house in Sopot in the belief that the village would not be bombed. Then he waited, until 4:40 A.M. on September 1, 1939, when the German battleship *Schleswig-Holstein* fired its guns at the Danzig fort at Westerplatte to signal the beginning. At dawn, an hour later, sixty Wehrmacht divisions blitzkrieged Poland with 2,600 Mark I and II tanks and 2,000 modern fighter airplanes. Abandoned without a tear by their allies, the Poles capitulated twenty-six days later.

Pieter waited at Sopot in great anticipation of a Nazi victory that would join for him the elements for which he had worked— the Ukrainian Nationalists, the oil interests in a united Ukraine, perhaps now even the implementing of Deterding's Dutch settlement plan, the award of his Sopot land, and appreciation from Abwehr. But if he had not heard by shortwave radio, he learned to his chagrin when the airplanes roared overhead and the tanks rumbled past the village that the Red Army—the *Soviets!*—was heading toward Lwów, entering Poland's back door while the Nazis battered the front. This maneuver—and its treacherous politics, which involved a last-minute alliance on Poland between Stalin and Hitler—caught Pieter Menten off guard. He soon understood that the invasion meant a Bolshevik occupation of Lwów and most of Galicia, including Podhorodse and Sopot, which spelled his doom.

He thought of running west into the arms of the Nazis, who stopped their eastward advance at the Bug River, but what was he to do then? Leave the valuables he had so cleverly brought to the house in Sopot from Lwów? He had no alternative but to remain and deal with the Bolsheviks as best he could, despite unprecedented dangers. He was a landowner, and according to rumor, the Bolsheviks hanged landowners. Whether his claim to ownership was valid did not matter now. He lived in a large, luxurious house; he had stables and a car; his Egyptian cigarettes and silver-topped walking stick did not fit a proletarian image. Moreover, his unpopularity among the peasantry bore witness to his status. Landowners by nature were unpopular. What was worse, the villagers would tell the new Soviet *komissars* about the Second Office's finding that he was an *agent provocateur* and had been jailed for his work with Abwehr. Nothing now—not even his Polish identity papers—could help him.

The Bolsheviks came soon after, as he had expected. He had not imagined that they would be Vladimir Pistolak and Petro Starzinsky from the village. On their own authority, they crossed the river with guns in their hands to order him to go with them to the prison in Stryj, where he had once been held by the Second Office. Menten did not try to reason with his captors. He waited until jail, then asked for a person in authority, but these Bolsheviks did not respond—at least not then—to the inducements of bribery with anything but anger. In his cell, Menten watched the guards humiliate Elizabeth, who had come with blankets and baskets of food. Unlike his Ukrainian Nationalist cellmates, a lice-ridden and hopeless lot, *he* saw the betrayal, even there in jail: the villagers of Podhorodse, more than the Bolsheviks or the Nazis or even himself, had brought this on. And he blamed Isaac for turning the villagers against him, for causing this misery and loss.

While he was counting up these hatreds, like a miser, the peasants of Podhorodse were forming a soviet, with Vladimir Pistolak in charge of redistributing the properties on the estates, starting with Menten's. Pistolak rode up aboard a Soviet tank. Mrs. Menten, Pieter's mother, shouted at the driver of the approaching vehicle from a window, "We are Dutch." The tank commander did not understand. When she repeated her noncombatant status, the officer said, "Holland is Hamburg" and ordered them out of the house while Pistolak searched "for weapons." Undoubtedly, he had never seen the likes of those carpets, framed paintings, and clocks, but he and the tank commander especially enjoyed the magnifying shaving mirror. Roaring with laughter, they passed it from hand to hand, inspecting their faces from different angles. When the laughter ended they had "liberated" the mirror *and* the paintings, clocks, candlesticks, figurines, porcelain, carpets, and tapestries—all the tank could carry.

After a brief period of calm Pistolak and Starzinsky moved into the house, sharing it with Russian soldiers, Mrs. Menten, and Elizabeth. (Dirk had returned to Amsterdam in his Talbot the week before September 1.) Soon the house was picked clean as new soldiers kept coming. After fourteen days the women worried that with nothing left to "give," the Russians would take the one "glitter" that remained, lovely Elizabeth. But Mrs. Menten held them at bay with her hauteur. *"Vagabonds,"* she said to her daughter-in-law. "They have no sense of civilization. So *that's* what the soldiers of the Workers' State look like—a complete degeneration. The word 'soldier' is too good for them!"

Meanwhile, the Ukrainian Nationalists slipped news of an escape plan to their fellow revolutionaries imprisoned with Menten in the Stryj jail. And soon after, on the appointed night, an explosion shattered the country silence and the cell wall fell away. Menten fled out of the rubble on foot to Sopot, where he bribed Pistolak with an old suit from a closet that was nearly bare. The suit so pleased Pistolak that he let them go.

Two nights later, with his mother and Elizabeth, Pieter drove his Chevrolet to their Lwów address on Piaskowa Street, which Russian soldiers had already plundered from house to house, room to room. Since the occupation, Lwów had been transformed into a plain of misery. The Mentens found a room and tried to make themselves inconspicuous in the hope that events might change their fortunes. Events soon did just that, but for the worse: the Soviet occupiers decreed that anyone remaining in their zone after January 1, 1940, risked forced transport to the Russian interior—to Kazakhstan and Siberia for the duration of the war.

The decree applied to foreigners, too, even those like Jacob Jan Broen, who enjoyed diplomatic privileges, as the Dutch Consul in Lwów. Broen made plans to leave Lwów by train for Cracow, and from there to Holland. Only a day or so before he closed the door to the Dutch Mission, he was visited by a desperate man with a story that he remembered, if only vaguely. His predecessor at the consulate, a Dr. Witowsky, had presided years earlier over Menten's change of citizenship. When Broen took over the consulate, he had read the correspondence, wondering why. Throwing away Dutch citizenship was at least bizarre, but Broen had long ago stopped questioning people's motives. And soon he forgot the episode. But now, the same man begged Broen, who issued him Dutch passport #154682 for "humanitarian reasons." Even more, Broen took Menten to Orbis, the Polish travel agency, for permission to cross the demarcation line into Nazi territory. With only four days to spare before the deadline, on December 27 they boarded a train as a group—Broen and his wife, Menten, Elizabeth, and his mother—with travel papers valid to Cracow, where they would apply to the Nazi administration for ongoing documents. Because of the urgency of their departure—and the permissible limit of 165 pounds per voyager—Menten carried only hand baggage. With tears in his eyes, he told Broen that he owned nothing now.

Aboard "cattle cars," they suffered bitterly when the temperature dropped to twenty-four below zero. When they demanded special treatment the Russians said, "A Pole or a foreigner has nothing to say, nothing to ask; he has only to answer." One and a half days later they reached the Bug River where the Germans received them in a manner that earned Menten's respect—with bowls of steaming pea soup, bread, and preserves. His belly full and his body warm, Pieter had never felt so empty. He remembered what the Russians had told him: "Your estate is now the property of the Russian workers."

He consoled himself in the opulence of the Hotel Cracovia, at Puszkina #1, the Ritz of eastern Poland. Broen, a simple and dutiful diplomat, could not understand the extravagance, or where the money came from. The consul applied for documents to continue their journey. But Menten did nothing, which Broen also did not understand until he saw that Menten was on good terms with the German occupiers. He told Broen that he wanted to stay to gain a foothold here in Cracow, the capital of the Nazis' General Government, the center of opportunity in the Occupied Territories, another boom town.

Respecting a boom-town axiom to look and act the part of what you want to be, with a gemstone from a soft leather pouch strapped to his waist, Menten purchased a brown double-breasted suit, a tan silk shirt, brown brogues with matching socks, a brown printed necktie, a checked brown foulard, and a brown felt fedora with a brown band. As usual his suits were cut in exaggerated patterns: the shoulders were too padded and the lapels too pointed. He was noticed as *too* elegant—dandyish. Once outfitted to his satisfaction, he bought an Adler coupé, in which he drove from the Cracovia down Manifestu Lipcowego through the Planty, finally to Rynek Glowny, the market square of Cracow around which Poland's art community—the dealers, brokers, advisors, experts, restorers, salonniers, everybody except the artists themselves—gathered in a warm embrace. The Glowny was the

oldest section of the oldest, and by far the most elegant, city of
Poland. Just off the Glowny, Menten knew from the many prewar
expeditions to Cracow in search of art, Horowitz had his gallery at
Braka #3/5 and Katzner at Wislna #2. The Old Town Hall
Tower, once a prison for thieves, faced Rynek Glowny #24, the
gallery of the number-one dealer, Joseph Stieglitz, a Jew like the
others with whom Menten now sought to renew an acquaintance.

He swung his legs out of the Adler, then ran a short distance
across the cobblestones, ducking from the cold into a narrow,
vaulted vestibule, and with his gloved hand he knocked on the
door. When nobody responded he peered through the glass and
noticed the discolorations on the walls where pictures had once
hung. He went back to the vestibule and tried the door; padlocks
hung on the frame like growths. He walked around the corner to
Wislna #2, Katzner's gallery. When he knocked, a head appeared
from the window above. "He threw away the keys and just ran,"
Mr. Katzner said about Stieglitz. Menten asked about the paintings, but Katzner did not know. Joseph Stieglitz had fled from the
Nazis. "He asked me, 'Do you know who this Frank is?'" Katzner said. "'I don't like him. I don't even need a premonition about
him.'" Menten knew the name—Hans Frank, the Governor General, *Reichskommissar*—but nothing more. Katzner said, "Stieglitz
thought there was more time to buy in eastern Poland. He was
stupid. Look at what he did. He ran from the Nazis to the Soviets.
Who is better?" Stieglitz had transported his family and many
paintings by rented car to Lwów two days after the German invasion. "I'm taking some good paintings," Stieglitz had told Katzner, "but life is more important."

Katzner revealed the news to Menten that the Nazis were "Ar-
yanizing" all Jewish businesses. The antique and art galleries
owned by Jews had not been assigned to *Treuhänderen* (German
"overseers"), but they were closed by order of the Governor General. Katzner had lost everything, he said, but Menten thought he
knew better. Even in the best of times, Jewish art dealers hid objects of great value—paintings, coins, jewelry, and carpets. Now
everybody was doing the same, and the more portable the better.
Menten thought how his own diamonds had saved him from

85

worse than penury. In times of upheaval portable wealth meant survival.

Menten returned to his car and drove northeast to a wealthy suburb of artists, intellectuals, diplomats, and businessmen. Grottgera Street faced a slope of grass and a picturesque stream called Mlynowska, now glistening with a crust of ice. Grottgera #12, as if designed by Walter Gropius, abutted the sidewalk with boxy shape. Its grated front window, like an oculus, dominated the platform over the door. A narrow, walled garden banded its sides and back. The house belonged to the Honorary Dutch Consul in Cracow, Joseas L. Debrouin, a sometime diplomat and the full-time owner of ORIZA, an import-export firm of cereals, grain, and rice. Ten years older than Menten, Debrouin's eccentric, long gray hair made him seem older still, belying his reputation as a womanizer who drank *jenever* and *schnaaps* as hard as he drove a bargain.

Debrouin liked the company of other Dutchmen so he could speak Dutch and really communicate as well as reminisce. That this other Dutchman was Pieter Menten was a bonus in Debrouin's view. Because of his family Menten had connections in Holland who could prove valuable to Debrouin in these uncertain times. More immediately, Menten was a good companion, a boozer, and a womanizer, too. At the moment, Debrouin and his "secretary," Maria Louise Olga Steengracht von Moyland, a thirty-four-year-old with large chocolate eyes and a soft, tremulous voice, lived in the house by themselves. The ORIZA offices took up the ground floor, and they had the second. The guest room—more than that, the entire third floor—was vacant. Pieter and Elizabeth would have all the privacy they wanted, Debrouin said, and the companionship could be fun. Debrouin insisted that they stay "for safety's sake."

Soon, after they had unpacked the hand baggage from the hotel, Menten listened carefully to Debrouin describe the new terrain. The consul had seen copies of public proclamations from Berlin, and he had made the acquaintance of the Nazi paladins in the Wawel residence of the Governor General and in the SS offices on Oleandry, Stycznia, and Monteluppich. "Chocolate eyes," whose uncle was the aide-de-camp in Berlin to the Foreign Minister, von

Ribbentrop, had helped him meet all the right Nazis. As far as business was concerned, Debrouin said, Hitler had told Governor General Hans Frank to turn the "economic, cultural, and political structure into a heap of rubble." The Governor General, who had arrived in October, informed his army staff officers that "Poland can be administered by utilizing the country through ruthless exploitation . . . [and] reduction of the entire Polish economy to absolute minimum. . . ." The second in command to Reichsführer-SS Heinrich Himmler, Reinhard Heydrich, had even circulated plans for the "housecleaning of the Jews, intelligentsia, clergy, and nobility" of Poland.

For a German, the pickings were abundant. Himmler had ordered the Main Economic and Administrative Department (WVHA) to assign German *Treuhänderen* to take control of Jewish businesses. The *Untermenschen,* the subhuman Jews, had already been registered, and everything was being expropriated from them. Debrouin needed neither genius nor insight, he said, to see into the future. A ghetto was going to be formed, probably across the bridge. Increasingly, the medium of payment was going to become loot—loot from the Jews and from Poles, from public and private institutions, museums, libraries, churches, synagogues, castles, from inside and outside industry. Certain *objets,* indeed, had already been removed to the Reich. The priceless fifteenth-century triptych by Veit Stoss, for instance, no longer loomed like some dark gate to another world above the altar in St. Mary's cathedral on Cracow's Glowny. But there was still plenty left, for Germans.

"And if you're not?" Menten asked.

"Hans Frank can make you anything he wants," Debrouin replied. Hans Frank, whom they called "The Dragon."

According to Polish legend, a dragon once lived in a limestone cave, at the base of the Wawel Hill in Cracow, that opened onto the Vistula like a mouth formed in anguish. Once, the dragon had eaten virgins. Since the Nazis had arrived in Cracow, Poles had reasoned that the dragon might not have slouched off and died as legend recorded. More demonic and insatiable than ever, it now inhabited the Wawel Castle, the former residence of Polish kings, instead of the cave. Poles now identified the bloodthirsty dragon as a Governor General, a Nazi plenipotentiary, as Hans Frank.

A dragoon in the Sturmabteilung (SA), Frank had begun his political career in the Third Reich by answering an advertisement for a lawyer to defend Nazi party members gratis. Later on, after he had done Hitler's bidding to change Germany's legal system in the early 1930s to something that was less "Jewish in spirit," he served as the first Bavarian Minister of Justice, then *Reichsminister* without portfolio, and on and on until the first week of October 1939, when Hitler charged him with the obliteration of Poland, an order about which he was wry enough to say, "If I wished to order that one should hang up posters about every seven Poles shot, there would not be enough forests in Poland with which to make paper for these posters."

Frank answered to Hitler alone in the General Government for all aspects of life and death, whether in the civil administration, the SS, or the Wehrmacht. No matter where in Poland, Hans Frank called the shots "to purge the territory of the Reich of Jews and Pollacks," "to get rid of either all the lice or all the Jews," "to make mincemeat of the Poles and Ukrainians," "to sentence 1.2 million Jews to death by hunger," "to show the Poles the hopelessness of their national destiny," "to destroy the Jews whenever we come across them." His authority was absolute.

Hans Frank knew that slaughter required incentives beyond honor and duty. And so, starting a few weeks before the Mentens' arrival in Cracow, on December 2, 1939, Frank activated the more reliable profit principle, saying, "This area is in its entirety booty of the Third Reich." A month later, he established the right to "confiscate all *private* property, except the most basic needs of a conquered people"—everything, as it turned out, but 600 calories per person a day. The week Menten arrived in January 1940 Hans Frank said, "Compensation could be given, but it would not be legally mandatory." Now the Nazis and their friends could steal.

While describing Poland as "a dung heap," the leaders of Nazidom all the same squabbled over the Polish spoils like children over toys. Reichsführer-SS Himmler reserved "all outstanding Polish art treasures" for *his* SS. Field Marshal Göring assigned Oberführer-SS Dr. Kajetan Muhlmann, a slimy figure who lurked in Göring's substantial shadow, to "confiscate" for Göring's castle Kerenhall "all outstanding works of art in Polish public institutions, in private collections, or belonging to the church." That covered most of the ground.

Hans Frank tried for purely selfish reasons to control this stampede of greed. He said, "We have, so to speak, become accomplices in a world historical sense; just because of this we must hold together and be in agreement with one another, and it would be ridiculous if we allowed ourselves to get involved in any squabbles. . . ." Göring and Himmler did not take any notice, which forced Frank to lay the matter before the *Führer*. From Berlin Hitler criticized the unseemly behavior of Göring and Himmler. To cut them out of Poland he ordered the exclusive transfer of all Polish treasures to Hans Frank's warehouse in Cracow. And he annulled the laws of sequestration and confiscation that Göring and Himmler had formulated earlier to make their plunder legal. Furious, they determined to get their shares of Poland despite the *Führer,* and, if necessary, behind his back, no matter how.

A man of no particular loyalty, Dr. Muhlmann now shifted into the shadow of Governor General Frank. Soon—too soon—he reported that the "safeguarding for all intents and purposes" was over. Frank and Muhlmann compiled leather-bound albums with photographs of the 511 most valuable works of art for Hitler's museum in Linz, Austria. How Dr. Muhlmann had identified and collected the art objects so fast he and Frank alone knew. In fact they had created a grand illusion. With the treasure out of reach in Hans Frank's warehouse inventory and headed for Linz, Frank's rivals turned elsewhere for spoils, long enough for Frank to identify and collect the art objects. The ruse had to last only long enough.

The job of Governor General was complicated, dangerous, and lonely. Hans Frank had a Bavarian mistress, but his wife, Brigid, a woman also with a well-developed sense of greed, obstructed Frank's path to happiness. Brigid was demanding and hard to please, but he spared no effort to keep her out of Poland and on their estate, Schobernhof, in southern Germany, so that his mistress could share his bed in Wawel Castle. At different times he bribed his wife with 200,000 chicken eggs, tonnages of sheep, a convoy of fruit, and various sculptures and paintings. But the eggs and fruit were nothing compared with what Frank had "bought" her from the Jew Apfelbaum: a priceless coat collection of black sable; Tartar sable; marmink; moleskin; muskrat; brook mink; muskutrine; electric beaver; polar seal; Roman seal; black marten; chinchilla; black, silver, red, blue, and white fox; Baltic leopard; ermine; genet; and shagreen.

Alas, finally even the pelts were not enough. While Frank was breaking "the backbone of the Poles for all time," Brigid decorated Wawel Castle with a plundered Rembrandt for the wall behind his desk (Frank once pointed out the painting to a visitor, saying, "We have here a handsome frame"), modern club armchairs with medieval furniture, paintings of Nazi social realism with a Da Vinci here and a codex or ancient embroidered chasuble there. She assigned her son, Norman, to the Polish Queen Yadwiga's historic bedroom and her other children to rooms the size of tennis courts. Weekends Hans Frank walked the castle's polished corridors wearing Bavarian shorts and a hat with a little feather, whistling Dvořák or Tchaikovsky, tuning his belief that "only men of a truly patrician disposition" ruled in the East, and thinking vainly perhaps that he looked a little like *Il Duce*. Power intoxicated Hans Frank all the more because it was of so fleeting a nature. But while it lasted, he wanted his personal, private coffers filled.

In the business of plunder the appraiser of art is revered almost as a god. His powers can make "gold" from base elements in nature such as pigment, clay, stone, and wood. The appraiser proclaims as genuine or fake a painting, sculpture, or vase from a particular school, period, or culture. He decrees a bottom line—worth in trade for other plunder or for gold, gems, or scrip. Because his art is imperfect, the alchemist can inflate prices here, deflate there, create and destroy markets, bestow "priceless" gifts on the ignorant merely by proclaiming their pricelessness, and make other men's priceless gifts seem as insults. In the topsy world in which he had become just such an "alchemist," Pieter Menten soon had power almost beyond his ability to measure.

Overnight, as if in a dream from which he did not awaken, the Nazis recognized him as an authority on art. He knew names and dates—the patter—from his days in Amsterdam. The Nazis adored him for the aura of respectability, of cultivation and culture, that he bestowed. They were thugs, morons, sadists and drunks, rapists and torturers, but with Menten's presence and benediction they were "art patrons and collectors." They were mostly ignorant about art and understood their shortcoming. The amazing thing was that everybody wanted to hear the gibberish in which Menten was more fluent than nearly anybody else in Cracow.

Hans Frank had learned that this new arrival, Pieter Menten, had once owned a "brilliant collection"; his family was patrician— Royal Dutch, Unilever, and all that. He was acquainted with Queen Juliana and Prince Bernhard. The credentials sounded spectacular. Clearly Menten knew the terrain, too. The one-foot-square, green-bordered late-eighteenth-century Thracian Kilim that he had given Frank after their first meeting testified to his expertise and the promise of better things to come. As "The Dragon" noted with pleasure, here was a man without loyalties in the Nazi universe. Menten as a Dutchman and a stranger in the General Government had no axes to grind, no political ambitions, no one to whom to tell compromising tales. Indeed, Menten was tailored for the job of *Treuhänder.*

Soon after in the winter of 1940, the Commercial Court of Cracow accepted the application *pro forma.* Jews exclusively had owned the businesses before the war, and now very few Aryans in Cracow knew better than Menten did how to take over and run them. The court did not question that Menten was not German. Germany and Holland were neighbors, and more than a little related by blood. Besides, and above all else, this application had the endorsement of the Governor General, which served the court nearly as a decree. Two months after he had fled utter ruin in Soviet-occupied Poland, Pieter Menten became the official *Treuhänder* of the Katzner and the Horowitz galleries, and the gem of the trade in Cracow, Joseph Stieglitz's shop at Rynek Glowny #24.

Menten's new association with Hans Frank suddenly made his acquaintance worthwhile to the higher powers in the Nazi hierarchy, and none among them became more devoted as a friend more rapidly than the Gestapo man, the second most feared man in Poland after Frank, Dr. Eberhardt Schoengarth, to whom Menten represented an island refuge in a turbulent sea of lawlessness, a haven from the insane duties of slaughter. Nearly everything about Schoengarth suggested the need for refuge from insanity. Physically, his moist gray eyes bulged in the sockets. Puffy and crimson, his face trembled just perceptibly under a sheen of sweat. A man at some emotional brink, he moved his large bearish body in jerks and spasms, and his words leaped and strained against the harness of self-control. In different times he might have been an object of pity—a gross, pathetic dipsomaniac; a person of deep, chronic depressions. But in Cracow, dressed in the plumage of the SS, he was a man to be more than feared.

A former professor of law at Leibnitz University and now the *Standartenführer*-SS of the Sicherheitspolizei (Sipo), an arm of the Gestapo, Schoengarth organized mass slaughter, hated doing it, and did nothing about his hatred but slaughter all the more. He uttered meager words attesting to his humanity, saying, "No people has ever before had to suffer such oppression as that being suffered by the Polish people," while ordering the same lamentable suffering and oppression. Schoengarth had the sensitivity to understand how guilt could make him feel human, when around him other Nazis seemed to feel nothing at all. Just as long as he could feel even depression, something salvageable remained of his soul; in the trembling of his hands he sought proof of his power to distinguish from madness.

After the tragedy of Germany in World War I, he had joined Hitler's NSDAP as an officer in the Geheime Statspolizei, the Sicherheitsdienst (SD), and later, the Gestapo. He had married a schoolteacher two years his senior and regularly attended the Evangelist Church before Himmler assigned him to the General Government as *Befehlshaber der Sicherheitspolizei und des SD*. Temperamental and proud, even vain, Schoengarth acted as though by his intellect and extensive education, he were superior even to Hans Frank, whom he openly called "a pseudo-king." He prudishly disapproved of the Governor General's misuse of army cars, government funds, courier mail, uniforms and customs regulations, and his extensive confiscation for personal profit. A small amount of graft was only to be expected, but what he saw was an industry of corruption, and the immorality of it sickened him. Above all, Schoengarth was a tidy person. At the Wannsee conference of SD-SS chiefs in January 1942, he had been an annoying advocate of bureaucratic terminology. *Einsatzgruppen* were to carry out *Aktionen* (actions), either through *Aussiedlung* (resettlement), *Säuberung* (cleansing), *Sonderbehandlung* (special treatment), *Ausschaltung* (elimination), or *Exekutivmassnahme* (executive measure). These terms created the illusion of a paper chase, not genocide. Schoengarth demonstrated a similar preference in art for the abstract over the concrete. He loved the designs and the pale colors of Chinese porcelain. The mistiness, the veiled and subtle aspects of a great, ancient, and unbroken civilization seemed to transport his imagination.

Schoengarth and his wife—and soon a baby daughter—lived a block from the Mentens in the big house on the corner at Grottgera #2. Elizabeth and Mrs. Schoengarth became fast friends and pillars in this transient society. During the day they ignored what must have been difficult to ignore happening around them—the rounding up of Jews and the disappearance of Cracow's intelligentsia. Menten and Schoengarth spent much of their time together at Lenartowicza #17, a plain, modern, five-story former apartment building that the SS and SD had requisitioned for an officers' "Casino," a place to unwind over a beer and *schnaaps* after a long day. They entertained guests upstairs in private rooms, and in the basement they lounged in a bar at one end of a restaurant "for men only" that featured imported *schnitzels* and *braten*. The place was richly, although hastily, decorated with large silver flashes of the SS, black swastikas on fields of red, and of course the obligatory photographs of the *Führer* and Himmler.

Soon, all SS ranks in the Casino deferred to Menten as more than Schoengarth's guest, as his "intellectual" friend. In this rich atmosphere, Menten learned about the basic SS attitude of "hardness." What Schoengarth and other new friends did not tell him, he learned himself. Schoengarth regarded the ideal SS officer as

93

impervious to all human emotions; he was contemptuous of "inferior" beings and arrogant toward most people who did not belong to the Order of the SS. However, as leader, Schoengarth had no one in whom to confide if he was always to appear unbending, as an example to the others. For letting down his hair he relied on the loyalty and friendship of an intelligent and prominent outsider—a civilian and foreigner. Menten was only too willing to forgive Schoengarth those trespasses, little "transgressions" and "foibles," as they called his occasional doubts about the meaning of the slaughter. As a *Treuhänder* Menten needed the SS to operate in the General Government where increasingly, he saw, nothing else counted, not even Hans Frank. If he was to steal from Jews, his "employees," Katzner and Horowitz, had to move freely in and out of the ghetto, where he was not permitted to go for the last of the Jews' valuables. Outside the ghetto, Katzner and Horowitz had to be exempt from wearing the Star. If the police "detained" them, they had to be let free on the authority of the SS. Practically, the SS engulfed "The Dragon's" civil administration, and Menten, quick to sense the relationship, soon became a major contributor to the SS Casino and host to important SS officers at the house at Grottgera Street, where he supplied them with women, food, liquor, the priceless luxury of privacy, and, from time to time, little bijoux of significant value. A Cartier watch, a Leica camera, a Chinese porcelain vase, a painting, a carpet usually fulfilled someone's secret desire. But soon the price he paid to the SS was not enough—it never would be. Of course the SS officers appreciated the gifts, but if Menten wanted a guarantee of their continued cooperation, he would have to give more besides baubles, and soon, they demanded more.

Himmler regarded himself, not Hans Frank, as the conqueror of the Slavs. A few years before, on July 2, 1936, he had entered the tomb of King Heinrich I, his namesake, the ninth-century Saxon conqueror of the Slavs, in Quedlinburg Cathedral, and on his knees he had vowed to complete King Heinrich's task. Himmler had furnished his lunatic fantasy at his Wewelsburg Castle in Germany to which he retreated for private weekends. Around an oaken table 100 by 145 feet he placed high-backed pigskin chairs inscribed with the names of his fantasy knights of the Saxony of old. In the cellar of the castle he built a Realm of the Dead—a stone crypt with five-foot-thick walls and twelve marble pedestals, on which he cremated the severed arms of any *Gruppenführer*-SS who had fallen in battle. Electric blowers ventilated the smoke of the burning flesh in a single column pierced by the rays of colored lights. He often communed alone in the Realm of the Dead, measuring his hatred of Hans Frank, whom he had to eliminate if he were to honor his sacred vow.

With the patience of the totally committed, Himmler sought to show the *Führer* how Hans Frank condoned—nay, encouraged by his own example—plunder for personal profit, a crime for which the *Führer* himself had set the penalty of death by hanging. Himmler assigned two trusted SS officers in Cracow, Obergruppenführer-SS Friedrich-Wilhelm Krüger and Schoengarth, to investigate and document a case against Frank for presentation to the *Führer*. The two SS investigators had no trouble eliminating Frank's underlings in the civil administration, men such as Dr. Karl Lasch, the Governor General of Lwów who was caught with a whole warehouse of illegal plunder. The first victim of Himmler's campaign, Lasch hanged himself in the SS's Monteluppich prison, and the circle around Frank tightened. There was now proof, but not yet enough for Himmler to make his case to Hitler. True, Brigid had accepted furs, stocks of tea, coffee, chocolate, tinned goods, textiles, and alcohol for her personal use. True, Hans Frank had appointed one of Brigid's three brothers to the Academy of German Law, another to a highly paid post in the General Government, and the third, a Swedish citizen, was given permission to enter the General Government for "business," which everybody knew meant plunder. True, Frank had accepted a rare Kilim carpet, and his wife had been delighted with the gift of a priceless piano from their dealer, Pieter Menten. But Himmler wanted still more.

By the winter of 1940, Menten had found himself in a position in the SS hierarchy of Cracow that went well beyond *Treuhänder,* and although he was only a foot soldier in the campaign to eliminate Hans Frank, Himmler wanted to ensure his continued participation and, if possible, his loyalty, too. The SS wielded the

95

power of destiny; if required, Menten could have been deported from the General Government or jailed, tortured, and killed. Himmler and his investigators, however, did not trust loyalty through fear, so they thought of psychological inducements that would bind Menten to their cause against Frank, no matter what.

General Schoengarth knew Menten coveted one painting above all others. Menten had told him so many times, when they talked of such things after hours in the Casino. Before the war, the painting had been right there in Cracow in the private gallery of the Czartoryski Museum, a collection of paintings, tapestries, gems, and armorial treasures matched only by the collections of Barycz in the Polish National Museum and the rooms of art owned by the Count Potocki at Krzeszowice. In all, before the Nazi occupation the Czartoryski Museum had contained fifty or sixty priceless pieces—goblets, monstrances, reliquaries and illuminated manuscripts, Gobelin tapestries, the splended fifteenth-century bishop's robe of Kmita, and, above all else, three paintings—Leonardo da Vinci's "Cecilia Galierani," or "Lady with Ermine," Rembrandt's "Landscape," and Raphael's "Portrait of a Young Man," without doubt the most beautiful picture that Menten had ever seen, he told Schoengarth, because contained within its frame he thought he recognized something personal, a reminder, a resemblance— the knowledge that this painting symbolized greatness.

At the invasion of Poland, the present Czartoryski prince, Augustus, had fled south to Spain with his wife, leaving the objects in the keeping of the museum curator, Mrs. Sophia Schmidt. Without any protection the collection was scattered within weeks. Two of the great paintings, the Leonardo and the Rembrandt "Landscape" had been on loan to Berlin's Kaiser Frederich Museum since weeks before the war. Why those two paintings and not the Raphael, Schoengarth's investigations did not discover. All he knew was what Menten lamented, that the Raphael seemed lost. But Schoengarth knew about the Czartoryski Museum, and through the resources of the SS, he had learned what Menten could never have discovered.

On a cold evening in the first week of December Schoengarth drove Menten up Florianska Street where the ramparts of the old city gate, the Baszty i mury obronne, formed a cul-de-sac. Together, as they entered Pijarska Street, Schoengarth stopped the car, got out, and rang the bell beside a high, ornate door. Soon an old woman, Mrs. Schmidt, invited them into a wide, enclosed courtyard decorated at one end with a marble statue of a reclining nude. Through yet another door, they entered a gallery which contained a staircase. With Schoengarth leading the way up, they climbed to the top. In the attic, electric lights revealed boards torn from the floor. Menten kneeled beside the shallow space and pulled out a tube covered in a protective cloth material. As he peeled off the cloth and slipped the contents from the tube, he knew from the border that this was the Raphael. Assuming the painting was a gift, he looked at Schoengarth. If Menten wondered at the price, he gave no sign.

Later that evening when he got home he showed the painting to Elizabeth before sequestering it from public view. But the painting did not interest her. Nothing did any longer. Exhausted by the tension in their relationship and horrified at last by what she could no longer deny was happening around her, she had by now ceased her rages. Anyway, nothing now seemed to make him notice her as a woman or stop him from carrying on with "chocolate eyes," the former in-house mistress of the Dutch consul, who had returned to Holland the previous May. In his absence, Menten had moved swiftly to seduce "chocolate eyes" under the same roof as his wife. Debrouin had asked Menten to take care of his business while he was gone. Menten could not resist that temptation either, and he asked his SS friends to name him *Treuhänder* of ORIZA. The house on Grottgera Street was part of the package that had included his new secretary-lover. At first they had only flirted. The more emboldened they became, the more obvious their mutual interest, the more Elizabeth had tried to compete. The harder she tried, the more she drank, partied, and, like "chocolate eyes," flirted with their SS guests.

Pieter now slept on the second floor. Elizabeth turned despondent. For hours on end, she would sit in the front window of the house, her dark hair shining in the sun, staring into space. She seldom talked anymore, but when she did, she spoke of mundane things such as flowers, the weather, her clothes and jewelry, as her grip on reality loosened. By almost any definition, she had lost

Pieter, and not to "chocolate eyes" alone. She now admitted to herself how he had changed since their arrival in Cracow, under the influence of new friends in the SS, the people whom he so obviously admired. He had become like those friends, and she hated and feared the change, because she hated and feared the friends.

She particularly hated ever to find herself near Otsch Kipka, a contact man in the SD whom Menten had befriended. Tall and thin with reddish-blond hair, he had a formal bearing and excellent, if exaggerated, manners, with which he partly tried to disguise a deformity. Kipka had no fingernails, and the truth of their absence—whether, as he said, an agent of the British Special Intelligence Service had pulled them out under torture, or whether they were a birth defect—did nothing to obscure their grotesqueness when he wrapped ten nubs of pink flesh around steins of special SS beer in the Lenartowicza Street Casino or dined with the Mentens. Once, when his girlfriend ridiculed the deformity, in a rage he emptied a machine pistol into the piano on which she played Chopin études.

Through Kipka, Menten met Untersturmführer-SS Wilhelm Rosenbaum, director of the Police School sixty miles south of Cracow in Rabka, a former tourist town of 6,000 residents where Rosenbaum maintained a villa, Magrabianka, on the grounds of the school. Despite frequent invitations to friends for country weekends, Rosenbaum rarely filled the villa's three guestrooms. Invitations to Magrabianka were never sought eagerly. Menten discovered why in the winter of 1940–41 when he joined Schoengarth and Kipka on a visit. As their host and guide, Rosenbaum was proud of what he had created at Rabka, which he likened to a real school. Students—Ukrainian, Polish, and German SS recruits—carried notebooks and studied for examinations. But Rosenbaum placed greater emphasis on the practical side. In one class attended by the visitors, an inmate from the camp nearby at Auschwitz lay on his back, an iron rod across his neck. The instructor, introduced later to the guests as Holz Apfel, balanced his full weight on the pole and rocked from side to side, until he had crushed the man's neck. With the fresh corpse removed, a new inmate was forced to sit with his hands tied over his upraised knees. With the iron rod threaded through the space between his knees and his elbows, he was lifted up as the two ends of the rod rested on tables. Exposed uppermost to the ceiling, his buttocks and bare soles were then clubbed with all the force in Holz Apfel's arms, so that the inmate "pinwheeled" on the impact. A gas mask over his head muffled his screams, and later, after he had fainted, his trousers wet with blood and excrement, he was revived with smelling salts and the process was repeated until he too died. Outside the classrooms on the rifle "range" children from Auschwitz were used as moving and stationary targets.

On their tour, Rosenbaum hoped to impress his guests. (He tried harder in most endeavors to overcome a fear of being mistaken for a Jew. He himself shot any Jew he found with the name Rosenbaum.) With his own hand, he showed the guests how to hack off human limbs with an axe, and, later in the afternoon, he demonstrated the techniques, only then being developed, of mass death—how to lay a wooden plank over a pit.

The Saturday night of their weekend visit, the guests ate and drank heartily in the large dining room at Magrabianka. They even splattered a service of Limoges dishware against the wall, a maid at the villa remembered, to celebrate the momentous announcement of General Schoengarth, who had returned only days before from Berlin with news that the decision had been made to kill whole categories of people without truce, without investigation, and without pity. Schoengarth told them that women and children were to be slain with the men. The instrument designated for this mass homicide was the *Einsatzgruppen,* "mobile formations intended for local and temporary duties." Einsatzgruppe A was to operate behind the Heeresgruppe Nord in the Baltic states; B to sweep central Russia; C to work the Ukraine and D the south. Nearly lost among these four *Gruppen* was a fifth squad, *Einsatzgruppe zur besonderen Verwendung,* or zbV, with 150 volunteers from Cracow and fifty each from Warsaw and Lublin. The commander of the all-volunteer zbV, Schoengarth had orders for his officers, Kipka, Rosenbaum, and Holz Apfel, to work compatibly with Einsatzgruppe C, led by Dr. Otto Rasch, with whom Schoengarth had earlier talked tactics. When the time came every

99

member of zbV had to "overcome himself." *Every* man had to kill or not be worthy.

One morning that spring, just a month before "the time" came, Menten as usual had entered the downstairs offices of ORIZA at Grottgera Street. Despite bloodshot eyes and a hangover from a late party the night before, he was actually excited, even cheerful. Elizabeth's gynecologist's son, Jan Garbien, whom Menten had hired as an office boy for the summer, looked up and smiled. Menten asked, "What do you know about estates?"

Garbien knew nothing and said so.

"Would you like to learn?" Menten asked.

Garbien wanted to study architecture, not land management, but he was flattered anyway by the offer and what it suggested about his abilities. He wondered what Menten had in mind.

"I'll teach you," Menten said.

"But nobody is allowed to cross the frontier," Garbien said.

Menten replied, "In a couple of weeks, maybe. I've got some things to do in Lwów, too."

"How long will you be gone?" Garbien asked.

"Probably two weeks, not more."

Weeks passed and Menten did not leave. The spring weather turned warm, advancing on summer, when on June 22, 1941, Cracow came alive with excitement of the long-anticipated invasion of Russia. In Cracow, trucks in endless convoys transported material east, and the sight of new tanks and artillery gave Cracovians the assurance that nothing could stop Hitler's advance to the Kremlin before the first snow flurries of winter.

The week after the invasion, Garbien had all but forgotten about their conversation, when Menten appeared in the office doorway behind the boy's back. Menten asked, "How do I look?"

Garbien turned around and, genuinely surprised, he blurted out, "Nice, you look nice." He stared at his boss less in admiration than in shock. Menten's German uniform had no insignia of rank, as if he were a mobilized reservist. However, only members of the SD wore this uniform. Garbien thought he seemed larger than life in this Nazi cloak, but he only repeated the lame compliment, "You look nice."

Meanwhile Menten tugged at the stiffness of the tunic, as if he wanted to make himself appear more a veteran. Such was his pride of plumage, he posed that afternoon, before leaving on the trip east, for photographs against the ivy-covered masonry wall in the back garden. He pushed the high-peaked hat down on his head, so that a shadow mysteriously hooded his eyes. Jauntily, he hooked his thumbs in the stiff black leather belt as the sun danced in the chrome buckle. In his wallet pocket he carried the new identification papers of a *Hauptscharführer*-SS with pay records (25 Marks per month) assigning him as a *Sonderführer*-SS translator to the zbV Einsatzgruppe of Eberhardt Schoengarth.

The main elements of zbV had reached Lwów at least a few days before, and Menten had to catch up. Racing in his Adler through the Wehrmacht roadblocks en route, when he arrived he found a city still in the grip of considerable chaos. The corpses of Ukrainians murdered by the retreating Russians littered the streets. For four days between June 30 and July 3, Poles and Ukrainians wearing blue and yellow armbands fell on Jews, whom they blamed for the Ukrainians' murder. Jews were dragged off to prison or, more often, killed on the spot. Together with officers of the SS, Poles and Ukrainians burned and destroyed synagogues and removed the headstones from Jewish cemeteries, later to pave roads, sidewalks, and floors, especially those for expanded prisons. Almost every civilian stayed indoors, listening to the crack of assassins' weapons from the execution courtyards on Zamarstynowska, Jachowicza, and Lackiego streets and the Gestapo headquarters at Pelczynska #59, where the courtyard walls were splattered up to the second floor with human blood and brains hours after the Germans arrived.

In his field headquarters of the zbV Einsatzgruppe at Bursa Abrahamowiczow, Dr. Eberhardt Schoengarth reviewed a list of twenty-five names and addresses. With satisfaction he noted how conveniently almost all the medical professors lived on Romanowicza Street and the professors from the Institute of Technology on Nabielaka Street, and so on. It made his orders that much easier: to arrest the men, search for those hiding, transport the men to Bursa Abrahamowiczow, and return for the women. He wanted the raid to commence at precisely 9 P.M. on July 3, 1941. The teams (two officers and two NCOs) already knew their assignments. One last minute change, though, accommodated a latecomer, Pieter Menten, who asked for one address in particular.

Yadwiga Ostrowski had a problem. Even her daughter had said so. She was not able to say no. But Yadwiga had barely stood still long enough to listen since the war began, much less respond to the warnings. Anyway, she was honored that the Counts Badeni and Yablonowski had chosen her to protect their valuables when they had fled. But her daughter had harped on it: "Our house looks like an art museum, and it will end badly one day."

Nobody, not even her daughter, could be impatient with Yadwiga for long. As far as most men were concerned, she was easily forgiven any oversight; she had long, dark-brown hair with curls that fell to her thin shoulders, and straight black eyebrows intensified the unusual blue of her widely separated eyes. By her open manner, moreover, she put women and men at their ease, often reaching out with a small, reassuring gesture, a touch, a compliment, a politeness. Her husband, Dr. Tadeusz Ostrowski, professor of internal medicine and director of the Surgical Clinic at Lwów University, served his Hippocratic oath "as his immortality," he used to say. Tall and dark with blue eyes, too, and an easy, reassuring smile, he was a friend to his students, who often discussed their ambitions with him. Medicine interested him, but his passion was the young people and their plans to change the world. Despite lectures and patients, a family, a social life, and a private clinic, once a year, usually in the summer, he had traveled to Western Europe before the war and, as an alpinist, climbed the shoulders of Mont Blanc and the Matterhorn and fished the clear waters that melted down from their peaks.

Rare among the intelligentsia, the Ostrowskis had dared to cross the rigid strata of Lwowian society—then a radical, if not dangerous, departure from form. They had always invited to their home Jews and the gentry, even the aristocratic Counts Badeni and Yablonowski. Kazimierz Bartel, the Prime Minister in Pilsudski's first government, was often their guest. The Jan Greks from the university hospital and the pediatrician Dr. Groer visited often. Through the Greks, they knew Tadusz Boy-Zelenski, the physician and author, cabaret actor, and translator of the French classics. Pieter and Elizabeth Menten had played bridge in their apartment at Romanowicza #5, a spacious, warm place with high ceilings and French windows that faced the street. The interior design reflected Dr. Ostrowski's position and Yadwiga's taste as an eclectic collector who derived pleasure from unusual art and antiques that Pieter Menten before the war had often helped her find. Sometimes Dr. Ostrowski tried to curb her enthusiasm, but so many objects had been available before the war—carpets, figurines, goblets, china, pictures, sculpture, coins, semiprecious and precious stones, antiques, furniture crafted in France and England, tapestries . . . Yadwiga had sought to buy them all on the pretext of investment. And soon, she possessed a Joshua Reynolds, a Canaletto, and the sixteenth-century busts of six Roman emperors.

Despite her relative youth, as the wife of Dr. Ostrowski, Yadwiga was the *grande dame* of the intelligentsia, and therefore she had a responsibility. When the Russians had occupied Lwów after September 1939, they shared their nine-room apartment with the Ruffs, a Jewish doctor, his wife, and a son with epilepsy. Life was difficult, but it was easier for the Ostrowskis and their friends than for other Lwowians. Indeed they were lucky to live anywhere in Lwów, considering how, as members of the intelligentsia, they should have been deported to Russia on the first trains. The Russians had exempted and treated them well after Dr. Ostrowski performed life-saving surgery on a powerful political *komissar*.

Some of the Ostrowskis' friends, however, had not enjoyed such good fortune. As soon as possible after September 17, 1939, they had fled the Russians, taking with them only what they could carry. The family of the Count Badeni, as minor royalty, did not need to wonder how the Bolsheviks would treat them if they were caught. On the eighteenth the Badenis buried some valuables on the grounds of their estate and brought the rest to the Ostrowskis, rather than risk confiscation if they were searched by authorities in Hungary, to which they fled. In the apartment Yadwiga hid the Badenis' two kidskin pouches that contained a superb emerald *en cabochon,* several large diamonds, and a necklace of small diamonds strung between each of 760 plump natural pearls that the count's father had purchased for 100,000 gold crowns in 1870 at the Paris Exhibition.

Pretty soon, as more and more fleeing friends prevailed on Yadwiga's generosity, the Ostrowski house had become a cask of treasure. But Yadwiga did not show concern. She did not even notice how people were fleeing Lwów for their lives. Yadwiga, and to a similar degree Dr. Ostrowski, carried on as if life were normal. Yadwiga asked, "What else can I do?" as she hung friends' priceless paintings on the walls and, like an Arab merchant, stacked Persian carpets thoughtlessly in corners of the rooms. If the Germans came, so what? The Russians had treated them well, and she remembered the gentleness of the occupying Austrian forces twenty years before.

Even as German bombs were exploding on Sknilow Airport, Yadwiga hosted dinner parties. On July 3, 1941, when the Wehrmacht had rolled through Lwów in pursuit of the retreating Russians, Yadwiga had gone to the kitchen to help her cook prepare food for a dinner party that same evening at which Boy-Zelenski had promised to read from his play, *The Wedding Reception*. However, the Greks next door and Boy-Zelenski had canceled. But Yadwiga determined to make something of the evening anyway, so she set the table with her best bone china, the silver candlesticks, two bottles of red Hungarian wine, and a stewpot—a "siege" meal, she said—with vegetables, potatoes, and meat. The light from the candles flickered as far as the damask curtains, pulled tightly in the blackout. Besides the cook, chambermaid, and chauffeur, the Ostrowskis had their resident "guests," Dr. Stanislaw Ruff and his wife, Anna, and their son, Adam; the Catholic priest Stanislaw Komornicki; and Katarina Demko, an American girl, who had been the Ostrowskis' children's English tutor for nearly five years.

At a few minutes after nine they heard a knock on the downstairs door. The chambermaid went to see who was there. Turning from the dining table toward the door, the diners first saw two German SS NCOs, one officer, and another man hidden in the shadows. The officer ordered them all into the downstairs foyer. As they passed out of the dining room, Yadwiga saw the officer slip an ivory figurine from the end table into his pocket. "Bandit!" she yelled at him.

The second man then came out of the shadows. "Shut up," he

said. And all at once they noticed Pieter Menten, their neighbor and, once, their friend. Immediately, before they could say a word, the officer, Holz Apfel, ordered the men in the apartment to follow him downstairs.

Yadwiga said, "Tadeusz, take a coat and hat."

Menten shook his head at her. "There's no reason," he said, almost kindly. "They'll be asked a few questions and returned immediately."

As the door closed behind them, Yadwiga went to the sofa and fainted. Ninety minutes later she heard another knock on the door. She told Katarina to take the pouches of jewelry from behind the bookcase while the maid went to the door. Now Holz Apfel and Menten pushed her aside and climbed the stairs at a run. Too frightened to move, the Demko girl did not hide what she was carrying. Menten took the pouches from her hands, and then quickly pushed the women and the servants downstairs into the van in the street, but not before he had locked the door of the Ostrowski apartment and pocketed the keys.

The SS teams and their female prisoners hurried now to Bursa Abrahamowiczow and the headquarters of the zbV Einsatz-gruppe, where they unloaded the van of its human cargo in the enclosed courtyard. Reunited with their wives in the hall of the building, the professors were told to stand with their heads bowed facing the wall. Any sound was answered with the butt of a rifle or the hard end of a whip. In the meantime more professors and their families arrived, including the Greks, Boy-Zelenski, and others from that house. Every ten minutes or so they heard screams and cracks of pistol shots from beneath their feet in the cellar. A German shouted after every shot, *"Einiger weniger"* ("one less"). While they waited, out the corner of her eye Yadwiga saw some-one fall to the floor, and she heard a sound of choking. Terror had triggered an epileptic seizure in Adam Ruff. Even before his mother, Anna, could relieve his suffering, a German officer shot him. Yadwiga and Anna froze, beyond fear. The German ordered them to wipe up the blood with Yadwiga's shawl, but her house-keeper pushed her aside and covered the boy's body. The German kicked her away and again ordered Yadwiga to clean up the mess.

Hours passed. Before sunrise the door opened and the professors and their families, including wives and children, stumbled into the courtyard. Professors Ostrowski and Ruff led the procession. Under SS guard they passed the gate and turned into Bursa Abrahamowiczow. Silenced by shock, the women followed their husbands into the night toward the Walecki Hills and the electrical generating plant where nearly everybody in Lwów went once a month before the war to pay his bills. Not too far distant from the city center and SS headquarters and yet isolated from public view, the hills were a perfect venue for slaughter. That day before dawn, the men of the zbV Einsatzgruppe executed the intelligentsia of Lwów.

The next morning—summerlike and warm—Pieter Menten prowled the streets of the city as an animal explores an old cave. Eighteen months had passed since he had evacuated this city as a refugee with Consul Broen; now Menten returned as a conqueror in a khaki uniform with the swastika band on his right arm. He knew there was little purpose in the gesture, but his curiosity overcame his judgment, and he told the driver of the staff car in which he was riding to stop at Slowackiego Street #3. There was no sound in response to the knock until, as he was about to leave, an older woman reached the door. Menten asked if the Pistiners— Isaac, Frieda, or any of their children—were at home. The old woman looked bewildered. She had lived in the house only since the Russian occupation. The name Pistiner meant little to her. Menten assumed by that that Isaac could be found in the countryside, in Podhorodse, where he would believe he was safe.

For the rest of the day Menten drove from house to house chosen from memory for confiscation. He had already decided to reserve the house with the graceful columns and the two small verandas outside the French windows, the Ostrowskis' house, for himself. On the doors of the other homes he had posted an official bonding order, a decree that made the house Reich property. The notice warned plainly in Polish and German that theft was punishable by death. Now he wedged his personal card in the door above the knob. Back in the street, he tore off the plaque under the bell for Dr. T. Ostrowski's Private Clinic.

Late that afternoon or the next morning when they returned to Bursa Abrahamowiczow, General Schoengarth ordered his zbV officers into the Walecki Hills. Past the SS guarding the road and the walls of the power station, they came on a secluded field of newly turned soil on which people were being executed as they arrived. At the first lull by the executioners for reloading machine guns and quaffing vodka, Schoengarth pointed out the precise, Berlin-designated dimensions of the burial ditches as he rattled off details of transport security, the varieties of execution, the placement of bodies in the graves, and the *coup de grâce*. The monologue lasted nearly an hour, the time scores of men, women, and children took to die. Holz Apfel, the primary executioner of zbV, volunteered a demonstration for the others who had not yet been blooded. He ordered a victim from the line to strip. He then searched for valuables, lined the man against the edge of the ditch, and neck-shot him. He then turned and gestured with the machine pistol to the next officer. One by one the officers ordered victims to strip, stand, and die. When his turn came, Pieter Menten showed that he too possessed the SS ideal of "hardness." The gun went off in his hand as if it were a thing with its own ferocious will; the buck of it against the pad of his palm surprised him. He had merely pressed the trigger, and the mechanism had done its will. It was easier to think that way because now he, too, had killed for the first time.

That night in the makeshift Casino, they celebrated the blooding. In the full blush of his complete acceptance as a "black Jesuit," as Hitler called his SS, Menten was effusive with praise for his comrades. When Holz Apfel bragged that he wanted to shoot one Jew for every year of the thousand-year Reich, Menten rose unsteadily to the top of a table and, saluting the ceiling with his stein, he toasted Apfel with the words, "And if you do, I hope you are awarded the Iron Cross."

The next day outside the Ostrowski house a man named Smolka saw Yadwiga. Before the Germans had occupied Lwów, Smolka worked as a technician in the laboratory of Dr. Ostrowski's private clinic. That morning Smolka had heard rumors that some professors from the university hospital had been shot the night before in an *Aktionen,* and he wanted to know if the Ostrowskis had survived. As he walked along Romanowicza, he tried to appear purposeful, as if he were striding toward someplace, and not just snooping around. When he neared the Ostrowski address, he saw a large truck backed up to the front door. He slowed his pace, risking questions. Workmen were carrying carpets, furniture, and paintings from the apartment. Smolka slowed down even more, and then he stopped, dumbstruck. He saw the beautiful image of Yadwiga's face in a workman's arms. The portrait had hung over the mantle in the main salon of the apartment. Smolka felt sick, as if he had seen a ghost, and he breathed deeply for control. They were dead, and every vestige of their lives was being plundered. A man came around the corner of the truck and said something to the workman with the portrait. He wore a khaki uniform with a swastika and seemed excited. He did not notice Smolka, who quickly turned around the block, where he waited, his heart racing, until the truck was gone. The Ostrowskis' door was locked, but Smolka read the card near the doorknob, in black lettering: Pieter Menten, *Treuhänder* of Antiquities, Rynek Glowny #24, Cracow.

A day or so after the trucks had transported the Ostrowskis' and other plundered valuables from Lwów to Cracow and from Cracow to the repository behind the barbed-wire fences of the Police Training School in Rabka, Menten sought to find someone he trusted to drive for him on other, more distant excursions for plunder. That morning as he left the Hotel George, where he was staying until he could move into the Ostrowskis', the clouds released a shower of summer rain. Under the front awning of the hotel, he grasped the elbow of a startled Mikhail Podhorodecki. Years before, Podhorodecki had been the owner of a town house and an estate in the country—and Menten's neighbor. Now, with the war, Podhorodecki had lost even his health. His emphysema was worse than ever, and his wife and children, whom he had sent away, offered no comfort. He had no money, not even for food, which he had taken to scrounging at the Institute for Deaf People. Bleak though the present was, the future looked worse. Most of the time he had nothing better to do than stay dry and out from underfoot of the newly arrived Germans.

Menten asked, "Can you still drive a car?"

Podhorodecki replied, "Well, as you know, I used to drive for a hobby, and that thing I had, the small one with the unpredictable engine . . ."

Menten said, "I need a driver, a chauffeur, for ORIZA."

"I can start immediately," he said, thrilled. They set out on foot in the direction of the garage.

The German military and police crowded the sidewalks of Lwów as if with the sun breaking through the clouds, a promenade was an order they could not refuse. Menten, noticing a tall man shamble toward them, slowed his pace. Like a scrap of paper that the wind had stuck to his breast, the ragged white patch with a bright blue Star of David explained why the man studied the pavement with such intensity, as if the cracks told a fascinating tale. Menten recognized him. Before the war Isaac Pistiner had introduced them more than once, and now he called out to him, "Hey, Leubel."

As if stung by the sound of his name, Jacob Leubel cringed. A Rumanian Jew and friend of the Pistiners who would soon flee to Palestine, Leubel was trying to reach the house of a friend in the center of the city, and he had prayed that the rain would leave his voyage uncharted. Although he had tried not to look, when the rain stopped he saw Germans appear on the streets in a dazzling and, for a Jew, terrifying display of uniforms. He saw how happy the Germans were, and how healthy they looked. They were fat, their cheeks rosy, their teeth strong and white, their chests thrust forward. When he heard his name, Jacob Leubel thought, This is the end of me.

Thinking again of the Germans, Leubel looked Menten in the face; Menten had that same hearty glow. Friendly and with a conqueror's boastfulness, Menten said, "So we meet again, Herr Leubel." He laughed. "But now things have changed, haven't they?" And then he asked, referring to their acquaintance, "Tell me, where can I find Isaac and his brother-in-law, Krumholz?"

"Why?" Leubel asked. Certainly Menten had forgotten about the hatred between them years ago.

"I need them, that's all. In Podhorodse I suppose?"

"I can't say," Leubel told him, but his heart leapt with a premonition. He knew where Isaac was hiding, but Menten was serving the Nazis, and although he knew Menten, he no longer knew whom to trust. He added, "Since we last met, the Russians and now the Germans have invaded this land. People are changing houses like clothes. For a long time I haven't seen either one of them." And while he waited to be dismissed, he thought he saw Menten smile.

The evening of July 8, 1941—one day after the massacre in Podhorodse—Frieda's heart beat faster when she heard the car motor die. What remained of her family in the Stewczyka Street flat comforted her as much as anything could, but now, with the sounds outside in the street, she did not know. Hastily, she made an accounting. The oldest boy, Lieber, lived across town. Isaac was hiding, and as long as he stayed underground, nobody would find him, although Frieda constantly wondered who or what would track him down first—Menten (Leubel had told them about his question that day in the street), the Nazis, or sickness. The Krumholzes—David, Malvina, and Marek—kept to themselves in their small flat on St. Theresa Street.

With so many people to worry about, there was little that remained for herself, and that suited Frieda just fine. This pogrom, this German slaughter of Jews, was difficult for her to fathom. As if some mindless machine were to roll over fertile land, crushing everything in its path, she could not fix an image of that machine in her mind, either as something to hate or to fear, any more than she could truly hate an aberration of nature, a hurricane, or a pestilence. Her emotions could not absorb any more, so much had happened these last two years. . . .

First the Soviet invasion had inched the Pistiners toward the abyss that the gypsy had seen in her tarot cards: the new local soviet had permitted Maria and Philip Wecker to remain as caretakers on the collective in Podhorodse, although they were forbidden to occupy Isaac's big house, which the soviet had commandeered as a rest camp for war-weary Red Army soldiers. Isaac had once owned the land, and in Leninist dogma, landowners simply did not exist. As "non-people" Isaac and Frieda had been ordered to take what they could carry and leave. They had taken Milusia, the infant daughter of Maria and Philip. And they had turned their backs forever on a way of life. They went to Lwów.

In the fall of 1939, the Russians had conquered 78,000 square miles in Poland and a hodgepodge of 13 million people of ten nationalities and five religions. The early experiments with a National Assembly of Western White Ruthenia and the Assembly of Western Ukraine had failed, so the Bolsheviks fell back on the tried-and-true policies of the eighteenth- and nineteenth-century czars. Some 3 million "troublemakers" disappeared into the vast Soviet interior. The NKVD had registered Esperantists and philatelists, restaurant and hotel owners, university professors, doctors, teachers, and "speculators"—a term for Jews—and given them an hour to pack up "clothes, footwear, underwear, bed linen, kitchen utensils, food for one month, and fishing tackle."

The Russians certainly had the freedom to do with Isaac what they wanted. The NKVD would surely have transported him to Russia if they had ever found him hiding without a passport in the apartment on Stewczyka Street, in which the Pistiners—three boys, Regina, and Milusia, the child—occupied three rooms, with the rest of the shared apartment sheltering other forsaken Jewish refugees. The only Gentile, a Russian pilot temporarily in one room, had carried a loaded revolver to the toilet as protection against whatever unspeakable evil he imagined the Pistiners and the other Jews might inflict when he had his pants down.

Two Pistiner daughters, Mara and Eva, had lived on separate floors at Pelczynska Street #26. Eva, her husband, Dr. Turek, and their eight-month-old daughter, Marisia, hid from the NKVD during the day, and they watched in the night for car lights that signaled a sweep for Jews by Russian police. One night in the winter of 1940, the lights shone and the police took Dr. Turek. The next morning, before dawn, the lights shone again. "You will join your husband," the police told Eva, who had packed food and clothes and what she needed for the baby, Marisia. "There is no reason to fear," they said to her. "Everything will be all right. You will go to a beautiful town in a lovely, vast country, and you will work in good conditions for good pay. You will have good food and you will become productive citizens."

When she reached the Lwów train station, Eva understood the tragedy. From all sides had come tens of police cars with women and children who had also been promised their husbands. On the train platform the police opened the doors of cattle cars. Eva was "asked" to enter a car with only women and children inside. The door was slammed closed. Horribly upset, her sister Mara had run to Stewczyka Street, where she poured out the tale to Isaac. Early the next morning, upon learning that the train would not depart for another day, Mara and her sister Regina returned to the station. Barred by a policeman from entering the platform, Regina got through to the end of the train where Eva had entered a car, and she called out.

"I am here," Eva called softly, peering from under the lid of the ventilation hole at the top of the car. "I lost all my milk. The child is dying."

Regina looked around her. "Throw the child to me. Quickly." And with the child in her arms she ran down the tracks to Mara, who was talking with the policeman. An hour later, they had returned the child to Isaac's.

The incident had shaken Isaac, who had aged a decade in the last months alone. With the last of the money he had saved for just such an emergency, he had bribed an official for a passport and papers identifying him as a "village peasant worker." Isaac had not waited for change to bring him good fortune. Events had already started to dim the last vestiges of hope for anything more than personal survival.

Sixteen months later, in June 1941, Jews ironically had sought passage out of Lwów by any means—even cattle cars—to any place, including the Russian interior, just to escape the Nazi invasion. Mara and her husband, Stanislaw ("Stash") Cygelstreich, had begged to board the same cattle cars that earlier had transported Eva. Mara went to tell her parents to flee as well because "this town will die."

"Why are you escaping?" Isaac had said. "Stay with us here. The Germans will bring order and all will be well again. You wait and see."

Mara had *not* waited to see. She had kissed her parents, brothers, and sisters, thinking it was perhaps for the last time. The next morning, Stash, Mara, and little Milusia, the daughter of Maria and Philip Wecker, headed east on foot toward Kiev. After

112

months of wandering and hardship Mara's family reached Kazakhstan, just as the gypsy had said, where they struggled to survive for the next three years.

Malvina Krumholz had told David she thought all this misery had been brought on by their move from the village. The heart attack after Bibi went to Palestine had embittered her. David had comforted her; there was still Marek to watch out for. The letters from Bibi had fueled David's desire to emigrate. He sensed that eventually the family would wind up in Palestine, if the British would allow it. There, certainly, Malvina's disposition would brighten.

When the Russians occupied Lwów the Krumholzes had been moved to a smaller and dirtier apartment, on the fourth floor, at St. Theresa #33. Malvina had made a small pullman kitchen into a workable space, and with fabric and imagination she had transformed the parlor. Despite that, David had looked longingly at the balsam-wood model airplanes that Marek lacquered so brightly. Now that the Nazis had come David wished to heaven that those little airplanes could fly them out of there.

Now, it had all come to this, Frieda thought, as she risked a sidelong glance out the window. A car had stopped. Three uniformed men in the street looked up at their building, as would architects surveying a design. Frieda knew the Germans had come for them, finally. Perhaps her voice edged harder, or her movements changed just so, because suddenly Marisia, the child of Eva and Dr. Turek, began to cry. As if the sound had shattered her control, Frieda stood rigidly watching the door for an instant before she scooped up the child in her arms. As the child's crying subsided, the door opened.

Menten crossed the threshold first, looking to Frieda as if something life-giving and human had been torn from his soul. There was an exhaustion and a wildness in his eyes that made her think, only for an instant. Wondering what he had done and why he was here, she thought to ask him—to greet him kindly and invite him to sit down. She had not even seemed to notice the uniform, it was

113

so out of character. She saw him more the way he had appeared to her those hundreds of times before the war and before the troubles over the land. When the uniform registered in her mind, contradicting her original thought, she had the feeling that he had not come to the house to help them. The men who accompanied him, also in uniform, went to search the other rooms, but Menten stayed where he was, near the door. He looked at Frieda and asked, "Where is Isaac?"

Her silence seemed to anger him. He pushed her into the back of the room and tried to snatch the child in her arms, but Frieda resisted with the strength of her body. Stronger, Menten grasped the child by the arm, like a doll, and again he asked her, "So where is he?"

Frieda probably did not hear, so intently did she watch the child, as Menten went into the other room, impulsively, and flung the child out the open window. Watching her fall, he drew the 9mm Parabellum from its holster and fired, missing. Frieda tried to stop him; just as impulsively, he turned the gun on her.

Two Pistiner sons, Japan and Dzionek, and Tadusz Zucker, the husband of the youngest Pistiner daughter, Saba, heard the concussions about the same instant that Holz Apfel and another SD soldier found them hiding. Once in the street, they waited in the car until Menten emerged from the building and impatiently ordered the Pistiners and Zucker into the car and told Apfel to drive off. Minutes later, the car stopped before a high arch with filigree iron gates that linked a masonry wall. On Menten's orders the Pistiner sons and Zucker ran under the arch up the path, past row after row of headstones, until they reached the middle of Lwów's large Catholic cemetery. Breathless with fear, the men knelt before three separate markers, and as they bent with their chests against their knees, Menten aimed the pistol at their napes. He shot Dzionek last.

Later that same evening Menten followed the aroma of cooking up the stairs at St. Theresa Street. This time the door opened on a scene of surprising domesticity. David Krumholz was seated at a table, his suspenders down and his shirt collar opened. Young Marek was reading a book. Startled, they looked up and froze in place. At the sound of voices, Malvina came through a curtain from the kitchen. She had lifted the apron to wipe her hands. *"Panne,* where are you taking them?" she asked Menten. When he made no reply she untied the apron and joined her son and husband. Malvina asked, *"Panne,* why are you doing this?"

They were driven to the area of the bright, bare lights—the electricity generating plant. Just as there were no answers to what was happening, there were no further questions. The Krumholz family was stood alongside a ditch to face the void. And with their hands clasped in front, not in prayer, but more in some final resignation, they died.

Even then, what drove Menten, whether rage or merely the desire to finish a task, had not exhausted itself fully. He dropped Apfel and the other soldier at the SD headquarters, outside the courtyard, and he directed the car toward Rappaporta Street, across from the synagogue, to a flat at #5. Although he seriously doubted if the man he wanted was there, he drew his pistol and knocked hard, and the sound of rapid movement came from within. When the door opened, Menten pulled the trigger on Dr. Sigmund Gelmann, Isaac's lawyer in the land case, who fell dead at his feet.

And still, it was not done.

That night, a cool breeze blew through the quiet darkness of the cemetery. Before he opened his eyes to the blurred white silhouettes, Japan felt chilled and rolled over on his side to press his cheek against the grass. As his mind struggled for clarity, he knew that the form beside him was his brother, Dzionek, dead. He moved slowly at first, testing the miracle of his survival; he touched the back of his head, outlining a wound that had bled before coagulating. He could not stand, or even try, he thought, as he rolled over again, on his back, dropping his head between his legs. Later, he crawled in the grass to the cemetery gate. The street was empty; nobody dared to violate the eight o'clock curfew set throughout Lwów. A car passed, but it was surely German. Somehow, he stumbled, crawled, and walked to Polish friends, who took him to a hospital that did not turn away Jews. He was treated so well by doctors and nurses that the wound did not in any way impair his memory.

While finding Isaac was not beyond Menten's means, he knew that Brigadeführer-SS Fritz Katzman, the Nazi police chief in Galicia, planned sooner or later to liquidate the Lwów ghetto, which would end Isaac's life with the same finality, if not the dispatch, of his bullet. He had watched as panicked Jews had rushed to meet the deadline: by the end of the first week of September any Jew found outside the ghetto was doomed. Those who had missed, if only by minutes, were hanged by the SS with electrical cord from lampposts until heaps of their dead bodies were piled up in front of the Judenrat offices on Jakoba Hermana Street. There in a light breeze dangled the corpses of the hanged, their faces blue, their heads tilted backward, their tongues blackened and stretched out. Luxury cars raced in from the center of the city, German civilians with their wives and children came to see the sensational spectacle, and, as was their custom, the visitors enthusiastically photographed the scene. Afterward the Ukrainians and Poles arrived by tram, with greater modesty.

Remnants of the Pistiner-Krumholz families—Lieber, the eldest son, and Isaac—stumbled under the Bridge of Death, the ghetto's antechamber, from which SS and Ukrainian police looked down like vultures on the Jews. Preying on the old, sick, and weak, these gatekeepers forced the rest under the bridge and down Peltewna Street into an area of huts that before the war had been the province of whores, robbers, and libertines. It was called the Kleparow ghetto, where hunger bloated bodies and scurvy, typhus, and tuberculosis soon struck a doomed community.

Soon, German military discipline transformed the ghetto into a *Judenlager*, or *Julag*. Inmates too weak for work went to the Sands execution pits or took "vitamins"—beams *(belki* in Polish) for vitamin B, boards *(deski)* for vitamin D, and bricks *(cegly)* for vitamin C, which they were forced to carry at a run from the Kleparow railway station to the camp. Often when the runners, exhausted unto death, reached the main gate, they heard the strains of Mozart, marches by Radetsky, and, ironically, Beethoven's Third Symphony. The gate itself was a dangerous place for a

Jew, a place of torment where selections were made for work details and, worse, for those special assignments that spelled certain death. Sometimes on spring and early summer afternoons, death arrived at the gate from a distance and without forewarning. That was when an officer of the camp guard and his family entertained luncheon guests on their balcony; when dessert and coffee were served, his wife raised a rifle to "toast" her guests with a dead or maimed *Julag* inmate. Clapping her little, chubby hands, their daughter applauded her mother's marksmanship with the abandoned glee of a child snuffing out birthday candles.

Through all this, Lieber Pistiner guarded his health jealously. Constantly in the work gangs outside the *Julag*, in the evenings he plotted to join a Resistance group that all inmates knew *must* be organizing in the forests. One night as the gang returned they were ordered to line up in front of the gate. (They had not heard the rumor of an inmate assaulting an SS guard—whether he was killed nobody knew. In retaliation, the SS general for Lwów, Brigadeführer Robert Ulrich, commanded the death of every tenth work gang inmate.) At first Lieber Pistiner saw what looked like a routine head count. Numbed by the brutality, he might not have noticed the Luger go off in the SS officer's hands, killing an inmate down the line. As the SS officer got closer, he did not stop. When he came even with Lieber, he raised the pistol and fired.

And finally, Isaac the Patriarch. He subsisted on bread that resembled mire, animal salt, groats, beet sugar, and vinegar. The older ghetto residents were easier prey to disease than to truncheons. The ghetto had one provisional infirmary but not a single pharmacy. Meager medications arrived from the Aryan quarter at prices that none could afford. Ten doctors tried at least to ease the pain and took preventive steps where possible, sterilizing clothing and practicing hygiene.

The memory of the "retaliation" killings was still fresh when the epidemic broke out. The disease, like the madness that condemned them there, ran its inexorable course. With twenty-five new cases every day at the epidemic's fevered height, Isaac became a statistic. The last words on his lips were *"Shema Yisroael . . ."* ("Hear, O Israel: the Lord our God, the Lord is One").

CHAPTER V

✖

"He planned with cunning. . . ."

IN EARLY 1942 IN German-occupied Poland, Pieter Menten was having a good time. With special SS license plates and his chauffeur "Teddy" Podhorodecki behind the wheel, his Chevrolet (made in Utrecht) swept through the police roadblocks, as he rode serenely in back, his arm around the delicate shoulder of his mistress, Irena Kostesteska, the Polish screen heartthrob.

Menten had *definitely* come up in the Nazi world. SS friends trusted him as an equal since the "trials" of last July with the zbV Einsatzgruppe, which Schoengarth had disbanded at the end of August 1941. Sharing, naturally, meant spoils, too. And business boomed so, he could barely keep up with the conquests of the Wehrmacht as it rolled through Lutsk, Rovno, Zhitomir, and finally Kiev and Riga, where only recently he had been summoned by Head of Division, SD Commander Bruno Streckenback, to appraise recent art "acquisitions." On that first journey to Riga, he had brought along Miss Irena, to whom he had made love, right there, in the back seat, beside a precious cello that contained pouches with gems. Making love on the move was almost a necessity. They were constantly on the road in the Chevrolet or the Adler, which were usually trailed by a Hartwig van that transported the loot back to Rabka and Lwów headquarters.

Once, passing nearby, they had taken the time to stop at the Sopot estate. Menten's brother, Dirk, who was visiting from Holland, came along. The chauffeur Teddy stayed across the river in Podhorodse to supervise minor repairs on the car. The blacksmith

118

who was helping to forge a cracked wheel asked him, "Do you know that he murdered people here?" And Teddy remembered that Menten had once said while they were driving, "I finished all my enemies, for everything." And now he knew what he had meant. As Podhorodecki talked with the blacksmith at his forge, he saw Pieter near the footbridge over the Stryj. A woman shouted at him, "You might as well have killed me and my children, because we are going to die of hunger anyway."

On the journey back Dirk and Pieter made much of their new money belts, which were more than three feet long and strapped to their midsections under their jackets. They boastfully showed the belts to Teddy and Miss Irena, who were suitably impressed by the large quantities of looted diamonds that the belts contained. Dirk, tall and slim, wore the pouch easily; Pieter, rapidly gaining weight in those good times, seemed stouter. Once back in Cracow from that same trip, after he had parked the car in the garage, Teddy Podhorodecki unloaded two metal containers, each weighing around nine pounds, filled with looted twenty-dollar gold pieces. "Don't bring them upstairs," Menten said. "Put them over in the corner," as if they were ten-penny nails.

One day, a blond, blue-eyed visitor with the chiseled, hardened look of an athlete came by appointment to Menten's house in Cracow. His tailoring was somber, befitting a dealer from the fashionable Wierzowa Street address of the *Treuhänder* for Warsaw's foremost art dealer. He had come to buy for his clients what could not be found in Warsaw. Boastful of his collection, Menten gave Jerzy Bieraszewski, as he called himself, a tour through the rooms of the Grottgera house. In forty minutes or so, Bieraszewski saw masterpieces—icons, great Russian art, objects he had last seen in Polish museums—and he flattered their owner. Then in one room, where Menten had stacked frames against the wall, like plates in a drainer, Bieraszewski thought he noted several extremely rare canvases by Maurice Gottlieb, the Polish Rembrandt. A portrait by Stanislaw Lentz nearly took his breath away. As soon as politeness allowed, he thanked Menten, promising to return before leaving Cracow, then rushed to the Central railroad station, where he passed the information of what he had just seen to a waiting contact.

119

Bieraszewski was an alias of the Polish Underground for a Jew named Marion Gutnayer, the grandson of the original owner of the famous Warsaw art gallery, long since expropriated by the Germans. The Underground had sent Gutnayer to investigate rumors of the Dutchman's commerce in Polish plunder, rumors now confirmed by what Gutnayer had just seen. Menten indeed possessed the stolen collection of Mieczyslaw Zagayski, the tycoon and founder of Drago, a conglomerate of mines, refineries, quarries, real estate, and construction. A Jew, Zagayski had passionately collected Polish art, especially Judaica, before fleeing to New York in the late 1930s, leaving everything behind. But the sight of Zagayski's extremely valuable collection had startled Gutnayer less than that portrait in Menten's house by Stanislaw Lentz. The white-bearded face in the canvas was Gutnayer's grandfather, the gallery's founder—a portrait that Gutnayer had last seen in 1939 over the mantle of the family's Warsaw apartment.

By the spring of 1942, Himmler felt ready to present his case against Hans Frank to the *Führer*. His SS investigators in Cracow had compiled a lengthy and incriminating dossier of corruption that even the *Führer* could not easily ignore. Himmler had expressed his praise for their loyalty to Krüger, to Schoengarth, and to Menten, who had anticipated the boost that Himmler's ascendance in the General Government would give to his fortunes. But Hans Frank was not that easily outwitted and removed. Before Hitler could do anything with the evidence, Hans Frank audaciously tried to resign as Governor General, but nobody resigned in the Reich unless Hitler said so. And Hitler had problems with the resignation. He did not want Himmler as the overlord of Poland; Himmler's growing power within the Reich had created a real threat already, so Hitler simply tore up Hans Frank's resignation and told him that this time he would overlook the corruption, as long as it did not continue. With this public show of confidence in the Governor General, Himmler, humiliated, tried to forget his sacred oath to Heinrich I. What helped salvage his honor was the new "higher mission" to which Hitler soon assigned him—the annihilation of European Jewry. Himmler withdrew his forces from the political battlefield. Höhere SS-und Polizeiführer

Friedrich-Wilhelm Krüger was transferred to Berlin. Another partisan, General Schoengarth, requested an immediate transfer to a Waffen-SS battalion in the Balkans—virtual self-banishment for a man of his achievements and education, but a post he had desired all the same to put temporary distance between himself and further political intrigue. Otsch Kipka faced trumped-up charges in Cracow's SS/Police Court VI of habitual drunkenness and of "defiling the race" with a Polish girl. The court forgave the drunkenness charges. (Kipka could not help himself, the court said, considering his role as executioner with the zbV.) And the Polish woman was later identified as a *Volksdeutscher*. When the court threw out the case, the Governor General threw Kipka out of Poland. A month after his transfer to Paris, the Underground assassinated him.

Eventually police loyal to the Governor General brought Pieter Menten to the dreaded cellars of the Stycznia Street SS Headquarters, where he stayed behind bars for his betrayal. In those summer days, condensation on the cell walls ran over last written words and prayers of former prisoners who had invited death before the further agonies of torture. Now, he, too, was tortured, but he did not betray General Schoengarth, against whom the interrogators sought evidence. From his cell, he boldly demanded and received pen and paper with which he wrote to Himmler, his ultimate protector against Hans Frank.

"I am a Dutchman," he wrote. "I am of the opinion that all Dutchmen are German and are as much German as the Germans are." Toadying mercilessly, he continued, "The Dutch are a Germanic tribe. Granted I may not be a PG [member of the Nazi party] and I may not be a member of the SS; yet I am an outspoken and enthusiastic supporter of the *Führer* and of his ideas and plans. I have always and at every turn, even before the war, acted in the interests of the movement as an honorable co-worker and have made myself available to that effect. The reorganization of Europe as the *Führer* sees it is my highest political idea. I wanted to give my estate to the SS; . . . on my estate I wanted to have a recreation facility built and furnished, all paid for by me.

"I so hoped to prove as the first Dutchman my sense of allegiance with the NS [National Socialist] movement, and in par-

121

ticular with the SS. *I was also the first Dutchman when the war broke out with Russia to make myself available to the Einsatzkommando zbV.* [Italics added.] Enclosed you will find proof of this," he wrote, hoping for rescue. "I am a merchant and like Dutchmen everywhere, I am one hundred percent a merchant. However, my business transactions have always been carried out with the approval of and in accordance with the highest police officials."

That August, Menten "escaped" from Stycznia—probably with the help of Himmler loyalists—into the mountains, through which he planned to enter Hungary. Elizabeth, alone in the house, had little to feel about his departure. She had already lost her husband to Miss Irena and before her, to "chocolate eyes." More than that, she hated the change in Pieter. He had not told her about his two-week absence in July 1941. But after he returned, he had wept at the slightest provocation and his nerves were raw. He had started to talk like the Nazis and to think like them, too; and he was drinking more than ever: his face was fleshy and she noticed signs of desperation in his eyes. There had been the Nazi uniform, which he had not worn since that summer. Now, they had arrested him—more evidence of unspeakable crimes. He had killed, she thought.

Later, in a Cracow hospital, she blamed the SS who had searched the house. Too much stigma attached to suicide and besides, the story helped *him* gain sympathy—look at the grievous loss he had nearly suffered. But the SS had not done this to her, not at all. She had taken the pistol to her room soon after the police had come in search of Pieter, and she had sat at the window as usual, looking out into space. Finally, she had turned away and, taking the pistol in both hands, had shot herself in the heart by pulling the trigger with her thumbs. The wound was not mortal, although it would be the cause nine years later of her death.

After the SS found Menten hiding out in the forest, they jailed him for a week in Monteluppich prison as an "honorary detainee." On his release, he was summarily ordered out of the General Government by Hans Frank, never to return. However, as a friend of Himmler and the SS, he was expelled luxuriously on January 31, 1943, aboard a plush, private train of four cars containing his household effects, furniture, antiques and paintings, one automobile, sixteen trunks, one Raphael, eleven suitcases, one gladstone with 575,000 zlotys (then worth nearly $110,000), Elizabeth, and his former mistress, "chocolate eyes." The train rolled out of Cracow Central station not to stop until, crossing all Occupied Europe, it reached the Dutch coast near Zandvoort, a home-coming for Menten with new dangers and newer opportunities.

More than ever in January 1943, the Dutch Resistance might have distracted the German occupiers from their wary gaze across the North Sea at Fortress Britain in order to sap their strength and ultimately ease an Allied invasion of the continent. But the Dutch Resistance had already aborted that logical mission, choosing instead to expend much of their energy against Dutch collaborators and suspected Dutch traitors—dangerously turning to battle not the Nazis so much as their enemies within. Directionless, without experience, disorganized, and ambivalent in their feelings toward the occupier, the Dutch Resistance, born in deformity, fought the enemy, if at all, only after 1943, once the Dutch honeymoon with Nazism started to sour in hunger and gross deprivations. But even then, the Dutch Resistance groups—and cells within groups—fought less to defeat the Nazis than for postwar political influence and material gain. Far from being a bright tower of selfless hero-ism, much of the Dutch Resistance was a squabbling embarrass-ment of self-interest and greed.

The Dutch had not flung themselves into the arms of the Nazis, but the courtship was nevertheless intense. Once Queen Wilhel-mina, the Princess and Prince, and the government had exiled themselves to London for the duration of the war, 9 million Dutchmen had wasted little time accommodating themselves to their German cousins. The largest newspaper in Holland, *De Tele-graaf,* was openly collaborationist and hired Anton Mussert, the head of the Dutch Nazi Party (NSB), to advise its editors on Nazi affairs. The civil administration worked side by side with the Ger-mans, as did members of the Supreme Court, except the Jewish president of the court and all Jewish law officers, who had been removed. Nearly half a million Dutchmen flocked to the Neder-landsche Unie, a mass movement that preached cooperation with the German occupiers. About 100,000 Dutchmen had volunteered to work in the Nazi munitions factories in the Ruhr, while at home during the early war years, business went on as usual, for most Dutch, anyway.

Before the Resistance was a twinkle in anybody's eye, 50,000 Dutchmen had marched off to join the Wehrmacht and the Waffen-SS to fight against Russia on the Eastern Front. The Dutch railway workers would indeed go on strike in September 1944 to help the Allied effort at Arnhem, but also because the jockeying for postwar positions of influence had heated up; they were also compensated for each day of the strike, including overtime and a Christmas bonus. Before then, the Dutch engineers and switchmen had knowingly run the trains with cargoes of strategic supplies for the Nazis, plunder, and, worst of all, Dutch political prisoners and more than 400,000 Dutch labor conscripts. With a loyalty to the occupying power that was sadly misplaced, Dutchmen had rolled the same rail cars east with cargoes of Dutch Jews destined for the extermination camps at Mauthausen, Bergen-Belsen, Theresienstadt, Auschwitz, and Sobibor.

For a community of Jews that had emigrated to Holland from Spain and Portugal in the fifteenth century to escape the Inquisition, destruction was swift and certain. In cooperation with Dutch banks, the Nazis confiscated Jews' assets and liquidated their businesses. Less than a year after the occupation, Higher SS and Police Leader Hans Albin Rauter had ordered Dutch Nazis to incite anti-Jewish riots in Amsterdam that resulted in the first deportations as "punishment" for Jewish resistance, and then had issued a "warning" to non-Jews who had briefly protested the transport. After that, the pace of annihilation quickened until the Germans had accomplished their objectives almost entirely. Of a total community of 130,000 Dutch Jews before the Nazi occupation, 115,000 were transported to camps and exterminated.

From the first, little more than an impulse existed for the Dutch to resist, but after Stalingrad, when the Germans conscripted Dutch labor and stripped the country's resources of foodstuffs, hungry people began to fight back, and some of their actions succeeded. On the night of March 6, 1944, a Resistance group in the south, emboldened by the certainty of Liberation, would decide to hold up the first passing German car on the road between Arnhem and Apeldoorn. As the moon rose they waited near the village of Woeste Hoeve in a drainage ditch, rifles pointed outward. Finally, as the chill touched them, a flashlight signal warned of an approaching BMW two-door staff car. (The commandos might have known that BMWs rarely transported enlisted men and lower-ranking officers.) As the car lights loomed the men of the commando cocked their weapons and once it came even, sprang the ambush. The BMW braked hard, and a firefight ensued. After several seconds the commandos fled across the dikes into the night.

A German patrol would discover the BMW at dawn and later count 243 bullet holes. Miraculously, one of the passengers survived, principally with his lower mandible shattered beyond hope of repair. A *Gruppenführer-SS und Höhere SS und Polizeiführer in den Niederlanden, Gruppenführer-SS und Generalleutnant der Polizei, Kommissar-General für das Sicherheitswesen in den Niederlanden,* Hans Albin Rauter was the victim.

In reprisal nearly 400 *"totenskandidate"* Dutchmen were shot dead in the drainage ditch from which the commandos had sprung the ambush. Those draconian orders came from the *Befehlshaber der Sicherheitspolizei und des Sicherheitsdiensts in den Niederlanden,* the second in command to Hans Rauter who was promoted after the shooting to *Höhere und Kommissar-General,* the chief policeman. Called "The Deputy" he had recently been transferred from a lonely Waffen-SS unit in the Balkans to Holland as a reward for his past loyalty to Himmler. In his new position, The Deputy reviewed the files marked *geheim* ("secret"). What he learned there surprised even him.

As a policeman in Zandvoort, which before the war had swelled as a floodtide with bathers in summer, Peter ("Pete") van Izendorn felt a moment's queasy disorientation that summer of 1943 as he watched the beach through binoculars. Now, construction, not colored umbrellas, webbed the dunes with concrete defenses against an amphibious assault from across the North Sea and farther in, with pads for launching fiery V rockets at London. From the back windows of his small beach house, van Izendorn saw not the gamboling of bathers but the swarming of workers and heard

125

muffled orders shouted by TODT-organization foremen, even from where he was standing. As a leader of Rolls-Royce, a Dutch Resistance cell of twenty men with an operational headquarters in Bloemendaal a few miles away, van Izendorn, tall and blond with an alto pitch to his voice that betrayed the massiveness of his build, reported to Haarlem, where he bicycled now. Lately he had been burdened by the unpardonable corruption within many Resistance groups. Van Izendorn recognized the temptations as immediately as the next man. If Resistance workers were stealing food only from collaborators who had grown rich from the war, he could understand, but as the son of a policeman, a stranger neither to corruption nor to probity, he did not condone the rest— the theft of valuable objects, or the bribery, extortion, and blackmail.

Soon after he parked his bicycle in front of the office and entered, a member of Rolls-Royce approached him with a story that immediately raised a warning in his mind. For months now, Rolls-Royce had "marked" collaborators for detention after Liberation—those who had flaunted their cooperation with the enemy. In a triumphant mood the man said, "We've got a new one, in Aerdenhout."

Van Izendorn thought by now that Rolls-Royce had identified the collaborators living in Aerdenhout, a millionaires' enclave of houses that everybody reverently called villas. What surprised him was that people rarely moved in or out of Aerdenhout. Because he feared the new mark was an innocent, wealthy Dutchman whose possessions were probably coveted by someone in Rolls-Royce, van Izendorn demanded a thorough investigation. But the more he heard about the new suspect in the next few months, the more he wondered. This man had moved into a villa with his mother, wife, and another woman, whom the Rolls-Royce agent identified as "beautiful." Most amazingly—and for van Izendorn, suspicious—they had arrived from Poland aboard a special German train. The man had bought a second villa near the one occupied by his mother. The neighbors whom Rolls-Royce had questioned said that the man owned numerous art objects: the second villa housed the overflow.

Van Izendorn said flatly, "I don't believe it."

"But it's true."

"How do you know?" van Izendorn asked, and before the agent answered, he said, "You can't get a train from the Germans, period. Even a German can't get a train from the Germans. And this man, you say, is Dutch? I suppose the Germans said to this Dutch stranger, 'Here's a train. Now collect your art and go where you want?' "

"I don't know," the agent answered.

"If you want me to believe you, go to the station. Someone there must have papers, a *laissez-passer,* something to confirm it. But I'm warning you, it's a waste of time." He thought that people would have talked about such a remarkable event if it were true. It would have gone no less unnoticed than if Himmler or Göring had arrived suddenly in this quiet corner of Holland.

In less than a week the agent returned. "It's true, what I said. All of it," he said and handed van Izendorn a bill of lading from Schenker and Company signed by Pieter N. Menten. The cargo manifest, van Izendorn saw, contained item after valuable item. "The stationmaster saw them remove that stuff from the train," the agent added. "Nobody else was aboard. He couldn't believe his eyes."

"Slow down," van Izendorn advised him. "We'll check it out."

In the months that followed, van Izendorn watched Menten with interest but not quite fascination. His house at Westerlaan #16 was indeed a millionaire's. Menten had traveled from Cracow across Europe with Nazi clearances. He owned art objects. But beyond that, there was nothing to report, nothing concrete to prove collaboration. Indeed, what he saw disappointed his expectations.

For the most part, Menten kept a low profile. He visited Paul Thiele, the director in Holland of Omnia, a quasi-statal Nazi company that auctioned properties confiscated from deported Jews. Listed as "a merchant in Aerdenhout," Menten bought apartment buildings in Amsterdam on the Apollolaan, in Cornelisstraat, Stadionweg, Holbeinstraat, and Murillostraat—the tempo quickening with purchases in Korteweghof and throughout Amsterdam, until the end of 1944, when the buying stopped. Meanwhile, he consigned sixty paintings to van Marle & Bignell, Auctioneers, in

The Hague: a Lorenzo Lotto (exhibited in 1934 in the Amsterdam Stedelijk Museum), a Lucas de Heere from 1557, a Palamedsz from 1634, a Thomas de Keyser from 1635, two paintings attributed to Rubens, "Bowling Farmers at an Inn" by Adrian Brouwer, a Piazetta, paintings by Codde, Costa, Coutis, Bourjuijnon and Magry, plus an Arij Scheffer. He hung more valuable paintings on the walls, stacked them on the parquet floors, and stored them with great secrecy behind disguised wall panels, in crawl spaces and underground recesses—a whole network .of caches built by a carpenter, W. H. Stokman, who slept nights in a spare bedroom of the villa.

From then on, Menten warily constructed defenses against the likelihood of a Nazi defeat and of his own prosecution for collaboration. He doubted with good reason whether anybody in Dutch law enforcement would ever discover what he had done in Poland; that did not worry him. But because he kept his eyes and ears open, he saw how the Resistance operated in Holland on its own profit principle, and he wanted to ensure the postwar safety for himself and his possessions. Even as a Menten of the noble houses of Shell and Unilever, he was not safe from the Binnenlandse Strijdkachten, or Forces of the Interior (BS). Ever since Sir Henry Deterding's death in Berlin in 1939, the ties with Shell and its banker Mannheimer had dissolved. Even more, now that the war was going badly for the Nazis, Shell wanted to disassociate itself from Deterding's fanatic devotion to Hitlerism. In his last years, Sir Henry had suffered from megalomania, at one point writing, "If I were the dictator of the world, I would shoot all idlers at sight." He embarrassed Shell's management and its stockholders. Certainly, Menten did not want to count too heavily on Deterding's successors for friendship and protection. He made lame attempts to ingratiate himself with the Underground, first by donating to *De Patriot,* one of many illegal newspapers, and later, to the Underground's general coffers—but the offers were refused. Clearly, Menten felt, he needed more guarantees than that.

He planned with cunning, first by alerting all branches of the Menten family of his return from nearly a quarter century of wandering in Eastern Europe. Therefore he was not surprised when the wife of his half cousin, Emile, came to him with bad news.

Close in age to Emile, Pieter still remembered the viciousness of his cousins' childhood taunts about his being inferior. But Emile had somehow escaped the family penchant for eccentricity, and he had been best known before the war for his charitable work with the Salvation Army. Despite the income from his father's oil royalties, Emile had worked as an officer with Pierson's Bank, and since the occupation he had been a brave and patriotic supporter of the National Relief Fund (NSF).

Emile's wife had come to Menten for help. The Gestapo had arrested Emile and his younger brother, Otto, for financing Resistance activities through the NSF, a charge that was certainly true and easily proven. After a summary trial, an SS court had sentenced the brothers to death by firing squad.

Agreeing to help, Menten first applied to the SS for a pass to visit Germany, as he explained, "to set up a German art business." "Chocolate eyes," in a note to her step-uncle, the aide-de-camp to von Ribbentrop, seconded his application, which Pieter knew would be scrutinized after his expulsion from Poland. He needed only three weeks' leave to travel, principally to Berlin, the home of the third Menten half cousin, Hubert, who had not escaped the family penchant for eccentricity. A collector of Oriental art and a dilettante with an enormous income from oil royalties, he called himself "Abu Ali." He had brokered a Rembrandt and a van Gogh to Walter Hoffer, the curator of Göring's Kerenhall Castle, and as a genuine follower of Hitler, he published pro-Nazi pamphlets at his own expense. As the elder of the three Menten oil brothers, Hubert served the family as patriarch. No matter what his eccentricities, what he decreed, the family obeyed.

If Pieter's intentions toward the imprisoned brothers had been purely humanitarian and loving, he needed only to have asked and something would have been arranged in Holland. But those were never his intentions. He had traveled to Berlin to negotiate something in return. They at once struck a deal that was never reneged on. From Hubert's point of view, the terms were cheap and acceptable, but for Pieter they were more precious even than his painting by Raphael. If he were somehow to find a way to secure the release of Hubert's brothers, he demanded full acceptance and recognition as a main-line Menten.

Soon after Menten returned from Berlin, the Gestapo set Emile and Otto free without explanation. In fact, they were set free with the same alacrity with which they had been arrested in the first place—at Pieter Menten's request.

In the meantime, Rolls-Royce continued to watch the house in Aerdenhout for concrete evidence of Menten's collaboration. Stories by neighbors of a vast art collection whetted the appetite of the Resistance, which dared go no further than surveillance. One day late in 1944, Rolls-Royce spotted a Nazi staff car parked in the driveway of the Menten villa, and they thought that now they had found their opening. Too wary either to photograph the car or to approach the house to identify the car's passenger through the windows, the Resistance men afterward questioned Menten's maid, a simple girl. "Did you see Germans in uniform, Nazi uniforms, German people?" van Izendorn asked her patiently.

"Yes," she replied, pleased with herself.

"Who?" van Izendorn asked.

"I don't know," she replied. She did not remember names, or much else besides.

Van Izendorn tried again. "Was he a general, a man of the Army, a man of the SS or the SD?"

"Don't know," she replied. But she knew that the man had visited the Mentens many times. "Mr. Menten used to get all excited beforehand," she told him. "He'd say, 'The Deputy is coming.'"

"The Deputy, in Amsterdam? In the SD, the SS, Haarlem?"

"No," she replied. "No, no, no."

The Deputy. The first time van Izendorn had heard the name, it had sounded odd. Although The Deputy could be anybody, The Deputy had to be a man of some influence in the Nazi hierarchy. If he were to discover the answer, he might then answer other, more disturbing questions about Pieter Menten. That Menten had important Nazis friends here in Holland was consistent with other facts known to van Izendorn—the private train, the Nazi clearances—and it gave a new credence to a story van Izendorn had heard only recently, a story that he had discounted because of its source, a deeply jealous man living in the same neighborhood as Menten. Joseas L. Debrouin had repeated to van Izendorn the story of how late in 1939 Menten had come to Cracow as a refugee from the Soviet occupation of Lwów and eastern Galicia, how he had befriended the Nazis, started as a *Treuhänder,* stolen Debrouin's business, ORIZA, and his girlfriend, the Baroness Maria Louise Steengracht von Moyland, and worn a German SD uniform. There were even photographs of Menten in the Nazi uniform. No, Debrouin did not have them in his possession, but he probably could get hold of them, if van Izendorn wanted, once the war ended and travel was again permitted between Holland and Poland.

Although the informant probably was a member of Rolls-Royce, nobody knew later who tipped off Menten to what Debrouin was telling people about the photographs. But one fact was clear: Menten wanted Debrouin dead. He had already threatened him. On September 14, 1944, he had knocked on Debrouin's door, Debrouin told van Izendorn. Smelling of liquor, Menten had waved a revolver in his face and demanded that he turn over the photographs. Van Izendorn listened patiently, and when Debrouin had finished, he thought for certain that he had stepped into the messy aftermath of a love triangle with the Baroness Steengracht von Moyland. Debrouin had lost the girl to Menten and wanted to destroy him purely out of jealousy, van Izendorn figured. No one had witnessed the so-called holdup, nor had Debrouin reported the incident at the time to the police, which would have been only natural. Before concluding the interview, van Izendorn asked if Debrouin knew the identity of a Nazi known as The Deputy. It was a long shot, and it failed. Later, when he had returned to his office, van Izendorn opened the looseleaf binder with the names and addresses of collaborators whom the BS (Forces of the Interior) planned to arrest after the Liberation. He wrote in the address of Debrouin. Besides Menten's name, he wrote, " + everything."

In the months that followed, the Dutch found themselves cut off from an early Liberation with starvation and disease worsening by the hour in what became known as the Hunger Winter of 1944–45. An acute shortage of fuel drove the city residents to denude parkland. The black market disappeared, and barter prevailed until nothing remained. Despite the reality of Nazi terror-

131

ism, starvation brought the most primal instincts to the surface. Hatred of the Germans and hope for Liberation survived, but the people aimed their bitterness at neighbors and relatives, at the once friendly shopkeepers around the corner. City foragers complained of the meanness of their well-fed country cousins. And the latter complained of the formers' greed. Nobody in Holland understood why they had not been liberated; they bitterly concluded that they were being sacrificed for some greater Allied goal. They blamed "American capital." Bombs from Flying Fortresses had leveled Dutch factories but conspicuously spared the Amsterdam Ford plant.

As one day dragged wearily to the next, anarchy spread through the larger cities. Authorities failed to distribute the meager stocks of food equitably, and most Dutch by now had become desperate, eating tulip bulbs and sugar beets when they could be found. Outside the church and certain areas of the Resistance, the law of the jungle prevailed. Formerly, many Dutch had remained respectable for fear of what their neighbors would say, but now the neighbors had started doing the strangest things themselves.

Mercifully, Liberation came in early May 1945.

BOOK II

CHAPTER VI

⊗

" . . . 'tis writ in the Law of Moses."

"Lieber KRUMHOLZ," THE young man repeated into the telephone, that morning in the first week of January 1945. "Yes, for *Ha'aretz."* And then, unwilling to resist the moment, he slid off his tongue with the ease of the smile across his freckled face, "It's the most *respected* paper in Palestine."

The remark sounded too eager, but Bibi Krumholz could not suppress the same pride in the newspaper that other people might have reserved for family, friends, or fraternity. *Ha'aretz*'s owners, the Schockens, early German Zionists, set high standards, and by reputation they employed journalists of only the finest caliber. Gustav Schocken himself had hired Bibi Krumholz away from the police, where he had still been assigned to the Ramallah slaughterhouse, less than a year before. With his police experience he was suited to be the newspaper's court and crime reporter; Schocken had chosen well. The young reporter's boast on the telephone mixed the yeast of enthusiasm, the perishable ingredient of youth, with experience of years as a policeman to produce the high-quality professional journalism that the paper demanded.

Enthusiasm benefited Bibi, too, because times were especially hard for him, and through the magic of enthusiasm, certain deprivations became easy challenges. Bibi owned one pair of pants, earned a few dollars a week, and shared a room in Tel Aviv since the job at the paper started, while Mala lived sixty miles away in Jerusalem to keep her job as a nurse at the Hadassah Hospital. They saw each other only on weekends when they both were free.

Even the separation, hard though it was, did not discourage Bibi. He had his health—he was a powerful man with ginger hair and light skin. One change was his blond mustache, the trim of which suited the fashion of the day. He had a family yet to build, a new country to believe in, and, probably sooner than later, to fight for, and practically a new career as a journalist to pursue. While he had nothing to speak of, Bibi carried himself almost as a conqueror.

Only the life he had left behind in Poland—and his family— stood in the way to total conquest. And he dwelled on that quite often. It was January 1945, and the war still engulfed most of Europe, even though the consensus in Palestine was that Hitler had lost and soon peace would prevail. Even now, refugees—the survivors of the Holocaust—straggled into Tel Aviv in pitiful numbers. Their tales weighed heavily on all Jews with families unaccounted for still in Europe. Bibi worried that the charnel house of Poland under the Nazis had consumed his family and close relatives, the Pistiners. When these lugubrious thoughts occupied his mind, he admonished himself. That anything had happened to them was unacceptable, and not just because he loved them. His break from Poland had been painful, especially for his mother. If they had died he would be strapped with an impossible need to change in his mind how things had been, and the burden of that guilt would weigh heavily on him. For now, it had accounted for only brief moments of depression, which he dispelled when he reported and wrote for *Ha'aretz* the sagas of how Jews had struggled through the war and survived, as though the stories captured on the pages of his notebook reflected his deepest hopes and fears. A romantic, Bibi tackled the assignments with an imagination that matched his enthusiasm whenever Gustav Schocken, the editor whom he revered, tapped him, as he had done now.

On his usual beat as a crime reporter, Bibi routinely witnessed nearly every form of hateful human behavior—British soldiers in Tel Aviv firing into a crowd of demonstrating Jewish boys and girls, Jewish shopkeepers in the Old City of Jerusalem shot by Arab terrorists at point-blank range. The violence had hardened him into a tough reporter, but he had not allowed himself to become dehumanized. That side of journalism made him feel alive but not necessarily good.

The person to whom he was boasting on the telephone about *Ha'aretz* was Dr. Hofert, who ran the Office for New Emigrants, a charitable organization for the settlement of Jewish refugees from the war in Europe. She welcomed Bibi's offer to write a story in *Ha'aretz*. She hoped, she had said, the publicity would reach refugees who otherwise might not know of the office's existence. Now, hearing her warm voice on the telephone and sensing her eagerness, Bibi felt positive for attempting to use journalism to help people's lives, rather than writing the usual crime reporter's run of bludgeonings and shootings.

Carrying an umbrella, Bibi left the Rehov Mazah offices of *Ha'aretz*. Dark scud of the Mediterranean sprayed the streets, as if Tel Aviv were a ship on a stormy passage. He looked up at the weather distastefully. Bibi was a Jerusalem man to whom this storminess was unfamiliar and bothersome. Gusts of wind tore at the umbrella, which he furled. He ducked down the sidewalk of Allenby until he reached Lillienblum Street and a converted frame house with a small sign near the door and an arrow that pointed up a flight of stairs.

On the first-floor landing he entered a room ringed with chairs. The place was small—it had a waiting room, a receptionist's desk, and an inner office—and shabby from constant use. The wooden floors were worn from the scraping of heavy shoes, and the musty smell of people who had been waiting long hours hung in the air. Soft bundles occupied the corners, the sole possessions of travelers under hard conditions. Fifteen or twenty men were dressed in tattered clothes. Remarkably, their hair was white, *completely* white, but their faces were not old. Was that from what they had seen? Bibi wondered. Their faces looked empty and unable to erase the memory of what they had witnessed. Some stared at the floor. Bibi couldn't shake the impression that they were all the same man. At the sound of his footstep they looked up, but as if he were in the middle distance, where the eye reads the mind. Bibi thought they had the look of death's companions. One man in particular reminded Bibi of his years in Poland. The man looked at the worn floor, but when someone said, "Mr. Krumholz, you can go in," breaking the silence, the man stared at Bibi with eyes clouded in confusion.

137

In Dr. Hofert's private office Bibi asked more questions than he needed for his article.

"Most of them survived the camps," she said. "Auschwitz, Sobibor, Treblinka—the Polish camps."

Those names sounded unfamiliar. "But why do they look the way they do?" he asked.

Obviously he did not know—really know—about the camps. "They lost their families, those who had them," Dr. Hofert told him. "Those who didn't lost themselves, left them there."

Bibi suddenly did not want to know more. His questions became perfunctory. He learned a little bit from Dr. Hofert, about why the office existed, about its funding, the staff and their work load, but he felt uneasy and wanted to leave. Something he had intuited about this place even frightened him. Something here was too close to home.

Dr. Hofert sensed that something was wrong, and she asked, "Is your family there?"

Bibi did not mind talking about that. He told her about his brother, Marek, his mother, and father, David, and the Pistiners. "I expect to hear from them any day." Lwów, he explained, was so far away from Tel Aviv that he had to expect delayed and interrupted communications. She said nothing, he thanked her, and again, sooner than he had wished, he found himself in the waiting room.

As he walked past the rows of chairs, the man with the confused eyes stood up and partially blocked his passage. "Lieber Krumholz?" he asked.

"Yes," Bibi replied, searching the man's face.

"From Lwów?"

What secret did this man know? "My family lives there," he said.

The man took an unsteady step forward, and Bibi was *deathly* afraid. The man hugged him so close Bibi felt his body shake. The other men in the room looked, but their eyes did not seem to register, as if this drama had been played many times before their eyes. Still hugging Bibi, the man whispered in his ear, "I am a friend from there." He paused for a second and said, "From Hell."

Fear made Bibi now feel as if he were floating on air. Instinctively Bibi sensed that the man knew. All those years and all the fantasies—his parents, his brother, his whole family, they were *living.* That they had not contacted him before this he took increasingly as a sign. Naturally they were alive. . . . They had fled to Kazakhstan or to Siberia. . . . Somebody had protected them. . . . It would be only a matter of time before they got in touch. . . . He would see them again soon. . . . They would be reunited . . . and happy. . . . They would live here in Palestine. . . . It would be like he had always imagined. . . .

Bibi looked over the man's shoulder. One man watched and tears ran down his cheeks. Bibi knew this was *his* moment. It was *his* turn, just as it had been for thousands before him and thousands who would come after—no one would remain untouched. Bibi said, "They haven't given me a clear answer. I wrote and went to the offices of the Vatican and the Red Cross."

"I am Jacob Leubel. I am sorry," the man said. "Nobody from there remains alive. You can do nothing for them but to say *Kaddish.*"

Bibi felt his legs weaken, and Leubel helped him to a chair, then sat beside him. "Nearly all the Jews you knew in Lwów do not exist anymore. It happened. All this is true. The Jews from there don't exist anymore." Leubel was crying now.

Bibi could not make a connection. He asked, "How can you be so sure, Mr. Leubel?"

Leubel waited a minute, then explained that as a Rumanian, and therefore the citizen of a German ally, the Germans had permitted him to leave the ghetto. "I heard and I saw everything there," he said, wondering how to start the complicated tale.

Haltingly he went on for a time, finally ending with a question, "Do you know who murdered your family?"

Leubel's lips moved slowly, as if he were having trouble forming the words, wanting to soften them. In that silence Leubel's very question seemed remarkable. "Do you know who is responsible. . . ?" Sure, Bibi thought, the Germans, the War, the Nazis.

Yes, of course, Leubel's face said, but there is more. For a long few moments he watched Bibi, fully aware now of the consequences for the young man of what he knew. Then he said, "Do you remember a friend of your family? Pieter Menten?"

139

Of course Bibi remembered him. He told Leubel, "I saw him the night before I left Lwów. . . ."

"*He* is guilty."

"How do you mean, 'guilty'?"

"I'm sorry," Leubel said. "He killed your family, and the Pistiners, too, all of them that I know of."

Bibi jerked his face away from Leubel. Friends do not kill friends, Bibi thought, certainly not in the manner that Leubel was describing now, cold-bloodedly and with premeditation. Wars changed histories, and wars changed people, too. Some people foamed at their mouths like animals. Yes, all that was true. But Leubel described something that for Bibi was far worse.

". . . Can you understand?" Leubel was saying.

"Is it *true?*"

"Everybody told what happened there."

"He was always a lovely man, a friend—*my* friend."

Leubel told Bibi of meeting that *friend* on the street after the Germans had entered Lwów, and how afraid he had been that day. And he told what he had heard from their neighbors in Lwów. "Two days after I met him he came to your parents' house. All the news was word of mouth, usually whispered. We were anxious to learn what happened. . . . He wanted Isaac."

By now Bibi needed to be alone to think, and excusing himself, but promising to see Leubel again later, he soon found himself walking in the rain toward Montifiore and the soot-gray walls of Beit Haknesset Hagadol Shel Tel Aviv, the temple that he had passed hundreds of times without thinking to enter. Someone at the door handed him a prayer book, and Bibi went inside, feeling the coolness and hearing nothing but the muffled automobile sounds from the road.

It is unbelievable what a man can change into, Bibi thought. Then he stopped himself. No, he had to find out for himself if what Leubel said was true, then how and why . . . *if* he were going to find out. And that would never be a foregone conclusion. For a beat of time he pondered: Thousands of Jews have lost family in the Holocaust, and they have only the Nazis to curse. Their families were "taken" in the camps or by *Aktionen* or even by "the Holocaust," a concept damnable in its vagueness, its inconclusive-

140

ness, its enigma. And forever, as long as they lived, their minds must contain doubt about who the murderers were, what they looked like, how they had committed the horrible deed, all the facts of a tragedy that, once learned in complete detail, can then be forgotten. They had nobody to seek out and punish, no single murderer at whom to point an accusing finger. But with Bibi perhaps it was different. Alone among the relatives of those millions who had died, he knew his family's killer; he knew him well enough to question Leubel's accusations, but he also knew him well enough to find a starting point in a search. What price, though, had Bibi to pay for success? Nazi Germany is falling, he thought, but a war, another war that may never end is just starting for me. The murderer must be confronted with his crimes to show that his victims are not forgotten.

Bibi opened the prayer book and tried to find the page on which the words of *Kaddish* were written. He found other words instead, and he read:

May God beneficently remember them, in conjunction with all other righteous ones of the world, and retributively avenge in our sights the blood of his servants that hath been shed; as 'tis writ in the Law of Moses, the man of God: "Ye nations, cause his people to rejoice, for the blood of his servants will he avenge; yea, he will wreak retribution on his foes, and cause his land and his people to be atoned for."

Closing the book, Bibi wanted to cry in this temple. Standing there stripped now of the fantasies that had guarded his past, he was left alone with revenge. He wanted to cry for what he had lost, but his grief was too large for tears, and it burrowed deep in his heart.

Leaving the portals of the temple, Bibi wandered down Allenby toward Jacob Leubel's lodging house. He thought about the words in the book: ". . . He will wreak retribution on his foes. . . ." And he realized a truth about himself for the first time, something that was more obvious to others than to him. All his life he had been running scared from pogroms and prejudice, hatred and brutality. He had sought out Palestine as a dream but

141

also as a refuge. Now, after the almost incomprehensible news that Leubel had carried from Lwów, he had to start up again, running faster and farther than ever before.

In the street, he asked himself the questions, Is he alive? Where is he, how is he living, did he return to Europe? Did he die for Hitler? How could Bibi ever find those answers? There was no precedent for hunting war criminals because there was no precedent for the horror of their crimes. There was no one to help Bibi. He thought, If this were an assignment, how would I begin? And he answered: First learn every part of the problem by studying in detail. The murderer had taught him that a hunter must learn patience and persistence, tenacity, doggedness, whatever it was called, to outlast and lull his prey. Become a hunter. Start with the memory of how and where it began. Reach back across the chasm of death and set yourself a goal, that no matter how long it takes, no matter what the frustrations and, more, the sacrifices, you will find your family's killer and bring him to justice.

CHAPTER VII

❧

"Let God stop *his* life."

THE MONTHS FOLLOWED in almost stunned silence, as much of the world recovered from the trauma of the war, but soon after, there were stirrings as life and duty imposed demands that were not to be ignored. New lives, no matter how shattered, had to begin; there were new attitudes and relationships to understand. And for most Jews, collective and personal grief, anger, retribution, and the demand for justice after the horror all had to be worked out.

In those months after Jacob Leubel had told his tale, Bibi struggled with an assortment of confusing and often conflicting emotions. Powerlessness conflicted with the desire to act, rumor conflicted with fact, and grief relentlessly blocked the impulse to go on with life. At first angrily, he swallowed his impulses for revenge, confused though they were, suffering the understanding, which he did not want, and even sympathy, which he did not need, of those people who heard his tale, including his wife, Mala, who said she knew what he was going through, but she did not really understand, not at all. Mala said, "Everybody has somebody who was killed—every Jew alive." Tired of hearing again what Leubel had told him, she repeated to Bibi what seemed obvious to her. "Everybody has the same, *everybody,* Bibi. Even me."

Of course everybody did not have the same experience. Their families had been the victims, but Bibi knew the name, the face, the history of the man who had killed his family. He said to Mala, "All I see is how happy the world is now that the Germans are

143

beaten. But, Mala, I am not happy. They were murdered like dogs in the street."

"Forget it, Bibi," she said. "Please try to forget it." But she knew the tenacity with which he held to an idea; she admired the virtue. As a man he stuck by commitments. If he was so rock solid with her, and she loved him for it, then she could not complain. Just sometimes, it was not easy for her to live with.

"I suppose I should forgive, too?" he went on. They had argued these points many times since Jacob Leubel's revelations. It got them nowhere, but developments in Europe constantly upset Bibi anew, and he brought this home. The Allies were trying a bare minimum of German war criminals at Nuremberg. The United Nations had solemnly pledged that "no crime will be left uninvestigated, not one criminal, whether directly or indirectly responsible, will escape punishment." The United Nations would see that retribution would be "swift, sure, complete. . . . There cannot, there will not be any pardon." But almost before the magnitude of the Nazis' crimes became known, the United Nations was reneging on its solemn pledge, ultimately to only equivocate. Bibi watched this closely. At first he believed that the Allies and the United Nations would honor their word. Later, he took out his frustrations on Mala. He said to her, "People are saying, 'We shall forgive them.' Mala, I can't say that. Pieter Menten must be punished."

"All right, but for now, Bibi, please think about the living," she implored. "Think about our people who are still lost—not dead, just lost."

She was right, and he knew it. He said, "But one day. . . ." And she nodded.

The two pursuits, he soon recognized, were not mutually exclusive. He did not have the benefit of hindsight. And in searching for any relatives who had survived—for example, what had happened to Japan, Mara, Maria, Gusta, and the two children—he would learn in general about the Holocaust and in a more detailed, legal manner, how Menten had turned killer.

Survivors reaching Palestine were telling what they had witnessed in Nazi Europe, and eventually he could learn from them, but for now, there were too few refugees to make a difference,

144

what with the cynical immigration policies toward Jews set by the British "protectors" of Palestine. Turned back from the shores and imprisoned in camps on Cyprus, the survivors could not tell relatives and friends in Palestine the news of the living and the dead of Europe, and unless the world woke up to tragedies like that involving the *Exodus,* the floodgates to Palestine would remain closed. If a Pistiner had survived, Bibi would help him begin a new life—if not in Palestine, then at least through Palestine as a way station. But for now, he heard nothing.

Meanwhile, he had his own reordering. Mala was pregnant with their first child, he had to find an apartment in Tel Aviv, and he had a new profession, about which he was more serious now than ever. All the romantic notions of journalism aside, *Ha'aretz* paid a wage, not a great wage, but a wage. And Bibi needed that income, now that Mala had quit nursing and the responsibilities of a family were dawning on him. Bibi knew he possessed no particular genius that set him apart from his colleagues—no gift for a subtle turn of phrase, no brilliant insights. But he had tenacity, which made him a slave to *Ha'aretz.* Nobody on the newspaper ever worked harder.

Also as a postwar reordering, great events were occurring in Palestine that swept up every inhabitant, whether Jew or Arab. Just after the war in Europe had ended, the war in Palestine began in deadly earnest. As the camps filled on Cyprus, the demand for an independent Jewish state in Palestine became even more urgent. Some Zionists argued for moderation, so as not to upset the British, while heated fighting broke out between Palestinian Arabs and Jews. The Jewish Agency and the Zionist Congress also argued against a valid armed defense, preferring to drown the British White Paper in a flood of illegal immigration. But these policies of patience sickened many of the younger Palestinian Jews, who ran wild burning British military installations, blowing up British Army Headquarters in the King David Hotel, ambushing British soldiers—all aimed at destroying the British will, already weakened, to remain in Palestine as protectors. These young Jews demanded a Jewish state now, already paid for with the lives of 6 million Holocaust victims. They wanted the state before the most important opportunity in their history was lost.

145

Through it all, Bibi did more than listen and watch. Nobody in Palestine in those days was allowed to stand on the sidelines. He did not condemn the timidity of the Zionists but the clarity of the terrorists' thinking suited him better. He worked sources for them within the British Police with which he maintained contact as a crime reporter, and he listened and watched, separating himself from the actual acts of Irgun's terrorist violence—his value to them was surely not in the smuggling of guns or the detonation of bombs.

On May 14, 1948, the British Mandate ended and the State of Israel was declared. Fighting erupted instantly between the Jews and all the Arab nations on Israel's borders—600,000 against many million Arabs. Only the present counted now, because it meant survival. Bibi took a leave from *Ha'aretz* to serve as press liaison officer in the Israeli Police. After one year, when the immediate crisis had subsided and the survival of the nation was temporarily assured, he returned to *Ha'aretz*.

On a Sunday soon after, *Ha'aretz*'s managing editor, Israel Finkelstein, called Bibi to his office. An Anglophile who sucked on paper clips and plucked crumpled copy paper from the wastebaskets to save *Ha'aretz* money, Finkelstein was a notorious stickler for details, demanding and imperious. He wanted a story about the new political department of the Jewish Agency. He assigned Bibi for no other reason than that he wasn't doing anything that day, and Finkelstein had seen him in the lunchroom in the basement. Finkelstein hated idleness almost as much as he hated waste.

An Egged bus took Bibi from Tel Aviv along the steep, treacherous Jaffa Road to the city he had prowled as a policeman and had learned to love. He walked to the offices of the Jewish Agency and asked for the political department. Introducing himself, he found the director to be helpful and pleased by the newspaper's interest in the activities of his small corner of the agency. He talked and Bibi took notes, asking an occasional question. Quite by chance as the interview was concluding, the director mentioned the smallest of all the department's duties. Just a few weeks ago it had started to collect information on war criminals.

This was the first Bibi knew of an effort in Israel, or anywhere else, to identify criminals in the war. There was still no Zero Six

Department of the Israeli Police, no Simon Wiesenthal Institute, no Tuviah Friedman. He did not expect any offers of help now, but he asked the director the question all the same. The response surprised Bibi. The director could not answer, he said, because the information Bibi wanted was secret. Bibi laughed in the man's face. "What can possibly be secret about war criminals?" he asked.

"Nothing is secret about them," the director replied. "But there are reasons. We hope to protect the people who identify the criminal. We are not a court of law here, either. The secrecy also protects the person who is accused. He may be innocent." The director considered Bibi's question again. His press credentials set him apart, and the director reluctantly agreed to check the card catalog. Then he went to a cabinet and pulled a file marked #4-1/4-386, dated May 10, 1945.

Bibi felt his heart race as he turned the manila cover and read, "Records of War Criminals, Instigators and Perpetrators of Crimes against Jews." There, at the top of a form, was the typed name, Pieter N. Menten. His eyes scanned the form. Yes, the name was spelled correctly, there was no question of two men with the same name. No Dirk here or any other Menten but Pieter N. Yes, and here was the nationality, Dutch, and the marital status, married—yes, how he remembered Elizabeth!—and children, none, which did not surprise him. Languages: Dutch, German, Polish. He skipped a few categories. Information for less than half of the forty-seven particulars was known.

He looked at the director. "This doesn't explain anything about him since the war ended," he said.

The director needed only to glance at the form. "Like a lot of them," he said. "He probably changed his name and went into hiding, maybe to Latin America, maybe South Africa."

"I don't understand," Bibi replied. The political department had received all this information, but they didn't know if he was alive, and if alive, where he lived? Nobody had even spotted him? The lines on the form that might have contained information relevant to Bibi's pursuit were blank. Just from listening to Leubel, Bibi knew more than this form told him. He read on, anyway. Under the category of Criminal Activities, someone had typed, "Owing to his intervention all members of the Pistiner family

147

were arrested and executed. In Podhorodse several Jews and local peasants were also arrested and part of them executed." Bibi read that again: "Podhorodse . . . several Jews . . . part of them executed."

Podhorodse? Leubel had said nothing about a massacre in Podhorodse. How could that have happened, and why? That was the village of his youth, of those memorable summers, the stuffed stag on the porch, the gypsy, the old house, the river and the forest, the hunting . . . with Menten. The village had served as his only memory of a place in Poland where he had felt relatively protected. Of course he had idealized the village, fantasized some of its features, making them seem better than they were, but that was part of memory, too. ". . . part of them executed," he read again. Part of what, he thought, the Jews, the Ukrainians, the Poles, or the whole village? What part? Whom in the village did Menten kill? Who had survived? These were questions that urgently needed answering.

On the form he saw, "Confirmed by Source No. 77." "Who is this?" he asked the director.

He shook his head. "We number those for the sake of source anonymity."

"I *lived* in that village," Bibi said, realizing it was unfair to get angry. The director was not responsible for this maddening dearth of information. What could the department do? Menten was not a big enough fish. "Are you sure you can't tell me?" Could Source No. 77 be Leubel? he wondered, but he eliminated that notion immediately. Leubel would have told him about Podhorodse. But who else from Lwów or that region knew what had occurred in Podhorodse, unless Source No. 77 was someone *from* the village who had survived the massacre. The director took the file back and replaced it in the cabinet. "Will you investigate this?" Bibi asked.

"That's not our function," he said. "We do not have the resources."

"Then who does?" Bibi asked, annoyed.

"I don't know. I am sorry."

Bibi started to leave. More to himself than to the director, he said, "If you put an ad in the newspaper you could find out more in two days than what you have in that file." Who would investigate Menten, who had the resources to put him behind bars? He answered his question right then. Alone, he would have to do this thing alone.

On the bus back down from the heights of Jerusalem, he thought, *really* thought for the first time. Menten would have sensed that the war was ending. He was too smart to mistake the signals. He surely would have remained alive and changed his name. Where would he have escaped to? Holland was the only logical place, but logic did not apply here. For all Bibi knew and all the resources he could muster, Holland could have been the dark side of the moon. He should visit Holland, but he could not quit his job, and who would pay his expenses? He had no money, and he could not work *and* travel. But, he thought, there might be a third way.

Soon after his return he visited the Press Center at the Hotel Ritz on Hayarkon Street, facing the sea. Scores of foreign correspondents from all over the world were covering Israel's birth and infancy, and the hotel served them as an office, spa, recreation resort, and place to live. Naturally, out of boredom and loneliness, they gathered in the bar, where they traded gossip, drank, told tall tales, nurtured grudges, and drank some more.

Bibi had friends among the foreign press; they made an effort for him because of the help he could give—the names of sources, facts, histories, and other helpful information that they could not find so easily elsewhere—and because Bibi was pleasant to be around. But he did not frequent the Hotel Ritz. There was too much work at the office—always too much work, Bibi thought, and he tried to devote every free moment to his family and their new apartment in the Yad Eliahu quarter of Tel Aviv. He didn't plan to give this inquiry much time, no more than a glass of juice at the bar and a few questions. Somebody there mentioned to him the name of a Jewish journalist who might be able to help—the correspondent for the Dutch socialist newspaper *Het Vrije Volk.*

Shortly thereafter, Andries Davids listened to Bibi's story, shaking his head as if he were permanently disposed to say no. But he didn't say no. He had heard something, he told Bibi, but he couldn't remember exactly what. Something about Menten tickled the back of his neck. Menten was a common name in Belgium, but not in Holland.

"All I want to know is if he is still alive," Bibi said.

Davids nodded. "Maybe I can help you," he said, promising nothing.

Journalists often scattered good intentions like chaff, and rarely made good on them with the excuse of deadlines and travel, Bibi thought, after he had heard nothing from Davids for weeks. Davids owed him nothing, anyway. People had their own concerns and problems. They were loath, Bibi knew, to get involved, particularly in conspiracies that involved the search for Nazi killers. Everybody had a mystery somewhere in his life that he wanted solved. Most of the time, however, solutions were not solutions at all, unless you could call them the unanswerable mysteries of Fate. Because Bibi knew better did not mean that others believed him. Even he admitted that the Menten story sounded odd, perhaps even delusional. He thought about Davids often, but he stayed away from the bar at the Hotel Ritz because he did not want Davids to feel uncomfortable for forgetting.

Bibi had nearly forgotten the original conversation when Davids called weeks later. After Bibi reached the hotel, Davids showed him a large manila envelope that his editor had sent from Amsterdam by surface mail. Bibi opened the clasp and tipped the contents onto the table.

"These are in Dutch," he said.

Davids laughed. "What did you expect?" They were stories clipped from Dutch newspapers.

"But I can't read them," Bibi said, upset to be so close to valuable information and yet so far.

Davids nodded. "Then you'll have to get them translated. If you do, I think you'll find answers there."

"Is he alive?" Bibi asked.

Davids laughed. "You'll see."

On an afternoon soon after, his managing editor, Finkelstein, assigned him to report the departure from Lydda Airport of an American diplomat. In the terminal lounge, while he took notes of the ambassador's parting statement, he thought how much he

150

wished he were leaving for Holland, particularly after what he had read in the translated clippings. Incomplete though they were, the clippings had presented Menten more immediately than ever before. For the first time, he had thought as he read the translations, Pieter Menten was more than a symbol of senseless death; now, he accepted that the man he had known so well had actually murdered his family. The man possessed the cunning of a killer; he had demonstrated that in Holland. Bibi hated the man so intensely that he now wanted to do something about it directly.

Still thinking of the flight, he went to the coffee shop near the departure lounge and saw that he would have to share a table. By unconscious design he set his coffee cup down on a table that was also occupied by a man in a uniform, a pilot, he told Bibi, for the Dutch national airline, KLM.

Bibi said to him after they had talked for a while, "I am sorry."

"Why?" the pilot asked, taken aback.

"It's just that I once had a friend from there."

"And that makes you sorry?"

"He killed my family."

The pilot, who lived in Holland, stared at him and answered, "No, I'm the one who's sorry."

As if the retelling were proof of progress, as though words could narrow the distance, Bibi repeated the story now. It was important. This man was Dutch; his profession of pilot symbolized the ease with which Bibi could reach Menten by air: he could travel to Holland and return during his two-week annual vacation from *Ha'aretz*. When Bibi had finished, the pilot asked, "What's his name?"

"Menten," Bibi answered, emphasizing the second syllable, as he would for the rest of his life, pronouncing the name like a curse.

"Wait a minute," the pilot said, suddenly animated. "I heard something about him."

Bibi nodded, "He's been written up in the newspapers."

"Didn't he have a trial? I mean, wasn't he tried for committing war crimes?"

"For collaboration."

"Not murder?"

151

Bibi shook his head.

"I don't understand," the pilot said.

"I don't really understand myself." Bibi knew he was being somewhat disingenuous. Murder charges had not been brought against Menten because there was not yet enough evidence to convince a prosecuting attorney anywhere on earth. Bibi, only a hearsay witness himself, needed an eyewitness. And there was another problem. *If* he found real proof, to whom would he present it? As far as he knew, Menten had not killed in Holland, and even if he had killed there, the murders of his family had taken place in Poland. And that probably meant a trial in Poland, which meant extradition to an Iron Curtain country.

The pilot was asking, "Aren't you worried he'll get away from you?"

"Yes," Bibi said. The outcome of the collaboration trial in Amsterdam had not been decided, but if Menten escaped punishment this time, he surely would disappear, if he hadn't already; he would change his name and emigrate to a country without extradition treaties. He had already tried something of the sort, the clippings said.

"How strongly do you feel about it?" the pilot asked.

Bibi did not exactly know how to respond. The answer was intensely personal. He said simply, "It's the most important thing in my life."

"Then what are you waiting for? Finish it yourself," the pilot said.

Looking at the pilot, Bibi wondered if this Dutchman had not been put there to make him face this choice, which he had scrupulously avoided until now. He supposed he had killed before, as a policeman. Back in 1938 during the Arab uprising, some of them had tried to sabotage the water reservoir in Jerusalem near where the Egged bus station was now, and he had shot into the night at them. He did not know if he had killed; he supposed so. But the Arabs had shot first. He had only defended himself, and the exchanges of gunfire had been impersonal noises in the night, with the occasional flash of a muzzle. Bibi had heard that anybody could kill in self-defense or passion. The premeditation of murder,

152

LIEBER "BIBI" KRUMHOLZ: On the porch of his uncle Isaac's "villa" in Podhorodse, the summer house that would become a cherished part of his memory, with the "rocking stag" (left) that the Prince Lubomirski had preserved for his children, and (below) with his parents, David and Malvina Krumholz.

ISAAC PISTINER: The failure of his businesses brought him in conflict over the ownership of the estates in Podhorodse (below) and Sopot; it also brought him in touch with spiritualism, which showed him the fate that awaited him and his family.

PIETER MENTEN (left): When he first appeared in Lwów, the Pistiners said that he epitomized Western culture—he smoked Egyptian cigarettes, carried a silver-topped walking stick, and spoke Polish with an endearing accent; his wife possessed a beauty "off a movie screen." *(Photo courtesy* De Telegraaf.)

SERGEANT KRUMHOLZ: An early émigré to Palestine, Bibi sent Menten a postcard from the Old City of Jerusalem, where he served in the British Protectorate Police through the Arab uprising of 1936 until 1943.

JOSEPH STIEGLITZ (right): An art dealer who worked with Menten in Cracow during the Nazi occupation, he would say later in court, "All in all, I have never heard anything bad about Pieter Menten." (*Photo courtesy ANP Foto.*)

PIETER MENTEN: In the uniform of the *Sicherheitsdienst* and with the rank of *Hauptscharführer-SS,* Menten supervised the killings in Pistiner's garden, "suggesting an actor in the wings of a theater, about to enter onto the stage." (*Photo courtesy ANP Foto.*)

HANS FRANK (left): No matter where in Poland under the Nazis, he "called the shots 'to purge the territory of the Reich of Jews and Pollacks.' " His authority was absolute, and his association made Pieter Menten a respected member of the Nazi establishment in Cracow.

EBERHARDT SCHOENGARTH: "In different times he might have been an object of pity—a gross, pathetic dipsomaniac; a person of deep, chronic depressions. But in Cracow, dressed in the vulture's plumage of the SS, he was a man to be more than feared." His friendship with Pieter Menten would last until the gallows.

HANS KNOOP (left): A tenacious reporter and the editor of the Dutch weekly magazine *Accent,* he confronted Menten with the charges of murder. Despite the odds against his succeeding, he followed the story to Podhorodse, where the graves were uncovered, and found Menten hiding in Zurich.
(*Photo courtesy ANP Foto.*)

WIBO VAN DE LINDE: The most authoritative and popular television journalist in Holland, he brought the crimes of Menten to a wider public and forced politicians to examine Holland's unenviable record in World War II.
(*Photo courtesy ANP Foto.*)

THE AMSTERDAM WAR CRIMES TRIBUNAL: Thirty-five years after the murders in Podhorodse, Menten (middle, seated at table) faced his accusers with haranguing attacks on the accuracy of their memories. The court was a "circus," he said, which the KGB in Moscow had arranged for reasons he could never adequately explain. (*Photo courtesy* De Telegraaf.)

DE HORN (below): The twenty-room house in a wealthy Amsterdam suburb contained Menten's $7-million collection of art. After the trial, an arsonist with a firebomb reduced the mansion to rubble. While he awaited the decision of the Supreme Court, Menten, along with his wife, Meta, lived across the street in the carriage house. (*Photo courtesy* ANP Foto.)

BIBI KRUMHOLZ (above): As he is today, in the garden behind his apartment
in the Yad Eliahu quarter of Tel Aviv. His
life was not complete until he had
punished his family's executioner. Now he
wants only to say *Kaddish* at the graves in
Podhorodse.

PIETER MENTEN: He tried every legal
trick to save himself, but finally his
brother, whom he had accused of the
crimes, appeared at the trial with incon-
trovertible proof of his guilt. In
maximum-security prison today, he has
run out of appeals, and only a royal pardon now could give him his freedom.
(Photo courtesy ANP Foto.)

however, was not a part of his character. He could probably take his police revolver to Holland, but what would that prove? he wondered.

Bibi said to the pilot, "If I kill him, then I will be a murderer, too. I will be like him."

As a former policeman, he respected the law; anarchy frightened him. Anyway, he said, "I doubt if I could kill a defenseless person, even him." Besides, there was a deterrent more powerful than his desire to see Menten punished. For whatever reason and no matter what justification, if he killed Menten, a court would have no other choice but to sentence him to ten or fifteen years in prison. He would waste his best years pitiful and alone in a cell, stripped of dignity, freedom to love Mala, and the joy of his family. And that, he thought, would only play into Menten's hands. If he were to kill him, Bibi would surely become Menten's last victim, destroyed by the Dutchman from the grave. "After all those lives he has taken," he said, "I won't give him another. No, I will see him in court."

But he knew that he had to act fast. The world was reneging on its promises to Jews. Bibi knew the words by heart. "No crime will be left uninvestigated, not one criminal, whether directly or indirectly responsible, will escape punishment." But he knew the reality, what the trials at Nuremberg did *not* show. At the end of 1946, nearly half a million Germans who had participated in mass murder and crimes against humanity were in guarded detention camps. By the late 1940s, fewer than 300 of these criminals were serving time behind bars. Bibi felt sick when Konrad Adenauer told the people of the new West Germany that the German Wehrmacht leaders had "had no mandate from the German people to submit to the terms of unconditional surrender." If the Germans truly felt like that, Bibi had thought, then what possible impulse existed in Holland, an occupied country, to prosecute war criminals of their own nationality? A Dutch court did not seem a probable choice to deal with Menten.

"Menten symbolizes the protected war criminal," said Bibi. "I want the Dutch people to know what one of their own people did."

"I don't envy you," the pilot said, and he almost laughed. "Everybody wants to forget, and I don't blame them."

"But before that, they should know the whole truth, shouldn't they?" Bibi asked.

"In a perfect world, but so much in Holland during the occupation brought out the worst; nobody now wants to know," answered the pilot.

"But it's a fact," Bibi said, seeing what the pilot meant—that facts were irrelevant.

"If you hurry, there's a chance," the pilot replied, offering a theory. In order to hide their role in the war, the Dutch—and other nationalities, too—created mythologies. The more unforgivable behavior required the more exaggerated myths. "If everybody who said they had fought in the Resistance actually had fought, the war would have been over before it began," he said. "That's an exaggeration, of course, but it contains a truth. If everybody who said they had helped Jews and hid them from the Germans actually did what they now say they did, those millions would still be alive. Take Anne Frank. Of course it happened, and it was courageous all around, but her story hides the truth that the vast majority of Dutch Jews died without succor. It could not have happened without the passive complicity of the Dutch. That's a burden. So there'll be a lot of resistance. You'd better kill him yourself."

In the days that followed, Bibi reviewed the conversation with the pilot again and again, and a tension of uncertainty developed. He did not know what to do, except to avoid a decision. And he found a welcome—a joyous—excuse in the return of loved ones from what he had believed was the dead, as if a fateful accountant had thought belatedly to change the ledger. First he learned that his cousin, Mara, the daughter of Isaac, her husband, Stash, and two children had survived. They had cabled from Paris where they had traveled from Poland en route to Tel Aviv. When they arrived in Israel, Mara brought news.

Once they had learned of Lwów's liberation by Russian troops in July 1944, Mara and her family had boarded a Soviet refugee flight from Kazakhstan, where they had spent the war, to Lwów's

Sknilow Airport. Mara had needed to summon the powers of memory to orient herself. Now, rubble filled the streets of Lwów. Bombs had flattened most houses. As Mara wandered the once familiar streets, she had searched the faces of displaced persons for a friend who could tell her some news of her immediate family and the Krumholzes. Russian soldiers guarded German prisoners of war near the center of the city, while Polish civilians, perhaps suspicious of the Russian victory, gave the Germans basic foodstuffs, candy, and cigarettes. Mara felt threatened by this gesture, and later she understood why, when the Poles tried to place blame for the destruction of the war on the pitiful few Jews who remained in Poland, and subjected them to new and terrible pogroms. Mara thought that Poland might never change, and she made the decision to leave as soon as she found the answers to her questions.

Now, they made rapidly for Pelczynska Street #26, where they had last seen Isaac and Frieda on the day that they had fled. Mara remembered how she had urged Isaac to leave, too, and how he had believed that the Germans would liberate them from the Russians, and all would be well. She realized that her father had clung to that belief to avoid the upheaval as a refugee in Russia. Mara believed that luck was with her now as she entered the street. The house was still standing. In the balmy weather residents rested on their windowsills and were listening to a radio broadcasting in Russian. She went up to the house and knocked on the same door she had entered a thousand times or more, and soon the building's concierge appeared, regarding Mara with astonishment. "You remained alive!" she exclaimed. The next words out of her mouth were, "The tragedy is enormous."

Frightened now, Mara ran toward Stewczyka Street #10, where the concierge said she last heard Isaac and Frieda had been living. Mara passed the same house, the same streets and sidewalks and shops, now utterly destroyed. As she approached Isaac's house an old woman in a tattered black shawl who looked "like a dog in search of its owner" stopped her. A Jewess and the neighborhood grocer, Frania had survived the war by daring to scavenge for food under the protection of night. On one of those nights, she told Mara, she had watched a German car stop in the

155

street. She had heard gunshots and watched as a child fell into the street, and later, she saw men entering the car. Watching from the shadows, she had seen "the nice Dutchman who had lived in Lwów before the war." Mara asked urgently if Frania knew what had happened to the child, Marisia. Frania said she had survived by a miracle.

They stayed in Lwów for a month, searching for Marisia, whom a relative of her father had taken to Katowice. Mara had asked nearly every Jewish survivor whom she saw for news of her family. She heard that Lieber had died, and so had her father, in the ghetto, and she was told about the Krumholzes, too. Japan had related his story of surviving Menten's cemetery executions, and although the people did not know his fate, they thought that he had fled into the countryside.

At the end of the month, with no reason to remain in Lwów, they moved to Bytom and waited for the British to change their emigration policies in Palestine. One day a stranger came up the stairs after her and handed Mara an envelope with the identity papers of Japan, a sad memory of a life on a card stamped "Jude" in blue. The Nazis had killed him in hiding. The stranger did not know how or when.

From Bytom they passed through Katowice, where they had found Marisia, seemingly none the worse for the harrowing experience. Now en route to Israel, the "family" stopped briefly in Paris, where Mara visited the Dutch and Polish embassies. She was shown every courtesy, even some sympathy. The forms were simple to fill out. On their pre-printed lines, she named the murderer of her family.

One night soon after, in their third-floor apartment, Bibi was trying to write a story for *Ha'aretz* that he could easily have put off. But he was alone, and writing sometimes distracted him from thinking about personal problems. Mala was gone. She had heard that her brother, Aaron, had been found near death in a northern Italian hospital, a miraculous survivor of Dr. Mengele's sadistic medical experiments at Auschwitz, and she had gone to see him soon after in Merano, high in the Rhaetian Alps. Bibi already missed her. He did not even have their baby daughter, Sima, to distract him; she was being cared for by friends in the neighborhood. Between the bits of the story he was writing, Bibi realized how important Mala was in his life. She was the best person for discussion about things that mattered. She knew instinctively the boundaries that he often did not heed. Bibi never understood how, but she had learned lessons that journalism, books, and interviews had failed to teach him. Until he found a better name, he would call it judgment.

Most residents of the Yad Eliahu quarter retired early in the evening. By around eleven o'clock the neighborhood was deserted and so quiet that the softest footstep on the stone stairs of Bibi's apartment building could easily have been heard. Only the occasional automobile with a ruptured muffler, or, overhead, the engine roar of an airplane on its final approach to Lydda punctuated the silence. Seated at his typewriter, Bibi heard nothing until suddenly, there came a rapping on the door. So unexpected was the sound that he looked first through the door's "peephole" into darkness on the landing. He wondered who this was, when the timed light switch illuminated the face of a man he recognized but could not identify by name. When he opened the door the man asked, "Are you Lieber Krumholz?" with a familiarity that suggested the shadow of an alliance.

Bibi answered, "Yes?"

"I am Samuel Schiff."

When he heard the name Bibi remembered. Schiff belonged to the sawmill in Podhorodse. "But I thought everyone was killed," he remarked, suddenly understanding how the Jewish Agency's political department had learned about the slaughter in the village. Schiff was "Source No. 77."

"Altmann and I were spared," Schiff said. Then as Bibi took his jacket, he added, "I've come here because I want to tell you about it."

After Bibi brewed a pot of tea, they sat at the dining room table, and Schiff said, "You remember, there were thirty Jewish families there. That day I was at home when a Ukrainian militiaman with a gun ordered me to go with him. I asked if I could go alone, and he said for me to take my family with me. . . . And we went up the

157

road to the Mayor's Office. All the Jews of Podhorodse were there, and from that office we were taken to the house on the hill."

"Uncle Isaac's?" Bibi asked.

Schiff nodded. "And I saw two SS officers on the veranda of the house. They were in uniform, and one of them was Pieter Menten, whom I knew well. In the yard of the house were more than two hundred people, Ukrainians and Poles, all dressed up like for a party. I saw that near Menten was the commandant of the militia, Philip Müller, who told me that Pieter Menten had ordered him to tell me and my family to go home. Then Menten himself told me. You would not believe, but I had walked only a few feet when I suddenly heard shooting, so we started to run to the house. Later, I saw women running down the hill with their children. They cried and shouted as they ran. From them I learned that Menten, along with the Nazi, had taken the husbands, the Jews, and ordered them to move on a plank, and then shot them when they reached the center. Later, I went back to the house and veranda where Menten had stood with the others. I saw exactly how they had fired their guns. On that day the daughter of Isaac Pistiner, your cousin, Maria, said to me that before her husband was shot she had clasped Menten's legs and begged him to spare Philip's life. Menten replied that he would return to Lwów and destroy all the Pistiner family. He hated Isaac."

Maria Wecker, the beautiful one, the last Schiff had heard, had fled on foot to Schodnice, and later died in one or another of the *Aktionen*. Schiff had waited a few hours after the executions, then fled with his family to Stryj to the house of Nachem Halpern, the son of the widow Halpern, owner of the Podhorodse general store. Then, Schiff told Bibi, "We must have looked dead. Nachem and I spoke quietly until the crack of dawn. I told him, 'Your mother, your sister, and her children were killed in Podhorodse. Before that, he killed all the men. Only Altmann and I were spared.'"

"The *women* and *children* too were shot?" Bibi asked.

"Yes," Schiff said. "The Ukrainians had dug another grave near the first one. Everybody said the same."

"Was Menten there that second day, too?" Bibi asked.

158

"I can't say," he said. "Nobody mentioned that he was. For myself, I don't know. But it was clear to me that I couldn't save my family much longer," Schiff went on. The night after the mass killing of the men, Müller had ordered a Ukrainian militiaman to bring Schiff to the Mayor's Office. Schiff told Bibi, "Müller looked at me for a long time and then said, 'I just wanted to see the Jew whom Pieter Menten permitted to live.' And like a miracle I was allowed to go back home.

"That same night," Schiff continued, "I decided to do a brave thing. I hitched horses to a wagon shaft and I fled to Stryj with my family. I do not understand the miracle. We drove the whole night, for seven hours, and nobody stopped us."

But the miracles soon ran out when the Germans occupied Stryj and assigned Schiff to a work gang. Together with Nachem Halpern and Uzik Nass, the son of the *melamed* from Sopot, he worked at forced labor, rebuilding a former Russian army camp that the Luftwaffe had bombed. Later that summer, he learned that his wife and daughter had perished. Without a family to protect, he had escaped into the forests with Nass. They headed back toward Sopot in the belief that the local peasants would give them food. They walked only by night, resting and hiding during the day. Finally, from the edge of the forest behind Sopot, Nass had told Schiff to stay put while he contacted Ukrainian villagers whom he had known for years. About half an hour passed, Schiff told Bibi, when he heard rifle shots and shouting. Suddenly, he saw Nass running toward him, his arms waving madly, as if in warning. Before he reached the edge of the field Nass fell dead. Schiff went deep into the forest.

"From then on," he said, "I lived like an animal." From time to time, he received scraps of food—potatoes, husks of bread, and gristle—from local Polish farmers, who otherwise had refused to hide him. He poached small forest animals and stole from the fields. After more than two years like this, he went to Schodnice, hoping to find a safe hiding place in the city. Instead, he found betrayal, and he was sent to the death camp at Mauthausen, where he survived until the Liberation.

Immediately after reaching Israel, Schiff told Bibi, he had reported the crimes to the Jewish Agency's political department. Bibi acknowledged seeing the report, but he said they could not rely on the Jewish Agency—or any other institution, for that matter.

"Whatever it takes," Schiff said, "I want revenge."

Bibi had already dealt with that question. Eventually Schiff would agree with him. He said, "No, my friend, not revenge. We will get justice."

Once Schiff had gone, Bibi did not sleep. He spent the next few hours at the typewriter, reconstructing as accurately as possible Schiff's story, with quotes, dates, numbers, and facts. As he typed what he remembered, Bibi thought first of Maria and the profound loss of his many friends in the village. It was tragic what Menten had done. And Schiff's account lent veracity to the revelations of Jacob Leubel; the two stories fit like pieces in a puzzle. Menten had killed Isaac's family, and David, Malvina, and Marek, for revenge—he had wanted them dead, as far as anybody knew, because of the land dispute. He could understand that logic, if nothing else about it. But why had Menten liquidated the Jews in the village, unless he had somehow blamed them, too? Nothing really explained such bestiality.

Bibi continued to work at his typewriter, once he had finished the notes of Schiff's story. He typed March 24, 1949, in the upper-right-hand corner of the stationery. If he had not known about the massacre in Podhorodse, the Dutch authorities did not know either. The Jewish Agency had not sent the form submitted by Source No. 77 to the Dutch Ministry of Justice, and Schiff had not visited the Dutch Legation office in Tel Aviv. So if they knew anything, they could know only what Mara had deposed at the embassy in Paris about the murders of the Pistiners and Krumholzes.

In the newspaper articles that Davids had given him, Bibi remembered the name of a prosecutor in Holland: Besier. After finding the clipping, he typed out the man's name and title, and then wrote down what Schiff had told him. He volunteered to send Schiff's complete testimony to Holland if the prosecutor wanted. He repeated the original point: Menten had liquidated human beings. Then, in such haste that he did not correct his grammar, Bibi sent the letter airmail to Bernhard J. Besier, the Attorney General for the *Bijzonder Gerechtshof* in Amsterdam.

He waited nearly three weeks for a reply. He thought Besier would want more information, but he had expected at least a telegram back in receipt of his letter. The Dutch had a reputation for efficiency and thoroughness. At the end of the third week, he wrote again, "Over three weeks ago I sent you a letter concerning the case of Menten. Meantime, I have collected some more evidence against Menten, evidence which might support your prosecution of his case. But to my regret, I have received no answer from you to my questions. How should I submit to Dutch authorities the material which is in my possession on Menten's participation in the murders of Jews in Poland?" This time Bibi signed the letter using his former police title, "Press Officer, Police H.Q., Tel Aviv," because he thought this would get a response.

Another week passed—too soon for Bibi's second letter to have reached Besier—and as he did every morning, Bibi checked his mailbox a few blocks away in the Yad Eliahu post office. There he found an official envelope from the Office of the Attorney General of the Special Court for War Crimes in Amsterdam. He opened it up, relieved that it was written in English. Dated April 25, 1949, with the File # BE-RS-6245 and signed by Bernhard Besier, it started,

In reply to your letter of March 24, 1949, which I received on the 2nd of April, I beg to inform you that the Special Court of Justice at Amsterdam closed the inquiry in the case of P. N. Menten on March 31 last so that *your information came too late.* [Italics added.] An inquiry in Holland into your complaint is rather impossible as I cannot have witnesses come from Poland to Holland and moreover you do not indicate me [*sic*] names nor addresses from witnesses. On the 14th of April my Court found Menten guilty of willful cooperation with the enemy and sentenced him to imprisonment for one year with deduction of custody time. The Public Prosecutor of Krakau [Cracow] too has a dossier concerning Men-

161

ten but most probably the Dutch Government will not be able to extradite Menten, who is a Dutch citizen, to Poland.

Yours Faithfully,

Bibi read the letter again, astonished. In so many words, Besier was telling him to drop dead. ". . . impossible . . . cannot have witnesses . . . closed the inquiry . . . information came too late. . . ." *Two days*—from March 31 to April 2—was too late to investigate charges of mass murder; these crimes were dismissed because of *days*. It was such an insult that Bibi refused to see the obvious—that perhaps the Dutch did not want to know that one of their own, an important man in their society, was a butcher.

Besier had proposed an insulting Catch-22. The Dutch would not acknowledge—much less prosecute—the crimes of murder because they had already tried Menten for collaboration, as if one in any way approached the severity of or canceled the other. Besier had asked him to contact the Polish authorities to request that they extradite Menten for trial. An extradition treaty did not exist between Holland and Poland. The Iron Curtain had recently descended between East and West Europe. Therefore, the Dutch would not extradite Menten for trial, no matter how clear the Polish jurisdiction, and they would not try him at home. Was that it? Bibi asked himself as he read the letter again on his way back to the apartment.

"What should I do?" he asked Mara later on the telephone.

She did not answer him directly. The fact dawned on her slowly, and she said, "My God, Bibi, the Dutch know—they have known all along, even before you wrote to Besier. They willed to ignore the murders, don't you see?"

"No, I don't," Bibi said honestly.

"Besier says, 'The Public Prosecutor of Krakau too has a dossier.' His file contains the accusations foremost that Menten murdered innocent people. The Poles know about murder, Bibi, because I told them, before we left Bytom and in Paris."

"Then the Dutch can't just ignore this," Bibi said.

"It seems they can." Mara asked him to read the letter a second time. Besier had written that he could not bring witnesses from Poland and "moreover you do not indicate me names nor addresses from witnesses. . . ." He himself said that was why he did not prosecute Menten for murder and why Bibi's complaint against Menten was "rather impossible." They would soon find out that it was true.

On his next free afternoon from *Ha'aretz*, Bibi went to the Tel Aviv District Court. A lawyer assigned to the prosecutor's office, Mr. Harpazzi, heard him out. He had often thought about the right course to advise for people like Bibi, and he shared those thoughts freely. First, he explained the hard truth about extradition. Even if a treaty existed between Holland and Poland or Holland and Israel—and none did exist—the process of extradition was cumbersome, requiring two complete and different trials: the first to determine if the crime warranted extradition and whether there was prima facie evidence to support the charge; but even after all that, the attorney general of the country holding the suspect could still refuse on political grounds. "Years and years might pass," Harpazzi said. He related other facts that Bibi hardly wanted to hear again—that the enthusiasm for justice had ebbed, starting in Germany. The new Federal Republic of Germany wanted—indeed *needed*—to forget the past. So did Holland.

Indeed, in Germany the men who had built and run the Third Reich now were serving to build and run *Wirtschaftswunder,* the "economic miracle" of the new postwar West Germany. The drift in the future was toward forgiving and forgetting their crimes and collusions because of their contributions to the "miracle." The British were cynical in allowing this, and the Americans tagged not far behind, soon to espouse the belief that a strong West Germany was the West's best bulwark in the Cold War against Russia. "From Israel we can do nothing," Harpazzi cautioned Bibi, "except offer our assistance to foreign governments *when they ask.* If they do not ask, we cannot make demands. I am sorry, but those are the facts."

An Israeli could point out to the Dutch the existence of a war criminal in their midst. Bibi had done that already, he told Harpazzi, in the letter to Besier. An Israeli could also assist with the testimony of witnesses to the crime of murder. But about witnesses Harpazzi cautioned, "You can never know. It is very, very dangerous. In the best of faith, you can testify against a person like Menten, identify such a person, and you may be quite wrong. The eyewitnesses can be wrong because they are working under so much emotional stress. It's not so much the imagination as the trauma these people went through. It creates a layer of things remembered which never happened, or maybe happened with entirely different people. It's a very tricky matter." He strongly advised Bibi to "forget it."

Bibi said, "Never, I can never forget it."

What he did next in anger took eight months, until the early spring of 1950. Some of the people he knew already. To inform others, he sent word through private channels in Israel and also placed an advertisement in the national newspapers, asking witnesses to Menten's crimes to come forward. And it worked. That spring he led a parade of these people in Israel before Judge Dr. Sussman of the Tel Aviv District Court, where, under oath, they deposed what they had seen. After Mara had repeated what she had already described to Bibi, Nachem Halpern briefly and poignantly told the judge under oath, "Pieter Menten was the murderer of my mother, sister, brother-in-law, and their children. On them may God bring quiet. Let God stop *his* life."

Outside the court, Bibi paced the long corridor as he watched the doors for new witnesses to arrive. As each one appeared, he asked beforehand what they planned to say. As best he could, he calmed witnesses' nerves. On the second day of the hearings he noticed a tall, formal-looking man in a gray suit seated on a bench inside the court. He had not seen him enter. During a break Bibi introduced himself. Mr. Jorissen, the secretary of the Dutch diplomatic legation in Israel, had been ordered to report on the proceedings for the Dutch Foreign Ministry. Later, Bibi invited him for a cup of coffee in a nearby café on Yehuda Halevi Street. Whether the diplomat knew the whole story, he did not say. However, he did say, "There is only interest in the big criminals—the ones whom the Americans and the British tried. Menten does not belong to that category. He is not a big man." But still, the Dutch had sent a diplomat. That had to signify *something*, Bibi thought.

The Tel Aviv District Court sent the testimonies to the Israeli

Foreign Office in Jerusalem, which in turn gave the court documents to the Dutch Foreign Ministry in The Hague. Worried, nevertheless, and suspicious that they would be ignored or somehow "lost," Mara wrote to Besier on April 23, 1950: "In connection with the statement which I gave recently in the District Court of Tel Aviv in the case of Pieter Menten, I take herewith the liberty to submit you [*sic*] a list of witnesses. . . ." She also sent duplicates of the official testimonies to Amsterdam by registered mail.

The same month, Bibi wrote Arie Tatakover, director of the Israeli section of the World Jewish Congress, asking him for support. Tatakover replied, "I sent a copy of your letter to the offices of the Jewish Congress in New York and London, and I asked them to get in touch with you if they decide for their side to do something in the case of Menten." Bibi never heard from them again.

Worried that the initiative might fail because of his inattentiveness, Bibi telephoned the Israeli Foreign Office, then followed up with a letter: ". . . In continuation of our telephone call of yesterday, which was interrupted because the telephone was suddenly disconnected, I am sending you a list of people who can give evidence and give testimony . . . to make a case against Menten. . . . I shall be thankful if you will give me the results of my appeal to you, and I place myself at your disposal."

A diplomat in the Israeli Foreign Office wrote back, ". . . All the names that you sent to us as witnesses, in case there is a trial against that man [Menten], we have sent to the Dutch authorities, as we mentioned. Our Consul in Amsterdam talked personally with the General Prosecutor there. . . ."

But Holland had already closed Menten's file. Authorities there did not *want* to open a new trial. As the months passed and nothing happened, Bibi felt bullied and insulted, as if the Dutch were defiling his family's graves. He had done everything in his power to help the Dutch, but the campaign had achieved nothing. He thought, Now it's time to "make a scandal."

Israel Finkelstein, the fastidious *Ha'aretz* managing editor, did not care much for stories about war crimes, particularly if the sto-

165

ries accused private citizens in his newspaper without the consent of public institutions, like courts. The stories forced him to perch on a thin limb of libel. If one of his—or Gustav Schocken's— favorite and trusted reporters burned with investigative zeal to expose an arch war criminal . . . well, maybe. But only after the lawyers had laundered every word. The *Ha'aretz* that Finkelstein had shaped was not sensational, and stories about war crimes often were. Anyway, in the lingo of journalism, the newspaper had "done" Nuremberg, and the Holocaust was more or less an ongoing feature. Finkelstein did not feel duty-bound to write about Jews during the war in the pages of *Ha'aretz* unless he felt that the story had implications that were either new or pertinent. There was plenty of news in Israel without old Nazis. This may have been callous and shortsighted, but it was the final news judgment of the managing editor.

Yet Finkelstein had to work with the only resource of journalism, people, which meant compromise—or best of all, Finkelstein thought, the *illusion* of compromise. He felt the same as most editors feel about their reporters, that they suffer from a hopeless but lovable immaturity which produces enthusiasm to see the world as fresh and exciting year after year. As managing editor he was the father figure to all this immaturity. He had to protect frail egos, and that was where the appearance of compromise came in. He often wondered how he succeeded so well, how he hoodwinked supposedly hard-nosed journalists, unless perhaps they knew all along and humored him as mice play with a clawless cat.

These assessments applied to nearly all his reporters, and none more than to Bibi. A tireless journalist, Bibi never complained when the work load separated him from his family—his daughter, Sima, was now nearly four. More than other reporters on the newspaper, Bibi seemed to substitute journalism for religion. His commitment, however, did not alter one fact. *Ha'aretz* wanted to be known as the newspaper of record in Israel—sober, serious, and objective. For his part, Finkelstein believed, Bibi had a weakness for what Finkelstein called "flashy, lurid things." This was not meant as criticism. Some people were drawn by what others found repellent. Finkelstein hoped that Bibi would continue to write for the newspaper the stories that the *newspaper* wanted written.

One afternoon in the late winter of that year, Bibi approached Finkelstein with his special request. He did so reluctantly and only after much thought. "I have a problem with a Dutchman," he said.

Finkelstein instantly saw the danger signs, but he listened with interest and indeed, for him, with sympathy. Krumholz was directly involved in this affair with all the power of emotion. But what did that involvement do to his objectivity, his ability to scrutinize facts, balance evidence, and all the rest? Finkelstein wondered if Bibi was the best person to report and write about his family's killer. And he answered himself, no. In his phrase, he was "too close to the story."

"Nothing has been done until now," Bibi pleaded. "I have more facts, and I must write all about it."

What was Finkelstein to say? He was not going to send Bibi to Holland; he rarely sent reporters outside Israel. Basically, Finkelstein thought, this was a personal vendetta that could require weeks of investigation and great sums of money. And for what? That one of his reporters would perhaps bring the killer of his parents to court? And one who was no Bormann or Barbie. How would the newspaper benefit? Yes, perhaps it would get a good story, but perhaps nothing. After all that expense in time and resources and cash, even if the killer was brought to justice, would it be anything more than another war crimes story? A lurid one at that? It all appeared to him a little unseemly.

"All right, show it to me," he said, by which he meant for Bibi to write up the notes. There was to be no more investigation, certainly no travel. And then and only then he would see what it was worth and make his decision whether or not to print it. He could not help being touched as he watched Bibi leave his office.

Late the following morning when he arrived at the office, Finkelstein saw the notes on his desk. For the moment, he set them aside, turning first to the more immediate demands of news. But later in the day, toward evening, as he read, his heart sank, more for Bibi than for anything else. Finkelstein knew that

167

Ha'aretz could not print such allegations without more supporting evidence. The man accused, he was reading here, was infinitely rich and resourceful, and also litigious. His lawyers would cannibalize this story, and an expensive libel suit would result. *Ha'aretz* could not win and if it lost, the price would surely be too high. Usually, Finkelstein asked Gustav Schocken what he thought on matters of delicacy, such as this. Now, he saw no need.

That left Finkelstein with a problem—the human side of the equation. This was no average story with an average involvement and interest. Bibi had identified a face and name, and what a superb achievement that was. But all the same, weighing the risks, Finkelstein jammed the copy on the spike, deciding to tell Krumholz nothing, unless he was asked, which he doubted, given the person involved. Bibi's answer to his silence would be an equal silence. Finkelstein banked on that. He wanted Bibi to assume that the story had been adjudicated evenly, like any other story. Managing editors never explained why they had killed a story. If Bibi wanted to go outside the house with it, he did not even need to ask. That was Finkelstein's compromise.

For all that, Finkelstein severely miscalculated the stubbornness of his reporter to see the story printed in *Ha'aretz*. The following day, as if it had risen from the dead, the story that Bibi had written again appeared on Finkelstein's desk, this time in printed galleys. Bibi had moved the story toward publication without his managing editor's approval on the assumption that no news from Finkelstein was good news. Bibi had forced Finkelstein to explain his decision. "You know," he told Bibi, "Menten is a rich man. I'm afraid he will make trouble for us."

Bibi replied angrily, "How do *you* know? Maybe *I* am right. Maybe he is the killer of my family. Did you think of that possibility? If he sues we will confront him with witnesses, and we will win."

"But who'll pay?"

"The newspaper will."

"The newspaper *won't*."

At last Finkelstein agreed—Bibi's anger had astonished him—

to an independent legal review of the article. If there was little chance of a trial against *Ha'aretz,* he told Bibi, then he would gladly go to press with the Menten story.

Two weeks later, the lawyer for *Ha'aretz* told Bibi, "I feel terrible about what I have to tell you. I suggest you don't print it."

The decision was final, but if it angered Bibi, he did not show it—at least outwardly. Complaining, he knew, did not change Finkelstein's mind, and Schocken rarely countermanded his managing editor's decisions. Besides, Bibi did not want to create dissension. He wanted the story accepted on its merits alone, not because he was a reporter writing about his own family. Somehow he thought that pleading cheapened their memory. He had gone as far as he could reasonably go at *Ha'aretz,* and that left him weakened but not without resources.

He went home and rewrote the story, simplifying it, cutting the flashy stylistic feature elements. He used the Tel Aviv District Court testimonies as a peg for a hard-news story, and when he finished, he took the copy to the offices in Tel Aviv of *Ma'ariv,* the afternoon paper and *Ha'aretz*'s competition, on whose staff Bibi had several reporter friends. They read the copy, and they too considered the question of libel, a judgment call that they thought minimal.

It did not appear on page one, but Bibi did not mind. Reading the truth about Pieter Menten in the pages of *Ma'ariv* made him feel that something had been salvaged, and maybe even more. He knew that journalists often moved in packs, at first with skepticism, then in a frenzy to get the same story, no matter what. The longer they delayed, the faster and more recklessly they tried to catch up with the journalist who had broken the story. As a press officer in the police, Bibi had seen the other side of the news. Perhaps he could manipulate that within the press. *Ma'ariv* gave the Menten story veracity. Maybe *Ha'aretz* could have given it more "class," but Bibi was not complaining. *Ma'ariv* had given him the bait to arouse interest in the story among the foreign correspondents at the Hotel Ritz. The effect would snowball, he hoped, and soon the Dutch newspapers would start to investigate the story in Holland.

169

At first the strategy went exactly according to his plan. On April 5, 1950, *Het Parool,* the Dutch daily, headlined an article, "SEVERE ACCUSATION IN TEL AVIV AGAINST MENTEN." The article echoed Bibi's story in *Ma'ariv.* "An official report has been drawn up by the District Court in Tel Aviv of an accusation made against Menten, living in Holland. It states that during the war in Poland Jews were sent to their deaths as a result of his doing. The accusation has been shown by the Israelis to the Dutch legation in Tel Aviv." The story quoted Mara and ended with the prediction, "This extremely serious accusation against a Dutch citizen will undoubtedly be investigated by the Dutch Justice Department."

Two months later Bibi received a letter from *Het Vrije Volk,* another Dutch daily. The paper's editor, E. Messer, wrote: "Mr. Davids [*Het Vrije Volk*'s correspondent in Tel Aviv] told us about your part in excavating the Menten affair. He intimated that you would be willing to write an article about this affair for our paper. If you are indeed, could you send us an article as soon as possible?" Bibi imagined that the Dutch newspaper would now investigate the Menten case on its own initiative, just as he had thought. Messer wrote: "Here in Holland we are very interested in getting to the bottom of this Menten business, especially as Menten is protected by a clan of reactionaries over here. If you could make it a *good* story, we are willing to accept up till 4000 words. Payment for such an article would be hfl. 100,—(providing it is really good!). We are not afraid of some 'human interest,' our daily being a paper for simple people."

For all the pleasure that the offer gave Bibi, one line in the letter worried him out of proportion. The editor had written, ". . . especially as Menten is protected by a clan of reactionaries over here." He asked himself, Was this why Besier had found Menten's prosecution for murder inconvenient? And if powerful "reactionaries" were protecting him, what was the use? As a foreigner and a Jew, Bibi did not count. If people in his own country could not touch Menten, then in Israel Bibi was tilting at windmills.

For the moment, he took heart. His tactic was working, Bibi thought as he worked at home evenings to recast the original story on a borrowed English-language typewriter. He broadened the story this time around, turning it back into a feature of human interest that would not fail to break readers' hearts and then enrage them, no matter who they were, what their religion, age, sex, or experience in the war. The story would then mobilize them. It was a story of justice—a fine story on its own, a great story with his personal involvement. He spent time polishing it, and once he had added a few finishing touches, he mailed the copy with a covering letter to *Het Vrije Volk*. In the letter he wrote, "I accept your proposal and submit you [*sic*] an article on Menten's crimes hoping it will also help us to stimulate the public's opinion and the authorities to bring the criminal on the accused's bench." *Now* the Dutch public will know, Bibi thought.

As time passed, the article did not appear. Bibi wondered why Messer had not written to explain the status of his story. After all, Messer had approached him. But weeks became months, as Bibi felt more and more humiliated. They had ignored a self-evident fact, and worse still, they had refused to print a phenomenal story, *his* story documented by *his* friends, a story that had been alive momentarily in the press and now was beyond revival.

"What can I do?" he asked Mala.

She hated to see him like this. Her impulse was to tell him to go to Holland. Otherwise he would not be content or allow her a minute's peace. But she could not give him that license, as she needed him there. More than that, how would they pay for a ticket to Holland? The answer was *Ha'aretz,* and she told him so.

"They've done what they can," he replied, feeling renewed bitterness at their timidity.

"Then you must wait," she scolded him. Some criminals did not pay for their crimes. Maybe Menten was one. "If he is truly guilty, Bibi," she told him, "then you will get your justice, maybe not now, but it will happen."

"When will it happen?" he asked. "How long do we have to wait?" He wanted her to see that the prosecution of Menten forced him to dwell in the past, and he was impatient for a more tangible reason. There were now eyewitnesses to convince a jury of Menten's guilt, if only a court would accept the case. In five years the same witnesses might be dead or scattered and lost. Every day

171

placed more distance between Menten and justice—a distance that soon seemed unrecoverable.

Just as these feelings of desperation were taking root, Finkelstein assigned Bibi to cover the opening of an air route by the newly established Israeli airline, El Al. Finkelstein knew what a plum assignment this was—a round trip by Super Constellation to Amsterdam that any of *Ha'aretz*'s reporters or editors would have been pleased to take. The trip was nothing more than a turnaround boondoggle with enough time for a visit to the Rijksmuseum and an overnight, but Finkelstein gave it to Bibi in the hope that it might compensate for the unavoidable wrong he had done to his hardest-working reporter.

On the long flight Bibi had many hours to consider what Menten had told him as a boy, that Holland in the spring was magical. Tulips everywhere in window boxes and private gardens colored the country with heart-stopping brilliance. The Dutch women, straightening into the midday sun, walked with a lightened step. Courting couples in the verdant Amsterdam parks watched the waterfowl chatter near the banks, as children played free of heavy winter clothing. But when he arrived Bibi was blinded to the magic, seeing nothing but imagined traces of Pieter Menten. He scorned the people for refusing to admit even the possibility of Menten's crimes. Cowed by his wealth and influence, they had overlooked the murder of Bibi's family and the Jews of Podhorodse as if their lives had meant nothing. Alone and miserable, everywhere he went, whether to a museum or a café, to the Leidseplein, the Dam, wherever, he saw Pieter Menten in the face of every second older Dutchman. At the Krasnapolsky Hotel on the Dam, the palace square in the heart of Amsterdam, Bibi locked himself in his room and looked down column after column on page after page of the telephone book for the name Pieter N. Menten, but he found nothing there.

He had brought a revolver, loaded with bullets, though its presence was absurd to him. Of course he had again contemplated murder, ever since the press campaign had failed him. He thought, I can kill, but killing as a personal business *is* murder. No, the revolver would stay in the suitcase, which forced him to consider whether or not to petition the Ministry of Justice, this time in person. In his pocket he carried the letter from Besier: The Dutch had turned him down. He would not give them the opportunity to insult him twice. Menten was too alert now to make a mistake, Bibi thought, but eventually he would grow slack and unguarded, and then he would make a fatal mistake. Mala had been right. The time also would come when a whole new generation in Holland would reach its majority, and as people who had not experienced World War II, they would respect a different honor. Suddenly, Bibi realized he faced the prospect of many years' wait, and he feared dying before Menten.

CHAPTER VIII

✖

"What in God's name has happened...?"

THE LIBERATION OF Holland in the spring of 1945 had created a situation for Pieter Menten of maximum danger, to which he responded in a characteristically daring manner. As soon as the Nazis surrendered, the BS (Forces of the Interior) had organized the former Resistance into a civilian police and paramilitary force to reinstate public order. To achieve a "moral character" after five years of occupation, the Allies in turn proposed to the Dutch to shoot "a thousand or more" of their traitors for membership in certain enemy organizations so that lesser collaborators would realize that punishment awaited them, too. But ultimately, a refined sense of justice prevailed. (Thirty-six traitors went to the wall. More than 100,000 collaborators were tried, but only half that number were eventually sentenced.) The procedures for dealing with Dutch war criminals gave rise to charge, countercharge, guilt and fear, and no small amount of corruption.

As soon as possible after Liberation, the BS had reviewed its considerable lists of suspected collaborators and made arrests, but in the part of the BS that had been Rolls-Royce, Pete van Izendorn was still not convinced of Menten's guilt and placed him in a category of "under house arrest," until the police found the time to consider his case more carefully or until more incriminating evidence surfaced against him.

In this rapidly changing atmosphere, Menten was at the peak of wariness, especially since in the ten days after Liberation several complete strangers had knocked on the door of the Westerlaan

174

house, then had run away when he answered. On the advice of lawyer Dr. J. C. Coeberg, he had decided to protect his valuables, which he feared the Resistance was plotting to "liberate." One spring day soon after, he laid out five "extremely valuable paintings," some 500 antique drawings, and a suitcase with nearly $1 million in cash and $152,000 in American stocks and securities for Coeberg to collect from the house and deliver to a bank vault. While waiting for Coeberg to arrive, Menten stripped off his shirt and stretched on a chaise longue in the springtime sun. Later, in the backyard, he heard the sounds of shattering glass, then a burst from a Sten gun, Elizabeth's scream, and men shouting. Before he could move, BS officers had surrounded him, then tied his arms and held pistols against his ribs. Minutes later they were driving to the internment compound for collaborators at Duinrust. For reasons of their own the BS said that they had changed their minds. Even if they did not know the identity of The Deputy, the important Nazi who had visited him, the accusations by the Honorary Dutch Consul Joseas Debrouin provided reason for an arrest, they said. Afterward, van Izendorn had sealed off Menten's house, which former members of Rolls-Royce then guarded. Oddly, the women—Mrs. Menten, Elizabeth, and "chocolate eyes"—were also taken away.

That night, Menten lay on a straw mattress in a cell without heat or blankets. A guard from the BS pointed a Sten at him and told him to stand against the wall. "Take off your clothes first," the guard taunted. "It's a shame to get blood on the clothes. We can always use those." Another guard approached the cell. The first guard said, "I'm not going to shoot him. You can see that. If the gun goes off, it's an accident." At one point later on, the guards forced him to pose naked for photographs with *moffemeiden*, Dutch women whom the BS had arrested for sexual "collaboration." The worst torture of the incarceration, though, was that he did not know whether the BS had stolen his valuables.

Van Izendorn made a thorough search of the Westerlaan house, then he gave Rolls-Royce permission to take whatever their families needed. The stocks that Menten had hoarded astounded and angered him. There was enough soap, bedding, and food to last a family for months, and only days before, while the Germans still

175

occupied the country, Menten's neighbors had been starving. What van Izendorn had found besides the stocks of hoarded goods confused him. He read signed copies of letters to Nazis with the closing "Heil Hitler" above Menten's name, and he saw photographs of Menten in uniform. What it all added up to, van Izendorn could not say. Menten had not collaborated in Holland, as far as he knew, and therefore his Polish collaboration presented certain jurisdictional problems. If he had collaborated, as seemed clear to van Izendorn, in Poland, then he had no power to act against Menten. If the Poles had a case and wanted to prosecute him, then they would ask for his extradition. Curious to know what he had stumbled into, van Izendorn went against police and even diplomatic procedures. He sent a telegram to the head of the Polish State Security Service in Cracow, who replied by mail many weeks later: "We are busy with the Menten investigation here. He was an important collaborator. He collected the possessions of Jews. Further details to follow." But further details never followed.

At about the same time, van Izendorn started to receive certain subtle—but all the same, alarming—messages that maybe Menten should be handled with great care. Nothing specific was ever said to van Izendorn, and he certainly received nothing in writing. Dimly at first, the message came from the Military Commission for Custody and Release, which weighed the evidence against suspected collaborators to determine whether or not their collaboration warranted continued incarceration and eventual trial.

One morning late in September 1945, Mrs. Catherine Koning-Stroink, the diligent chief of the commission's bureau in Kenaupark, fingered through the day's mail to discover one envelope in particular that gave her a start. She ran an opener through the crease and pulled out the stationery. Prince Bernhard had indeed written the letter, as she had guessed by the seal and the Z.K.H., for His Royal Highness, on the envelope. He was requesting the release of one of the commission's detainees, P. N. Menten. A little annoyed by the high-handed manner, she wrote back immediately to tell the Prince that her office was processing the case of P. N. Menten through normal channels. Whatever Mrs. Koning-

Stroink's feelings, her superiors on the commission obeyed the implicit order. Less than two weeks later, Menten went free, soon to accuse van Izendorn of stealing more than soap and food from his house.

By the time Menten went free and returned home, van Izendorn wanted to forget about the investigation, which had failed to turn up evidence of his collaboration in Holland. The word had spread that friends of influence could destroy the career of a policeman who would not leave the investigation alone or could even help a young policeman who dropped the case. Until he found more concrete evidence, van Izendorn decided to leave well enough alone.

Yet, no matter how he tried, the Menten case refused to go away. Menten's accusations of grand theft stung van Izendorn. Then one day late in December 1946, as he sat with his feet up on his office desk, a man with a strong European accent entered and introduced himself in broken English as Mieczyslaw Zagayski. He told van Izendorn that he had fled Poland before the war, leaving everything he owned behind, then had reestablished himself in the United States. By the time the war ended, he counted his fortune in the millions, just as he had done in Poland. One day only a few weeks ago in New York, where he traded on Wall Street, he had received a telephone call from Marion Gutnayer, a recent refugee from Poland who related *his* tale as a member of the Polish Underground—that he had seen paintings from Zagayski's prewar collection hanging on the walls of Pieter Menten's house. Two days later, Zagayski had boarded a Pan Am Clipper for Europe, and had traced Menten as far as Haarlem and the office of Pete van Izendorn.

"Yes, Menten *was* in jail," van Izendorn told the neatly tailored man.

Zagayski asked to visit Menten's house that same night. Van Izendorn thought for a long minute, then finally said no. Maybe the stolen art was there, but he did not have the authority. The theft, if it had taken place, had occurred in Poland. Van Izendorn said, "But . . . I will go with you to the house, and you can ask to see inside."

When they reached Westerlaan, Elizabeth, not long released from detention camp, explained that Pieter "was out." Van Izendorn introduced himself and Zagayski. "I have nothing to do with this," van Izendorn told her. "If you want to let us look, fine, but I can't force you."

"That's all right," she said, motioning them inside.

"Mrs. Menten, if you say no, it's all right," van Izendorn insisted. "We won't bother you."

But by now she did insist. Once inside, Zagayski said, "That's mine." He pointed to a painting, then another and another. He went to a hall table and lifted up two candelabras. "These are mine, too," he said.

Van Izendorn asked, "Can you prove it?"

To van Izendorn's astonishment, Zagayski showed him an inventory of his possessions made before he had fled Poland. The inventory contained the names and descriptions of the items, along with their code numbers.

Zagayski pointed to an oil painting on the wall by Maurice Gottlieb, the Polish Rembrandt. "If you look at what is written on the back," he told van Izendorn, "you will find the numbers 'AB . . . 7204.' "

Every time, Zagayski was right, but to take the art back to New York with him he needed the permission of the Beheers Institute, an office set up by the government after Liberation to confiscate and redistribute the possessions of convicted collaborators. Soon, after van Izendorn had handed over the objects to the Beheers Institute, they wrote to him: ". . . Mr. Zagayski found four paintings recognized by him as his property. Since Mr. Menten was absent, his wife voluntarily gave him the four paintings, recognizing the fact that they indeed belonged to Mr. Zagayski. . . . The paintings were given to Mr. Zagayski by this office [the Beheers Institute] on December 27, 1946."

A day later, Zagayski returned to New York with a small but valuable part of his collection restored.

Soon after, in Germany, the British President of a Military Court in the British-zone city of Burgsteinfurt, said to the defendant in the dock, a gray-haired man with watery eyes, "Eberhardt Schoengarth, the Court sentences you to hang until dead." Schoengarth, who had "looked like a pleasant, well-mannered ski teacher" to the Canadian soldier who had captured him in the SS redoubt in The Hague, was being returned to answer questions about his activities in Holland, before the court sentence was carried out back in Germany.

The Dutch newspapers that covered his trial referred to Schoengarth by his last official title, "the deputy to General Hans Albin Rauter," duties he had assumed on a temporary basis while Rauter was recovering from the ambush on the road. Schoengarth, who had ordered the reprisal killing of 400 Dutch citizens for the attack on Rauter, had been transferred to Holland in 1944 from the Balkans, and before that from Poland. And now the Dutch wanted him returned to Amsterdam for interrogation.

Weeks later, van Izendorn took a tram toward Amsterdam's Ould South, about a mile from the Dam, which was an area of new public housing. Getting off at the Havenstraat, he looked south to the Olympic Stadium, where the 1928 Games had been played. To his right, eight tall overgrown evergreens almost completely obscured the portals of a brick building, an edifice that had once sent fear through the hearts of many Dutchmen. As the Gestapo jail in Amsterdam, a prison without a name, its architecture suggested no other function. Beside the front meshed iron doors, *Je Maintienderai,* etched in marble, permanently exhorted keepers to guard society against violators of one law code or another. Beneath, the Roman numerals MDCCCXC seemed a conceit, a coy manner to tell the building's vintage.

Van Izendorn checked at the front administrative office, they were expecting him. An officer accompanied him across a gravel exercise yard the size of a basketball court on which thirty-six barred windows stacked in four stories looked down. The prison was shaped like a cross, a slim replica of a Gothic cathedral, with the nave, choir, and the crossing a warren of small doors. In place of a choir, eight cells, larger than the others, fanned outward in a wedge, providing prisoners with just enough room to exercise in winter. Near those cells were four special "solitary" rooms usually reserved for unruly prisoners, one to a soundproofed cell. The card in the copper slot beside the lock of one door announced the presence inside of Eberhardt Schoengarth, recently arrived from Burgsteinfurt. The guard–officer pulled back the bolt and pushed open the heavy door. Van Izendorn entered, thinking that this probably was going to turn out to be the biggest mistake of his career. It had been a long shot from the start, but now that he had used influence to get this interview, he had to carry through. The idea had originated with a newspaper report he had read only a few days ago in which the return of Schoengarth was mentioned. Van Izendorn, his interest piqued, remarked as he had shown the article to his police assistant, "A *deputy* who served in Poland? Menten. Poland. Maybe. Let's try."

Seated on the cot at the far end of the cell, Schoengarth wore his black SD uniform, stripped of all insignia, so that he could have been either a general or a private, if van Izendorn had not known better. He looked up with a shy, downhearted expression. A moment of embarrassment followed in which van Izendorn could not decide how to address the prisoner, as "general," "Herr," or "doctor." He chose his most recent title, "general." He said, "I am a policeman from Bloemendaal. Have you ever heard of it?"

"No," Schoengarth replied.

"The name of the municipality is Bloemendaal, but there are five villages, and one of the five is Aerdenhout. Have you heard of that?"

"Yes."

"Did you visit there?"

"Yes."

"Did you visit a good friend there?"

"Yes," Schoengarth answered, then again, "yes . . ."

Van Izendorn held up his hand. "Please, stop," he said. "When I show you a photograph, will you recognize that special friend?"

"Yes, sure."

Van Izendorn had brought with him the photographs found in Menten's house during his initial search; he had received from Debrouin the photograph of Menten in an SD uniform, taken that

180

spring day in 1941 in the rear garden of Debrouin's house on Grottgera Street, and he showed that, too.

Schoengarth said, "That is Pieter Menten! How is he?"

"Quite well, quite well," van Izendorn said. "Now, I'd like you to tell me the whole story."

It took the rest of the day, covering the whole period from Poland to then. Yes, Menten had been a *Treuhänder* of three Jewish art businesses, and yes, he had served as a member of Schoengarth's staff in early July 1941, as his zbV Einsatzgruppe had carried out its orders in Lwów; Menten had worn an SD uniform and yes, he had provided certain services that included translating and familiarizing the zbV officers with the local terrain. When Schoengarth had been transferred from the Waffen-SS unit to Holland late in 1944, he had indeed visited Menten as an old friend with many shared experiences "several times and warned him in no event to get involved with any German institution," Schoengarth said. When van Izendorn had finished his questioning and closed the notebook in which he had written the gist of the general's answers, he asked, pointing to the notebook, "General Schoengarth, it's the truth, the *whole* truth?"

Schoengarth replied, "You know, I have only three weeks to live. That's the whole truth."

Then, as he was about to leave the cell, van Izendorn asked Schoengarth to sign the back of the photograph of Menten and the pages of notes van Izendorn had written. Then van Izendorn satisfied a strange curiosity. He asked, "Do you remember the moment you knew the Germans would lose?"

Without hesitating, Schoengarth replied, "Yes, March 1945."

"Come on—March 1945? And you a general? Until March you thought Germany would survive?"

"At the beginning of March, Hitler told me that secret weapons were coming."

As he rode the tram back to the Amsterdam Central Station, van Izendorn was truly elated. He had finally learned who The Deputy was and more. He knew he had enough in his notebook to ask the Public Prosecutor of the *Bijzonder Gerechtshof,* the Special Court for War Crimes, to bring formal charges against Pieter

181

Menten for (1) serving in a foreign army and (2) assisting the enemy. Murder was not mentioned because it was not yet known.

Before his return to Burgsteinfurt to hang, Schoengarth welcomed yet another visitor into the cell—someone whom he had not expected to see again this side of the bar. With a rap of the inner, soundproofing door of the isolation cell, the guard announced Pieter Menten's arrival. By what authority Menten had reached him there was a mystery. He had probably used his influence or had successfully bribed a high-ranking official in the BS, but even if that were true, the circumstances were truly strange. The prison authorities had doubled Schoengarth's security, as one who had "ruled" in Holland after Rauter as a ruthless Gestapo leader. Many Dutchmen, in and out of prison, would have enjoyed nothing better than to have killed him themselves as an act of patriotism. Despite this awareness, the prison officials admitted a virtual unknown without official authority. Menten was accompanied to Schoengarth's cell by neither a lawyer, nor a BS investigator, nor anybody from the *Bijzonder Gerechtshof*. Because of these circumstances the meeting between the two men suggested an urgency; the content of what they discussed went well beyond the grave. With the guards and prison officials respecting their privacy, this was the most important discussion either man would have in his life.

They had not seen each other for more than a year; Schoengarth looked younger (he was forty-three) and healthier, probably due to abstinence and prison regime. Menten did not know what to expect a man condemned to the gallows to look or act like. He had read the newspaper accounts of his trial. By an odd quirk, Schoengarth had been convicted of the murder of one single Allied airman downed near Enschede; his other crimes in Poland and Holland had not entered the Allied court's proceedings. Perhaps the British military tribunal had found the less complicated case of one man's murder easier to try than crimes against humanity.

Before Schoengarth had been found in the SS redoubt, while the war was ending Menten had discussed with him the certainty of a Nazi defeat. As a former jurist and doctor of law, Schoengarth knew what fate awaited him if Hitler's so-called secret weapons failed. Resigned at his war crimes trial, he had not defended himself against the charge; there was no point. The president of the court had asked him, "If you received an order from Hitler or Himmler that you were to disregard the rights of prisoners of war, would you as a Doctor of Law have felt bound to obey that or not?"

He had answered what he felt. "I would have had to carry out this order, as an order has to be carried out even if it cancels any existing laws."

They had asked another question, and he wanted his answer on the record. "Which are you prouder to be, a *Brigadeführer* in the SS or a former Wehrmacht officer?"

He had stiffened a little. "I am proud about the two."

Back in their days in the General Government, as close friends Menten and Schoengarth had promised to take care of each other, no matter how it turned out. Drink had stimulated a lot of that Casino talk, but for some reason—perhaps friendship—they had pretty much kept their word. Schoengarth had asked Himmler for Menten's private train transport from Cracow to Holland. He had seen that Menten received the priceless Raphael. Now in return for those favors he wanted a promise that Menten would keep no matter what.

Schoengarth saw himself as a family man, not a good one, or even very attentive to his wife, his sons, and his daughter in Frankfurt, but then, few men of his meteoric rise to power in the Reich had found the time to indulge those impulses. His sons had died fighting as young officers on the Eastern Front, which made him feel the worse about Ermuth, born only five years ago. When he added up a balance sheet of sorts, he had not given Ermuth much of a head start, or much of himself, and, now, he was bequeathing to her a legacy as the daughter of a convicted and hanged monster who had shot and killed a pilot in cold blood. The Allied occupying forces and any reconstituted German government would surely cancel the army pension due to his survivors. And so, he was not even leaving Ermuth enough to provide for food and shelter, let alone her education. *His* fate seemed better, unless . . .

The time they had together now was limited; the guard at any moment could have separated them for eternity, and there was still much to discuss. Straight out, Schoengarth asked Menten to "watch over" Ermuth and ensure that she did not suffer for his crimes. If that meant paying her school fees or, later, her university tuition, then would Menten do that? Would he become Ermuth's "uncle"?

Menten responded, "Yes, of course."

Suddenly, Schoengarth became businesslike. He repeated from memory the questions that van Izendorn had asked him, and what he had replied about Menten. The penalty for collaboration was death, but Schoengarth had information that would keep Menten alive and, more, keep him free to watch over Ermuth. In the next few minutes, according to what Menten later revealed publicly, Schoengarth poured out those secrets he presumably had learned as the Gestapo general in Holland, plus some information from secret files acquired in Berlin on that final visit to the *Führer,* but most of what he told Menten he had learned from a colleague, Major Hermann Giskes of Abwehr. With these powerful weapons, Menten could easily buy his immunity from prosecution or extradition for anything important, because if he were not immune, he could just as easily incriminate—or blackmail—the Dutch establishment, up to the Soestdijk Palace. . . .

. . . The story presumably had begun in that instant when a camera hidden in a chandelier captured on film two naked men between the upraised, parted legs of Benita von Falkenhayn and Renata von Natzmer, young wives of officials in the new Nazi Ministry of War. The photographs were to guarantee the women's cooperation with one of the men, a former Polish cavalry officer whom well-bred women in Berlin admired for his horsemanship, chivalry, dashing good looks, and sexual stamina. On February 27, 1934, Abwehr had arrested the man, Captain Jerzy von Sosnowski, the frequent guest of the Nazi Reichswehr SA and ladies' man par excellence. To the astonishment of socialites who had given him their favors and their husbands' secret papers, von Sosnowski was a Polish spy.

After the arrest Abwehr had discovered the camera. The developed film gave them the identity of the second lover, who was working for the Polish spy. Once Abwehr arrested him, the forty-five-year-old retired colonel in the Czar's Grodno Hussars Regiment with a chic ten-horse equestrian school in the Tiergarten of Berlin readily confessed to espionage. Alexis von Pantschulidzew, known as "the equestrian" and "the man with the white mustache," never looked back. Easily "turned," he became an active agent in Admiral Wilhelm Canaris's Abwehr. From then on he spied exclusively for the Nazis.

Ever since he had escaped his Russian homeland, von Pantschulidzew had alternated his year between Berlin and Reckenwalde, Germany, where he taught equestrian skills to the family of Prince von Lippe-Biesterfeld. Soon after the prince's death in 1934, von Pantschulidzew married the widow, the Baroness Armgard von Sierstorpff-Cramm, a frivolous, pipe-smoking woman nicknamed "Crazy Lola" for her colorful behavior in Berlin of the 1930s. For his influence over the family people called von Pantschulidzew "The Second Rasputin" and "The Dishonorable Stable Man."

The new prince and the eldest son, Bernhard Leopold Friedrich Eberhard Julius Kurt Karl Gottfried Peter zu Lippe-Biesterfeld, who adored his new stepfather, had descended from a lineage peopled by a Saint Bernhard, whom a pope had canonized for converting Baltic infidels to Catholicism; and a Bernhard grandfather whom the Kaiser had decorated for distinction in battle with two Iron Crosses and the Bavarian Order of the Crossed Swords. The late prince had drilled his successor to "become a knightly German and a Christian," an exhortation that the boy had taken very much to heart. At the University of Berlin, which was a hotbed of Nazism in the early 1930s, young Bernhard experienced a remarkable conversion. Formerly a mediocre student, he now completed with flying colors the law course of the *Referendaris-Juris,* the legal equivalent of a Ph.D., and passed the final examination, which most candidates failed at their first try. The conversion from indifference to application was not unrelated to the young prince's membership at the time in the Sturmabteilung, the SA Brownshirts of the *Führer's* National Socialist Party (NSDAP), in which he participated in the League for Air Sports, a Göring-run training school for future Luftwaffe pilots. After the Night of the Long

185

Knives, in which Hitler organized the murder of Ernst Roehm and most other leaders of the politically threatening SA, Bernhard abandoned the SA for the Schutzstaffel, the dreaded SS, the up-and-coming organization for an up-and-coming young man to which his stepfather, von Pantschulidzew, by then an Abwehr spy, had introduced him for the promotion of a career that was more than any royal diversion.

Despite dashing good looks and an extroverted personality that captivated young women, "Benno," as he was called, had a problem that plagued him his life long. He was poor, especially then, in the 1930s, when princes—even princes from lowly royal cadet lines like the Lippe-Biesterfelds—were never poor, at least never as poor as Prince Bernhard. Everybody treated him with some deference because he was a prince, yet he did not have the money to maintain the life-style without working like a commoner. Other royals shunned him, almost as if he were an impostor, or worse, a leper, only because he could not pay the bills. What remained for him were the minor royals and the society riffraff whom he was forced to entertain for his dinners in Paris and Berlin. Desperate and eager, while still a devotee of Himmler's SS, and pushed forward by his stepfather's guiding hand, he found a solution that satisfied both his financial problems and his political loyalties. He became a valued employee of I. G. Farben, the mammoth German chemical firm.

I. G. Farben was not just any chemical company. One of its subsidiaries produced Zyklon B gas, which was later used in the death camps that worked Jewish "slaves" until they died. Now, when the company directors hired "Benno," I. G. Farben was setting up a private worldwide Intelligence and industrial espionage network with direct links to Abwehr and thus to the Oberkommando der Wehrmacht (OKW). I. G. Farben's field personnel or, as they were called, *Verbindingsmänner* ("contact men"), transmitted to Frankfurt surreptitious political as well as economic data collected worldwide that served Nazism's military ambitions and the aspirations of the company's shareholders. In 1936, with the coming *Anschluss,* I. G. Farben began an aggressive search for stockpiles of strategic war supplies, oil and metals, for the New Order. In close coordination with Abwehr, I. G. Farben's new

Intelligence division worked out of the seventh floor of the north-west corner of the company's Frankfurt headquarters, which earned it the name "Department NW7."

Of Germany's several neighbors, none was richer than Holland in the strategic supplies that the Wehrmacht needed to give Hitler military victories. The Treaty of Versailles that had settled World War I had stripped Germany of its colonial sources of strategic materials. But Holland had possession of its colonies in the East and West Indies—Sumatra, Borneo, New Guinea, and Aruba—with their bountiful supplies of crude oil, kapok, rubber, coconut-palm oil, tea, tin, sugar, and coffee. More important even than these, Holland had Royal Dutch Shell.

Abwehr and NW7 saw the obvious. The House of Orange-Nassau presided over this cornucopia. The original founders of the Dutch East India Company, the house had participated in commerce for hundreds of years. Although the constitution took away the Dutch royals' absolute political power, their commercial influence prevailed. The most dazzling—but by no means the only—diamond in its crown, a 5 percent majority shareholding interest in Royal Dutch Shell worth more than $2 billion alone, made the House of Orange-Nassau the wealthiest royal family on the planet. From the point of view of Abwehr and I. G. Farben, the House of Orange-Nassau had all this and one thing more. It had an aging Queen with a young, eligible daughter, Princess Juliana, who was first in the line of succession.

I. G. Farben's corporate managers in Berlin had promised Bernhard a directorship—unprecedented for a twenty-five-year-old—if he maintained what they called his "passion" for his work in their NW7 Intelligence section. Their appreciation of his talents heightened at the 1936 Winter Olympic Games at Igls in the Bavarian Alps, when a German banker of I. G. Farben introduced him to Princess Juliana. Back in Paris a week later, Prince Bernhard asked a friend, "What would you say if I were to become engaged to Princess Juliana of Holland?" The friend knew how Bernhard was dependent on his brains and I. G. Farben's goodwill, but he said nothing. A short time later, Juliana and Bernhard were engaged to be married.

Quick though it had been, the arrangement seemed to satisfy

Queen Wilhelmina. The marriage of her only daughter had frankly been a worry. Tall, awkward, homely, and lacking in glamour and poise, with light-brown hair, blue eyes, a large nose, and a big-boned comfortable figure, and under the eye of a domineering mother ("The Princess will remain as God and I made her," said Wilhelmina when Juliana had asked to try makeup, pointedly ignoring her husband Hendrik's contribution; and when Juliana, a student at Leiden University in 1927, won the prize for the university "song of the year," her mother had said to her, "Don't get excited. They gave you the prize because you are the Princess"), Juliana had grown up shy and hesitant, not the least with suitors. Despite all that, she was seen as one of the most eligible girls in the world. Newspapers, always excitable around eligible royalty, linked her unfairly with Prince Charles of Sweden, the Prince of Wales, and the Duke of Kent. Despite her fabulous wealth and the position she would inherit, suitors were not overwhelmed, until Igls and the dashing Prince Bernhard.

As part of their official engagement, Prince Bernhard signed the "Treaty of Weissenburg" with terms of marriage that sent him "underground." He changed his citizenship to Dutch and "resigned" from I. G. Farben. His boss in NW7, Dr. Max Ilgner, arranged for him to join Hollandse Koopmans N.V., an Amsterdam bank with strong ties to I. G. Farben. From there he moved to Nederlands Handels Maatschapij, one of Royal Dutch Shell's banks. Soon after he signed the treaty, he met with the *Führer,* who noted that Bernhard had "cringed and scraped like a gigolo," while the *Führer* recalled that Prince Hendrik, Juliana's father, earlier had approached him ". . . for a loan of seven and a half million guilders, in return for his assurance that he would then do all in his power to increase German influence in Holland."

Bernhard had one last fling on the Rankestrasse across from Ciro's in Walter Wunderlich's restaurant, where strains of "Deutschland Über Alles" and "Horst Wessel Lied" drifted into the night. Wunderlich, the restaurant owner and the commandant of Bernhard's former SS detachment, shouted to the clientele that night that he had reported Bernhard's serious breach of SS discipline to the Reichsführer-SS Heinrich Himmler. "You have broken the betrothal law of the SS," Wunderlich said. "You failed to apply to me, your superior officer, for permission to marry, and to bring proof of your wife's Aryan ancestry." Bernhard looked stunned. "What your punishment will be I cannot say," Wunderlich went on. "Maybe expulsion from the SS; maybe promotion; maybe both." Roars of laughter, handshakes all around, more backslapping, more beer, and then Bernhard departed for Holland and the public announcement of the marriage, about which Joseph Goebbels's newspaper, *Völkischer Beobachter,* reported: "This event is greeted by the German people with great joy. . . ."

Some Dutchmen were not so thrilled. But the vast majority of the Dutch did what came naturally—they minded their own business. If the Nazi connection caused them to wonder, the German connection did not. Juliana's father Prince Hendrik had been a German, and he had been harmless enough. And who could forget the blood, cultural, and emotional ties between Holland and Germany? They were even recorded in the Dutch national anthem with the words *Wilhelmus van Nassouwe, ben ik, van Duitsen bloet* ("I am William of Nassau, of German blood").

The wedding adhered closely to tradition. The couple exchanged vows in a fifteenth-century church before Royal Navy cadets and "100,000 Dutch girls." Dr. Max Ilgner of NW7 looked on, as did Walter Wunderlich. Stepfather Alexis von Pantschulidzew represented the German Abwehr, and for Bernhard's brother, Ashwin, this was the last big social outing before he joined a Waffen-SS *Himmelfahrtskommando,* a Nazi suicide squad. Before the altar, resplendent in a uniform of brass and braid, Bernhard took interlocking if not conflicting vows—as a man, to the Royal Dutch throne's heiress, and, as a *Verbindingsmann,* "contact man" within the House of Orange, to Abwehr and I. G. Farben.

Soon after, the honeymoon had commenced when the train chugged out of The Hague's Central Station bound for Igls, where the couple had met. Many hours later, after a local Austrian band, waiting on the platform, struck up a brassy rendition of the Dutch national anthem, the royal couple failed to emerge from the train. The anthem was played again, this time with more oom-pah-pah. The Igls mayor and his councilmen had shivered in the cold, crossing and recrossing their arms. Finally, after they were told what had happened, they were not amused in the least: to put journalists off the scent, the newlyweds had sent the train empty, while they traveled in a different direction to a destination well off the beaten track. Oddly, considering the hundreds of secluded and scenic places from which to choose, they had chosen Krynica, an average, unchic, untrammeled ski resort in the Polish Carpathian Mountains, where they stayed in the Villa Patria of the famous Polish singer Jan Kiepura.

The choice of Krynica caused a sensation. Poles were thrilled, if not bewildered at first. In such seclusion, Lula and Benilo, as the couple had pet-named themselves, held the press at bay. Naturally, guests were limited to not more than a handful, including Pieter and Elizabeth Menten, who invited the Prince and Princess to their "hunting lodge" in Sopot. Bernhard could not deviate from an itinerary that next included Vienna, but Pieter Menten's invitation helped to forge a connection that would bind the men, often painfully, for all their days. . . .

In the prison cell, Schoengarth skipped over much of this material. He assumed that Menten was aware at least of some of the background, and time was now the most important element of all, according to what Menten later would recall of the conversation. This information concerning the Prince's past, both men knew, was not as important as a description of the events of the war. . . .

. . . The silk of Wehrmacht parachutes had pocked the sky over Holland at dawn on May 10, 1940, as Prince Bernhard in The Hague was preparing to shave. As legend recorded, he cinched a bathrobe around his waist with one hand and cocked a machine gun with the other, firing recklessly from a veranda of the Huisten Bosch royal residence at a Luftwaffe fighter overhead. He handed the smoking weapon to a sergeant, who fitted in a fresh clip as the Prince continued his ablutions.

Hours later, Bernhard led his family—Juliana, and their young daughters, Beatrix and Irene—to a waiting Bank of Netherlands armored car. A box with the Crown Jewels accompanied them. A month later, Princess Juliana and the girls were bound for Canada on the Dutch ship *Sumatra,* while Bernhard and Queen Wilhelmina stayed in London to oversee the Dutch government in exile. Despite misgivings ("A leopard does not change his spots," said the British Air Marshal at that time), Queen Wilhelmina promoted her son-in-law forcefully with the Allies. By the autumn of 1940, having been denied the right to fly aircraft for the Allies, he took an assignment at MID-SOE, Dutch Military Intelligence Division of the Special Operations Executive, Churchill's "ministry of ungentlemanly warfare."

The invasion of Holland had hardly surprised Bernhard, who had received warnings seven months before from "family relations"—his brother, Ashwin; von Pantschulidzew, his Abwehr stepfather; and his I. G. Farben contacts. Bernhard had warned the GS-3 counterespionage division of the Dutch Army, which was skeptical. The Germans had spared Holland the cruelty of invasion in World War I, while crushing Belgium, their neighbor to the south, so why this time? Bernhard sent similar warnings to King Leopold III of Belgium. Just as he had hoped and failed to do in Holland, Bernhard planned to pressure Leopold to surrender his country in reaction to the threat of invasion alone, thereby saving the Wehrmacht the effort and expense of military conquest.

Meanwhile during those months of what came to be called "The Phony War," von Pantschulidzew promoted a scheme in Berlin known to Abwehr as "Enterprise 3-F," or "Three Fraus"— for Juliana, Bernhard's wife, Armgard, his mother, and Wilhelmina, his mother-in-law. Von Pantschulidzew had wanted to trade Hitler the Dutch Army in return for his naming Bernhard a *Nationalstatholder,* also sparing the Wehrmacht a military conquest and occupation. As one who had complained bitterly since his marriage that the people of Holland saw him as a "necessary evil," Bernhard as *Statholder* would have enjoyed plenipotentiary powers. . . .

. . . Now, Schoengarth was nearly finished, but there was one more thing before he called for the guard to show Menten out. In all that he had said there was no concrete proof. Evidence of conspiracies existed all right, but that was not going to help if the BS tried to prosecute Menten for collaboration, as Schoengarth suspected from the drift of van Izendorn's questioning. Menten

191

needed something concrete and near to hand, and Schoengarth knew exactly what it was.

He described a woman in Amsterdam whom Menten should contact at the Cavalo Bar on the Leidsestraat. Leonie Brandt-Pütz was a Dutch spy whom the Bureau for National Security had sent to interrogate Schoengarth. By now, she would have made contact with a former double agent, Gus van Reede, who had in his possession, Schoengarth knew, a copy of a handwritten letter to Hitler, dated April 24, 1942, signed by Prince Bernhard. The letter had offered Holland to Hitler as a federated entity of the Reich in return for a *Statholder*'s position. The letter was written in the full confidence of 1942 that the Nazis simply could not lose the war. There were two or three copies floating around, and van Reede's was for sale or exchange. With the letter in his possession, Menten could fend off prosecution, if his friendship with the Prince suddenly dissolved. The threat to the monarchy would dampen any prosecutorial zeal.

When their meeting ended, they stood up, facing each other. Schoengarth went and rapped on the door of the cell, and the guard came. Menten turned and shook the general's hand, knowing this was for the last time.

Once he had left the prison, Menten disappeared, as if from the face of the earth.

For a time during the occupation, the Dutch had stood up to the Nazis most courageously in the pages of *Vrij Nederland, Het Parool, Ons Volk, De Waarheld, Je Maintiendrai,* and notably in *Trouw,* which lost 120 reporters to Gestapo firing squads. Some other newspapers straddled a fence, while others, including the popular Amsterdam daily *De Telegraaf,* supported the Nazi occupation both out of ideological conviction and as a means to continued profitability. The owner of *De Telegraaf,* Henri Holdert, dining on *belon* oysters throughout the war at the Georges V in Paris, had wanted the income from the newspaper no matter what editorial policies it had to pursue—even if the board had to appoint a full-blown Nazi as editor in chief.

At Liberation, the authorities put *De Telegraaf* out of business and punished its reporters and editors by prohibiting them from practicing their skills until they had been "rehabilitated" for a period that ranged from months to several years. However, *De Telegraaf's* star reporter, Henry Lunshof, convinced the post-Liberation review board of the correctness of his behavior during the occupation, and he turned his skills to the pages of *Elseviers,* a weekly Dutch-language newsmagazine. His skills were unique, for Lunshof often liked to substitute fiction for news features out of laziness and the sincere belief that the poet's touch made better copy. Once, assigned to report on a shipwreck off the Dutch coast and unable (or unwilling) to reach the scene, Lunshof invented the story of the ship's sinking. When Queen Leopold of Belgium died in an automobile crash, Lunshof had described in print how the sun glinted light off the brass buttons of King Leopold's tear-stained navy blazer, when the King had worn a sober, black suit on that overcast day of the Queen's burial. His editors never seemed to mind. They even enjoyed his little quasi-literary confections.

Not long after he joined *Elseviers,* while the *Bijzonder Gerechtshof,* the Special Court for War Crimes, continued its investigations of Menten's collaboration, Lunshof received a call from an important member of *Elseviers'* board of directors, Emile Menten, the half cousin whom Pieter had saved from the Gestapo firing squad. Emile asked Lunshof to "check out these rumors about theft" from Pieter Menten's house in Aerdenhout. For his part, by exposing corruption in the Resistance, Lunshof was mitigating crimes of collaboration by *De Telegraaf.* By "rehabilitating" Pieter Menten, in a real sense he would be excusing a man, a newspaper, and even to a degree a nation all too willing to be excused of its war record. If anything did, *that* end of rewritten history justified a sprinkling here and there of fantasy, and Lunshof set to work at his typewriter with genuine commitment.

"The Menten case is a story of the times," he wrote. "One sees all the elements of injustice crystallized in it, injustice that has reigned since Liberation, which is a continuation of the injustice that the Germans introduced here. . . . This is a story of greed, betrayal and cunning. Fundamental notions have been turned upside down. Perjury has been committed. All in all it's not unlike a

193

muddy little pool that one stirs up with a stick. That all of this has to be said of Holland is a bitter and sad matter. Doing justice to one man can only do the society good."

In part one of the eight-part series, Lunshof plumbed to what he perceived to be the heart of the matter, when he wrote, "At Liberation, Menten had the reputation of being pro-German. Not just that, but a collaborator, a murderer, a thief, a profiteer, a jackal of the battlefield created by the Germans in Poland. People needed this psychological background to justify the real crime, the robbery of . . . valuables which they [the former members of Rolls-Royce] succeeded in stealing." Later, in part three, he itemized that theft. " . . . two leather satchels with 700 white brilliant stones and 800 colored stones, five paintings by Memling, Hobbema, Lochner, Botticelli, Cranach, 500 drawings including some by Dürer, Terborch; table settings by Meissen, 100 paintings without frames, three paintings by the Polish master Gottlieb, an amount of 350,000 guilders in bills. . . ." In total he accused Rolls-Royce of stealing 3.5 *million* guilders from Menten, but he offered neither proof nor testimony. He wrote, "It's a sign that something is wrong, something is gnawing but watch out, watch out. Don't let it gnaw further. . . . What in God's name has happened to the Holland we once were proud of? This case is a knock on the door, soft and slow, but very penetrating, and the hand that is knocking is called 'decline.' "

If only Menten's lawyers had left his defense alone, the case against their client certainly would have disappeared, like a neglected animal. Lunshof's newspaper series gave pause to the *Bijzonder Gerechtshof,* which felt that its prosecutors could more profitably turn to other cases of collaboration besides Menten's. Foolishly, Menten's lawyers did not feel that they had earned their retainers until they had picked at issues, conceived of and tested defenses with writs, motions, affidavits, depositions, and more. Menten had employed the best legal minds sympathetic to his crusade. Dr. J. C. Coeberg from The Hague was now joined by an eloquent lawyer, L. G. Kortenhorst, a Catholic from the south who did not understand the nature of collaboration in war and so could not conceive of the charges against Menten. Kortenhorst felt messianic about these issues. He represented Menten in court in what amounted to a full-blown political case while at the same time representing the Dutch people as president of the lower house of parliament without feeling a conflict of interest.

With Menten coaching from hiding, the lawyers' accusations flew like counterpunches. Their defense tactics changed at every turn: Menten had joined General Schoengarth's zbV Einsatzgruppe as a translator? Their client did not speak either Polish or Russian. The manner of van Izendorn's and, later, the *Bijzonder Gerechtshof* prosecutors' questioning of Schoengarth in prison had conformed to Article 187-SB of Dutch law? Neither Menten nor his legal representatives had been present to hear the questions and record the general's answers. It did not seem relevant to Menten's lawyers that the *Bijzonder Gerechtshof* had been unable to find Menten or that Schoengarth could not be late for a gallows' date. After the fact, the lawyers pointed out that Menten had been willing, if only the men of the *Bijzonder* had located him, to attend the general's interrogation. Next, the lawyers charged that the Schoengarth interrogation transcript had been altered. The final draft quoted General Schoengarth as saying, "During the advance [toward Lwów in July 1941], he [Menten] did various work as an interpreter including among other things translating documents that had been confiscated by us." In the margin, the interrogators had penned in, "During the advance he translated confiscated Russian documents." But Schoengarth had not initialed this change. What were these transcripts, the lawyers demanded to know, but simple, amateurish forgeries? If anyone doubted the accusation, Menten demanded, let him ask General Schoengarth.

Dead? Schoengarth was *hanged?*

Now, the lawyers admitted, maybe their client *had* worn an SD uniform, and maybe he *had* performed some services for the German officers, but in Poland and *strictly under duress*. Later they produced what they said was a spoken gallows' statement from Schoengarth: "Men," they quoted him saying as the noose was lowered on his neck, "I'm going to leave you. They brought me to Holland, and the Dutch wanted statements from me about Menten which are in conflict with the truth. Menten never stole anything in Poland, and he suffered under the Germans, including arrests, questionings, and kidnappings. I would like to add, there

195

was an investigation going on against Menten . . . since Menten was suspected of espionage against Germany. Facing death, I declare this to be the truth."

The lawyers pressed on, while political friends of their client applied relentless and effective behind-the-scenes pressure. Menten had every chance to win, except for one obstacle—a feisty, none-too-imaginative, sparrow-breasted man with a mustache as wide as his initials were long, F. P. Th. Rohling, the investigative attorney for the *Bijzonder Gerechtshof,* who often hid behind long silences during which the ash from the cigarette hanging from his lip tumbled down the lapel of his mottled suits, as if he hoped to camouflage himself from intruders. The case involving Menten was his first since recently joining the *Bijzonder.*

Frans Rohling had kept abreast of the case, but he had not put his frail shoulder behind the prosecution. Of course he doubted the innocence of a man who could not be found during an investigation; he also wondered why Menten's version of the story had suddenly changed to correspond with Schoengarth's—about the uniform and services for the officers. Yet, for all that, the case was not a priority in Rohling's quiet, mousy world—not until Menten's lawyers attacked his integrity as a man, lawyer, and civil administrator. Annoyed, Rohling "dug even deeper into the case," even as Kortenhorst in a letter dated March 5, 1947, was asking the *Bijzonder Gerechtshof* to drop the warrant for Menten's arrest, if not the charges, because Menten had suddenly lost the mental capacity to defend himself, according to a psychiatrist, Dr. Edward Hoelen, who produced a psychiatric report to that effect. The arrest warrant per se was not dropped; but now, the court permitted Menten to turn himself in to Dr. Hoelen, "who will keep him in his institution as if he were a prisoner," the *Bijzonder* stipulated.

On April 8, 1947, Menten emerged from hiding and entered the Ursula Clinic of Dr. Edward Hoelen for a "sleeping cure" to settle his nerves.

Meanwhile, Frans Rohling questioned the stepdaughter of Dr. Ostrowski from Lwów, who was passing through Amsterdam en route to Belgium. Visiting the clinic Rohling then interviewed Menten, who repeated his story, except for one slip. "In Poland at

196

the time *everything was possible,"* he said. Suddenly curious about Poland, and wondering what Menten had meant by "everything," Rohling asked the Foreign Office to order the Dutch ambassador in Warsaw to open an investigation. The Poles, the ambassador later reported, were interested in Menten as a collaborator, but he was not high on their wanted list. Rohling then asked the Russians to explore the Lwów end of the story (Lwów had become a Russian possession after the war). Nothing came of that initiative.

By now, Menten was near panic. (Dr. Hoelen called his state of mind "disturbed.") He could defend himself against dead men and Dutchmen, but if Rohling continued to ask questions in Poland, there was no telling if the murders might somehow be revealed. Such was Menten's concern, he risked a day trip from the clinic by rental car to find a sympathetic witness from Poland. When Rohling heard about this violation of the detention ground rules, he felt intense pleasure. Obviously Poland had cut very close to the bone; and now Rohling had every right to order Menten placed in a real prison.

Policemen armed with a search-and-arrest warrant arrived a short time later at the Ursula Clinic. In his room, before he went anywhere with anybody, Menten demanded to speak with his psychiatrist, Dr. Hoelen. As they waited for a guard to get Hoelen, Menten complained that he felt hot and sick, and he asked to open the window. The policeman nodded his assent. Menten now complained of nausea, asking permission to go to the bathroom. Finally Dr. Hoelen arrived. As Menten feigned sickness, Hoelen made a scene, screaming and carrying on, then pompously demanded to see the identification of the policemen. Behind their backs, Menten crept from the bathroom and flung himself through the open window, 11.5 feet to a roof below.

He hit the ground on all fours, but he was up and running for cover in the same instant a pistol shot rang out, then another. The impact of a bullet on his shoulder knocked him to the ground. He coughed and spit. There was no blood; the bullet had not pierced his lung. He looked back; the policemen were taking the long way around, giving him enough time to reach the edge of a nearby canal, which he dove into and swam. When he next looked back from the opposite side, he saw that the police were standing there refusing to cross the canal.

On October 28, 1948, in the Fourth Chamber in Amsterdam of the *Bijzonder Gerechtshof,* Justice Ruys presiding, Pieter Menten was tried *in absentia.* After the first day, Justice Ruys expelled a stenographer whom Menten's lawyers had hired. He then told them crabbily to join the crowd of spectators in the public gallery. They walked out and the empty chair reserved for the defendant spoke eloquently for the prosecution. The Attorney General asked the court for a sentence of one year, minus the five months already spent in preliminary detention at Duinrust. Justice Ruys found the defendant guilty, then read out the sentence of three years, minus five months, to an empty chair.

The hands of Catholic nuns nursed him—and not his wounds alone—even months after the shooting. Pieter Menten had arrived in a terrible state of distress at the Westeinde Hospital, to which he had walked after his escape. While Dr. Hoelen at the Ursula Clinic jabbered into a telephone about an "assassination attempt" that had reminded him of "four years ago when the SD picked up Jews," Pieter Menten was being x-rayed in the emergency room of the hospital. The wound, while messy, did not threaten his life. The bullet itself could remain where it had lodged, the doctors agreed. Yet the night after he was admitted, Menten was operated on, all the same. Instead of the area of his chest wound, the surgeons worked their scalpels to alter the shape and profile of his telltale nose. The attending nun in the surgical theater knew that he was "Menten from Aerdenhout who had lived in Poland for many years," but if her suspicions were aroused by the circumstances of his arrival or the surgery, she said nothing for the eleven months he remained at the Westeinde, hiding, devising a reason for his visit. He told Elizabeth, who stayed at the Aerdenhout villa, during a visit, "The Attorney General in Amsterdam had an attempt made on my life. Two policemen with revolvers came after me. I jumped out of the window of the second story, and when I hit the ground, I scraped my face on the gravel. One policeman shot at me and I was hit in the back. It was then that I again scraped my face even further on the gravel. I managed to escape, first swimming through a small canal. Because of my face—the whole skin on my face had come off. Because of the skin on my face, my nose was bandaged."

The verdict of the *in absentia* trial alarmed Menten. He had assumed that the prosecutors of the *Bijzonder Gerechtshof* were backing away from his case, because people who "would be in trouble" if he told the secrets were starting "to shake and shiver." However, something in his strategy had failed, and he now faced a bitter future—a long jail sentence, the permanent confiscation of his property, and, because he had served in a foreign army, the loss of his Dutch citizenship. There was nothing left but to appeal the court ruling. At the very least he wanted to disprove the foreign army charge. If he were to lose his citizenship, the Dutch government could then extradite him to Poland, where by now the authorities surely knew of the murders.

Having once escaped from the police and refused to attend his trial, Menten now gave himself up and complied with the court order to remain in the Vujht Detention Camp, a place of meager comforts compared with the Westeinde Hospital, until the appeal was heard. However, Kortenhorst did not see the need for his client to remain in the camp and wrote to the Minister of Justice that he "would appreciate it if you could expedite Mr. Menten's release from prison as soon as possible." In the same letter, he pointedly mentioned his government position as president of the lower house of parliament in the same KVP Catholic Party as the Minister of Justice. Dr. Hoelen's newest psychiatric analysis that Menten's sanity would deteriorate in jail worried him. Soon after, the Minister of Justice signed Menten's release order with his own hand.

Rohling and van Izendorn now were certain that the fix was in, and from now on, the case was "political." Indeed, the minister's support of Menten served as a warning. When Rohling learned of the minister's decree, his initial incredulity turned to stubbornness. Menten's detention and release were none of his damned business, he told the minister, and Rohling adamantly blocked Menten from walking out the camp doors. By now, the minister must have dreamed of those desolate, venomous archipelagos

199

once called the East Indies to which people like Rohling were formerly banished.

For all the sameness of the appeal trial proceedings, convened in February 1949, it was new stuff to Menten, who now occupied the defendant's chair as a fulminating sea captain, hurling orders at recalcitrant lawyers. When the prosecution submitted the SD uniform photographs as evidence, Menten said angrily, "There is no other area where things are tampered with as much as photography and film." The nose in the photograph was larger than the nose on the defendant's face—reason for the court, ignorant of the plastic surgery at the Westeinde Hospital, to disregard the photographic evidence. Kortenhorst said, "Many abnormal things like this occurred in this case, and the most abnormal was that Schoengarth was questioned in the absence of the suspect."

The Presiding Judge: "We were not able to find him [the suspect, Menten] at the time. Save that for your plea."

Kortenhorst: "We are forever making incidental pleas!"

The Judge: "This is all going quite strangely."

Kortenhorst: "I protest!"

The Judge: "Please be quiet. You do not have to pound the table."

From time to time, the defense lawyers tried to trick the court with sly definitions—Menten had not joined a foreign *army* because the Sicherheitsdienst (SD) was a Nazi *party* organ. As the trial progressed, the defense lawyers now feared with good reason that the verdict would be the same as before and the sentence probably even more severe.

On the last day of the trial, they pulled a *coup de théâtre*.

As he took the witness chair, the star performer played his part with consummate skill. He cringed as if before a lash; he spoke with apology accenting every word; his rounded shoulders sagged in resignation. Like a creature of the dark, the witness for the defense wore a charcoal-gray suit, white shirt, and black necktie; he was funereal to the softness in his voice. There was nearly an invisibility to the plainness of his round face. His brown eyes like windows made his appearance even more remarkable. One emotion especially shone through: his eyes had the power to give voice and even a scent to an enormous fear. They cringed, and a look there made people feel embarrassed for what they saw. His eyes cast a spell of reluctant humility on the court proceedings, as if this one Jew were grief itself.

At the outbreak of the war, Joseph Stieglitz had run the family art and antiques gallery located at Rynek Glowny #24 in Cracow that Menten had taken over as a *Treuhänder* for the Germans, while Stieglitz survived the German occupation hiding in Lwów. Before the war he often told flatterers softly that his reputation as an art dealer exceeded his ability. Often in the same breath, however, he mentioned that the largest museum in Warsaw had spent 80 percent of its annual budget for new acquisitions through him, and that he had brokered a collection worth 350,000 zlotys, a vast fortune in the early 1930s. Unlike anyone else in Poland, Stieglitz had been sought out for his discretion: what he knew he did not tell. He traded without homage to provenance, an oversight, perhaps, that Menten had demanded of Stieglitz in most of their dealings.

During the German occupation, Stieglitz had worked for Menten in Lwów, just as the other two former gallery owners, Katzner and Horowitz, had done his bidding in Cracow to stay alive, by collecting valuable art objects from the private collections of Jews whom the Germans had forced into the ghetto, and later to death camps. However, given the German appetite for plunder, it hadn't been long before little of value remained uncollected. Stieglitz had stayed alive because of his art expertise, but by 1941, even Jews whom the Germans had once found useful were disappearing. Stieglitz had been arrested once for nine days and tortured until Menten had intervened through General Schoengarth for his release. That any Jew was freed on the word of an SS general was a "miracle." Stieglitz had been arrested again and Menten had again saved him. By then, Stieglitz had read the signals, and with death dancing before those fearful eyes, he had told Menten that he wanted out, and Menten had suggested a plan. Together with Otsch Kipka, the three men had planned to go "hunting" in the Silesian forests, and when they neared the border, Stieglitz would run across to the other side, but for reasons of trust, Stieglitz had declined the escape plan. Instead, he had "sold" Menten $20,000 worth of art, coins, and jewelry. Menten promised reimbursement once Stieglitz had reached a safe haven, a prospect that both men doubted, but Stieglitz had little choice. If he were to survive to collect the debt, he had to travel light. He had bribed a contingent of Italian soldiers, who took him across into Hungary disguised as an Italian officer. Years later, he had emigrated to Palestine.

Since then Stieglitz had kept abreast of Menten from his humble, inconspicuous "antiquities" shop in an alley off Allenby Street in Tel Aviv, from which he sold Judaica to important Jewish collectors in Israel. He had written to Justice Frans Rohling in July 1947 and then again five months later in December, he had explained that Menten owed him money in lieu of the art he had left behind. "All in all," he had written a last time, "our agreement was made in 1941 and is still valid. . . . I know how attached Menten was to his collection. Obviously I would be willing to accept other items of equal value as a form of payment."

Now, he faced the court, ready to help Menten go free so that he might finally collect the debt. Before he answered questions, Stieglitz told the court how his grandfather in Tel Aviv was even now lying on his deathbed. Stieglitz had known that his duty was to testify for Pieter Menten, but his reluctance to travel such a distance to Holland was understandable. However, his grandfather had insisted with his dying breath that Joseph had to save Pieter Menten. "If a person saves the life of one Jew," the old man had uttered, Joseph told the court, "he saves the lives of *all* Jews."

Prosecuting Attorney: "It's a miracle you survived the war."

Stieglitz: "It is indeed! Mr. Menten performed that miracle."

Prosecuting Attorney: "What was his reputation?"

Stieglitz: "Of someone you could trust one hundred percent." Then, "Menten helped several Jews who were in danger of being picked up. In Lwów, an acquaintance, Mrs. Karlin, was arrested, since she had not been wearing the yellow star. . . . I turned to him [Menten] and asked for his help. He got in touch with someone and succeeded in her release. A certain Mr. Wohl and his family were also helped by him. I know several other cases, but I cannot remember the names. He was always willing to help, and it was not always successful, obviously. All in all," Stieglitz concluded, "I have never heard anything bad about Pieter Menten."

From that moment, a grain of doubt buried itself deep in the courtroom. Emotions entered the deliberations with colorations as unexpected as they were brilliant. In his summation, the Attorney General desperately tried to return to the evidence. "You can achieve anything with money, but thank God that justice cannot be bought," he wishfully told the court. In the statement of the defense, Kortenhorst waxed eloquent if not original, borrowing liberally from the text of Lunshof's newspaper series. "Menten is a victim of absurd gossip in which he is depicted as a common thug, a murderer, a thief and a jackal on the battlefield created by the Germans in Poland." He cast Menten as a "Dutch pioneer in a foreign country, a great businessman as we only know from the American business world," who "only wanted to help Jewish friends with their antiques stores—people like Joseph Stieglitz, who has come to Holland, all that way, to claim that Menten saved his life."

On the morning of April 14, 1949, the court read out its verdict: Menten had acted as a *Treuhänder* "to help Jews and Jewish businesses." Maybe he had been a "member of the staff of General Schoengarth's group zbV," but that position did not necessarily constitute serving a foreign army; indeed, the court could find sufficient evidence to support only the accusation of willful cooperation with the enemy. It sentenced him to one year, minus the time in preliminary arrest, minus the time in the Ursula (psychiatric) Clinic—all in all, minus a total of one year.

Now, out from under the threat of further prosecution, even the threat of the murders' revelation in Holland, Menten recast himself, expunging the unsavory impression from his record. He blocked a halfhearted Polish application for his extradition to stand trial in Warsaw. He had the temerity to demand *Wiedergutmachung,* damage compensation from the government of Holland for what he called "the largest robbery in the past fifty years." Demanding nothing less than 3.5 million guilders, he received a first installment of 250,000; his political friends tried to get him even more compensation, but the Secretary of State told parliament, "I'm compelled to question any further payment. *That* amount was a lavish settlement for linen, clothes, food, soap, and household articles that were indeed taken from him and given to hospitals." The courts doubted if Menten had ever owned certain other goods reported stolen. "This pertains to diamonds [*claimed* to have been hidden in a car tire in a hiding place built into one of the walls], American bonds [of which there were absolutely no records], and finally, a number of works of art whose existence, nature, value, and fate—despite detailed investigations—have remained mysterious." The Minister of War awarded Menten a further 300,000 guilders, then another, final check for 70,000—a total of more than a million guilders from the public treasury.

Emboldened by the Dutch windfall, Menten next sued West Germany for damages under the Nazis in Poland. In the Munich *Wiedergutmachung* court, Menten built his case with statements from three Jews. Adolf Sonderling, a resident of Tel Aviv, had sworn in a statement, "One day I ran into Menten, and he did not try to avoid me. Being a Jew I had already experienced disappointments with old non-Jewish friends and acquaintances who pretended they didn't know me. He invited me to his house that same evening and offered to let my family and me hide in his house if needed. I was moved by this. It was dangerous, hiding Jews. If I had not been able to hide in his house my family and I would definitely not be alive today." After this preamble, Sonderling's statement went on, "I got to know the house as a small private museum. In the long, weary hours we were hiding, I, who could appreciate art, found solace and hope in the collected art works there—hope in my almost hopeless situation." Sonderling even remembered the artists represented in Menten's (formerly Dr. Tadeusz Ostrowski's) apartment. Stanislas Lenz, also from Tel Aviv, had sworn, "Menten saw I was wearing the Star of David, and he still greeted me; I felt very good. All my other Aryan friends did not associate with me any longer. We talked. I asked his advice and for help. He offered me his house immediately, so I could hide there, if needed. He told me that other Jews already hid there from time to time. I repeatedly hid my wife and child there during raids. On those occasions I admired his art treasures." Joseph Stieglitz, once again rising to Menten's defense, swore that "Menten felt it was his humane duty to help Jews and Poles, disregarding the danger this entailed. In the spring of 1942, Menten asked if I would come . . . to help him make an inventory of his art collection and furnishings in Lwów . . . the inventory and my statement that his collection was indeed of high quality took three days to finish. He bought only first-class objects." Stieglitz appended the inventory made that day, a list with which he said he had escaped all the way to Palestine from Nazi-controlled Europe.

Weeks after, Sonderling and Lenz succumbed to the terminal diseases from which they were in the final throes when they had made the statements. When asked later, the widow of Stanislas Lenz said with an air of incredulity, "My late husband never mentioned to me that Menten saved our lives." And that was a bizarre oversight indeed unless Menten had bought the lies of dying men.

Menten next offered the German court testimony of a witness to his "suffering" in the General Government, someone who was not a Jew, someone who spoke from firsthand experience of how the Nazis had stolen from him. He daringly chose the former director of the Rabka Police School, Untersturmführer-SS Wilhelm Rosenbaum, who told the Munich court that he had "heard the orders given to confiscate from Menten." Stating in its judgment that Menten "had been treated [in Poland] like a Jew," the West German court for *Wiedergutmachung* agreed with his claims and awarded 550,000 Marks, which in those years was a fortune.

The outrage that Frans Rohling had felt at the reading of the verdict and the sentence of the *Bijzonder Gerechtshof* matched the bewilderment of Pete van Izendorn. As men of conviction, they were not prepared to accept the court's finding, but before they could act, their careers were destroyed—in Rohling's case, utterly, as a warning to anybody else who might stubbornly try to ignore the signals. Rohling had wanted to serve on the bench, but he never again was even allowed to practice law. Later, he found a minor position in the Department of Education—the modern equivalent of the East Indies. Pete van Izendorn fared only slightly better, probably because his ambitions were more contained. Years later, before his nomination as commissioner of police in the township of Zaandam, he needed the approval of the Minister of Justice. During the interview, the minister opened a thick file. He said, "If you were to become commissioner wouldn't you fear the national press?"

205

"Your excellency, for what?" van Izendorn had asked.

"Ummmmm . . . Menten, for the Menten case." He flipped through the file and said cryptically, "It's possible."

"But why should I fear and not you?"

A short time later, van Izendorn received his promotion.

Despite the judicial defeat, their belief in Menten's guilt remained, more steadfastly now than ever. Van Izendorn felt that he had walked into a conspiracy. "But who? Why?" he asked Rohling, who said a time would come when the Menten case would again surface. To prepare for that eventuality, they duplicated photographs, letters, sworn testimonies, names, and addresses used in the Menten investigation, trial, and appeal. These were their insurance policy.

Duplication of the evidence, though prudent, was illegal. And possession of the documents now constituted a danger. There was no telling what Menten would do to ensure that they were destroyed. With the assistance of a former member of Rolls-Royce, van Izendorn and Rohling drove to a dike near the Dutch coast, and in the vault of the earth they buried the documents inside an airtight, waterproof shell box. Van Izendorn said, "It's ended. For now."

CHAPTER IX

❦

"... The bloody monster, how *dare* he?"

HENRIETTA BOAS RAISED her feet a little too high off the ground when she walked, as if she feared she might stumble, because her thoughts usually were elsewhere, on times gone by, on images in Greek and Latin classics, on terrain where she would rather have been, for example, that day in May 1976 than crossing the intersection near her house in the Amsterdam suburb of Badhoevedorp. As usual that spring morning, she looked as if she were hastening to turn a page in her mind before she entered the bungalow where she lived with a cat named Puss.

As she did every morning on her return—her voyage to the village for the newspaper adhered to practically the same course and schedule—Henrietta produced a key from the copious pocket of her tweed skirt and turned the lock. She placed the newspaper on the telephone table near the door and she called out to Puss, somewhere among the old books, magazines, and newspapers heaped in the living room like stalagmites.

Henrietta was no longer youthful, but neither was she old. However, her appearance suggested less about age than a broad eccentricity. A wild—and to some, frightening—shock of gray hair sprang from her head, as though it were a badge of her eccentricity. The gray made the black of her heavy eyebrows all the more prominent, perhaps even pretty. Occasionally she permitted herself a quick glance in a mirror, a primping of that wild shock, but rarely anything more. She avoided makeup, and in general lived a quiet spinster's existence.

What had driven Henrietta Boas into that cave of her solitary dwelling, only she knew. A Sephardic Jew whose family went back centuries in Holland, she had a doctorate of classical literature from the Sorbonne and was a teacher of Latin and Greek. In fact, she had been a young student of the classics in Paris those twenty-six spring seasons ago when the German invaders approached the gates of the city. With the distant rumble of artillery in her ears, she had fled south, first to Poitiers, then Bordeaux, before boarding a steamer for Southampton. In England for the duration of the war she had lived in Bloomsbury and translated for the Dutch Service of the BBC and Radio Orange.

After the war, she had returned briefly to Holland, destined for Israel, where she provided for herself by writing for the Jerusalem *Post*. Like many early Zionists, she soon decided that young Israel presented "insurmountable" hardships; housing shortages and the constant pressures of war and terrorism were too much for her. So she returned to Holland where she taught the classics in high school, and, on the side, continued with the Jerusalem *Post* as its Dutch correspondent. The writing barely paid expenses, but "this hobby" gave her an excuse to get out into the world, while allowing—indeed, demanding—an emotional distance. The other, full-time Dutch reporters amused her. None had her education, but she respected them for the bluster and extroverted behavior that she could never exhibit. She knew that they saw her as an eccentric, a dabbler, but she did not agree that they were any better journalists or worked harder, particularly when the stories dealt with the war, the Holocaust, and Israel, the country of her heart.

In 1968, Henrietta wrote a series about Friedrich Weinreb, a Dutch Jew who had cruelly extorted money from fellow Jews during the German occupation by promising them exemption from Nazi "transports," while in reality exempting nobody. Henrietta pursued the story in the pages of the Jerusalem *Post,* and such was the quality of the journalism and the unusual nature of the story that occasionally a Dutch newspaper picked up her reports. In Israel, the managing editor of *Ha'aretz,* Israel Finkelstein, who by now was nearing a well-earned retirement from the paper, read her series. Impressed, he wrote to her, and in their correspondence, he learned that she maintained a small apartment in Tel

Aviv, which she used one month a year during her annual teaching vacation. Finkelstein asked if she would stop in to see him that summer. Perhaps, he ventured, there might be a place for Henrietta on *Ha'aretz,* as their Dutch part-time correspondent, or stringer.

Age had not dulled Finkelstein's memory. That summer, after he had flattered Henrietta into accepting the stringer's job, Finkelstein again remembered the terrible slight to his friend, Bibi Krumholz, so many years ago—it was like another lifetime. Bibi was by then the senior correspondent for *Ha'aretz,* a truly seasoned political reporter and war correspondent close to, and maybe even a little past, his prime. The previous spring he had distinguished himself and the newspaper as the first journalist to enter the liberated Old City of Jerusalem at the end of the 1967 Six-Day War. He still worked harder than all the other reporters, even the ones young enough to be his sons.

Bibi had not forgotten Pieter Menten, but the light of passion in his eyes burned slightly dimmer, ever since he had reached the painful understanding with himself that all his best, most honest efforts had failed—that something more powerful than truth protected Menten. Bibi had stopped talking about it to Mala, who was thankful to see the change in her husband, and he had not described the murders to his daughter, Sima, and his son, David, who were old enough by then to understand. Only on occasional visits to the house of his cousin, Mara, and her husband, Stash, was the name Menten on his lips. As if it were again 1945 and he had just finished hearing the story from Jacob Leubel, Bibi now did not know if Menten were alive or dead; living in Holland or hiding out, perhaps in a Latin American country, under an assumed name; rich or poor.

When Finkelstein had finished with Henrietta that afternoon, he walked her around to Bibi's office, near his own in a pecking order that began with the office of Gustav Schocken, still the editor. Bibi graciously asked Henrietta to join him for coffee in the basement canteen. Across a Formica tabletop, he said to this complete stranger, "Something eats at my heart." Then he described what it was.

When he had finished his story, he saw that Henrietta was sympathetic and perhaps willing to help. He said to her, "And now it's time that something more is tried. After all these years, maybe the young people in Holland have enough courage to face this man." He then asked, "When you go back, will you find out if he is still alive?"

Uncertain of herself, Henrietta said, "I'll try, but I can't promise anything." Honestly, she did not hold out much hope because she had no experience whatsoever as an investigator. She probably could not even find out if he was still alive, and if he was, what then?

Back from Israel a week later, she wondered where to start. She had not lived in Holland immediately after the war, so she had not read the celebrated newspaper series about Menten by the journalist Lunshof. Menten probably lived in Amsterdam, Bibi had told her. But when she looked in the telephone directory, she found no listing for him, and she figured that he was either dead or living outside Holland. More logical still, he was using an alias. A friend who worked for the Amsterdam municipality checked the death register, and again, the name Menten did not appear. With a thoroughness that was characteristic, she wrote to Bibi promising him to check a few other leads when she had the time. Later, she looked up the name Menten in the directories for The Hague and Rotterdam, but his name did not show up there either. Menten had disappeared so totally that she wondered if maybe he wasn't a figment of Bibi's imagination.

As she knew, the Rijks Institute for War Documentation housed tons of relevant war material. Set up and paid for by the government, the institute employed several historians to sift through the mass of documents to make sense—and in some instances, to make revisionist *nonsense,* fantasies, and myth—of the war and its aftermath in Holland. Thankfully, one historian at the institute, Johannes ("Hans") van der Leeuw, had agreed to help, when normally someone like Henrietta, without an academic reason to use the institute, would have been politely turned away.

On the telephone, she had asked, "Have you ever heard the name?"

Van der Leeuw had actually laughed. "We have a file on him like that," he said.

"Like what?" Henrietta had asked.

"To the ceiling," van der Leeuw had replied. "He lives in Hilversum."

That day, September 1, 1969, Henrietta had typed a progress report to Bibi. She wrote, "This time I have better news for you. I've discovered Mr. M's address, which is some 25 Km [sixteen miles] east of Amsterdam. . . . His telephone number is 11004. I've now asked a young relative of mine, a freelance press photographer, to go there tomorrow and take a picture of the house, if possible with the nameplate. I did not tell him for what purpose." Now excited by the investigation, Henrietta continued, "As my main daily work is that of a teacher, I shall be free to go to the Institute for War Documentation only on Wednesday afternoons; the Director told me I would need several hours to read the material."

For the next two Wednesdays, Henrietta studied the thick file brought to her in the third-floor reading room of the Rijks Institute, and when she had made photocopies of the most important documents, she mailed them to Tel Aviv.

Now that Finkelstein had just retired, an age-old obstacle had been removed at *Ha'aretz,* Bibi felt. With Henrietta's material they would write an article under a dual by-line to appear first in the pages of *Ha'aretz,* and then, translated, in a Dutch daily with which Henrietta would make contact.

When it arrived, the envelope contained photographs of Menten in Nazi uniform and details from his trial for collaboration that Bibi had never known—for example, that Joseph Stieglitz, with an office not half a mile from *Ha'aretz,* had testified in Menten's defense. Bibi sat down and, occasionally referring to now-yellowed copies of his earlier efforts, again wrote the story of Pieter Menten. When he had finished and was proofreading the copy, he realized how identical this article was to the one written for *Ha'aretz* nearly twenty years before.

With every reason for optimism, Bibi submitted the article for the scrutiny of Finkelstein's successor, a brash, young, and antagonistic editor named Yair Kotler.

On November 16, 1969, Henrietta wrote Bibi, "I've still not seen your article on Mr. M. Has it not yet been published?" When she did not hear from Bibi, she wrote again, this time without mentioning the article. She told him about a recent story in *Het Parool* about a tenants' strike in an Amsterdam apartment building owned by Menten, who had turned off the heat and electricity when the tenants had refused to pay the rent increases he was demanding. "He must be a millionaire," Henrietta ventured.

She continued to write him. "About M. himself there is no news," she said in a letter that November. "His name has disappeared from the press again." She offered Bibi the suggestion that he contact Simon Wiesenthal, the celebrated Viennese Nazi hunter; he had a reputation for success. (Henrietta did not know that Wiesenthal and Bibi had been boyhood acquaintances before the war, in Lwów.)

Finally, Bibi wrote back to her, angrily. The suggestion that Wiesenthal was better equipped to hunt Menten had stung him. Kotler had spiked his story, on the old grounds of libel, and that had hurt Bibi enough. But Henrietta and her mention of Wiesenthal was the last straw. He wrote, "I don't know what he can do better than I. He has no power. He will go to the Dutch, and they will tell him to mind his own business, just like they told me to do. As a policeman and a journalist I am better trained for it than he is. So why would I seek his help?" Partly because neither of them wanted a reminder of their failure, Henrietta and Bibi broke off nearly all contact; even when she visited Israel on vacation she did not stop in his office. When the article wasn't published, there was nothing else, except New Year's cards. Henrietta had nearly forgotten all about Pieter Menten, even about Bibi. . . .

. . . Until this spring day in 1976. She went to the comfortable chair near the front window, where Puss, stretched out on the sill, was purring in the warmth of the morning sun. She spread out the newspaper, quite honestly not expecting to find much of interest. *De Telegraaf* had taken a turn toward tabloid sensationalism and, after lurid murders and sex scandals, not much space remained for news of political or cultural substance, especially on weekends, and this was Saturday, May 22, 1976. The newspaper contained mostly advertisements and fluff features of a timeless nature. Wetting her fingers better to turn the pages, Henrietta skimmed the

212

columns. She had actually turned past the page—a story about an art auction—when she realized. Suddenly, she flipped back, saying out loud to herself, "That's *him,* the killer."

She leaned closer and read, "GREAT DUTCH COLLECTORS ARE A DYING BREED," then, "The taxes here are so high that only a few people can afford to own collections like those of Mannheimer, Dreesman, Van Bevningen, De Geus van den Heuvel." The story heralded an important auction in a month's time at the Amsterdam showrooms of Sotheby–Mak van Waay, the most prestigious art auctioneers in Holland. A mixture of fact and fiction written by Wim van Geffen, the art and antiques editor of *De Telegraaf,* the full-page story reported, "In 1923 he [Menten] purchased 4,000 hectares [9,884 acres] of property with 320,000 square meters [383,00 square yards] of trees and oilfields in East Galicia from Princess Maria Lubomirska. . . . Menten's oil activities ran parallel with those of a great-uncle, also with the name Menten, who was chief engineer for mining in the Dutch East Indies. It was he who initiated the founding of the 'Bataagsche' Oil Company. A certain Deterding was *his* bookkeeper; this Deterding would later become chairman of the board of Royal Shell. . . ."

Henrietta could barely believe how the journalist described Menten, whom he called "PM." "In between world wars, PM not only got acquainted with the businesses of great people, but also with their art collections. Mannheimer of 'Bankhaus Mendelssohn' was Menten's banker and he taught the young enterprising Dutchman a lot about the art of collecting." The Germans confiscated the collection that Menten had built with purchases from famous estates of Mannheimer, Otto Lanz, Dreesman, Rijkens, Dooyes, and the exiled Italian monarch King Umberto. The article continued, astonishing Henrietta more as she read, "Due to lack of servants he [Menten] was forced to give up his large apartment on the Apollolaan in Amsterdam. . . . Pieces were added to his 'apartment inventory' from the collection at his estate 'De Horn.' This was probably due to new problems with lack of space for all his possessions."

It sounded to Henrietta that Menten was auctioning off only a part of his collection—the few pieces from his Amsterdam *pied à terre* in the Apollolaan for which he did not have storage room in the mansion he called De Horn.

Henrietta thought, these paintings—some of them, anyway—represented innocent blood. But she wondered if Menten was really so arrogant as to publicize the Sotheby auction like this without any safeguards. She looked again at the article. Audacious, yes; foolish, no. A page-wide photograph across the top of the newspaper showed Menten's house, De Horn, in all its twenty-room vastness—a magnificent three-story mansard, thatch-and-brick traditional Dutch dwelling. The lawns seemed to spread forever with leafy trees sheltering the front windows. There, barely an inch high, dwarfed by the enormity of the place, beside the awnings over what looked to be a patio, was the standing figure of a man, his leg jauntily cocked on a low brick wall, his hands in his pockets. His facial features were indistinguishable—a *total blank*—as if anonymity had nearly, but not quite, overcome hubris.

Without a moment's hesitation, Henrietta dialed the telephone number for the PTT (Post-Telephone-Telegraph). The telegram she sent Bibi advised him of the art auction. Then she typed a letter, short and to the point. "I happen to know the present Director of (Sotheby) Mak van Waay, Mr. J. P. Glerum, a young man." He had been a favorite student in her classics class several years ago. "I shall not contact him unless you approve, as Mr. Menten might thereby be forewarned," she wrote, then enclosed the newspaper article and sent the envelope by Express Mail to Tel Aviv.

The next afternoon when he telephoned, Bibi said excitedly, "He has finally made the mistake. He's exposed himself where he is vulnerable," but only if they could publish an article about the real Menten in a Dutch newspaper. He asked her to write the story in Dutch, alerting the country to the meaning of the art auction—that Menten was selling paintings plundered during the war. Bibi said, "I will try to get the same piece published here. Let me know."

Henrietta stood there with the telephone in her hand, a little frightened. She did not want to disappoint him now, and she did not want to tell him that she did not have that kind of access. She could not do what he had asked alone. Her recent contributions to the local press had been letters to the editors and an occasional story in *The Jewish Weekly*. After all, she was a stringer for Israeli papers, not a local editor or reporter. Even if she were, this story was too important, she thought. She and Bibi needed a journalist with a reputation, someone who was certain to get the story published. She thought about the journalists she knew in Amsterdam, then their publications. She eliminated *The Jewish Weekly;* it did not print news. Next, she considered Philip Mok, the foreign editor of *Elseviers,* the Dutch weekly newsmagazine. As foreign editor, he did not decide what went into the magazine. Menten was a domestic story and out of his jurisdiction anyway. She crossed Mok off her list. Then she thought of Hans Knoop, the editor in chief of *Accent,* a struggling general-interest magazine. A former police reporter, Knoop was tenacious, young, ambitious, and Jewish. Decided, she asked Knoop on the telephone if they could meet on her next free day off from school—the following Tuesday—for tea around 4:30 at the Apollo Restaurant. She did not tell him why, but Knoop brusquely agreed, to Henrietta's mild surprise.

That same morning, May 22, 1976, Jan Pieter Glerum, the director of the auction house Sotheby–Mak van Waay, wore the hunted look of a man who thought he was supposed to be somewhere else. Generally, nerves propelled him through the hectic days of dealing with idiosyncratic art collectors, with the several thousand details that together made an auction, and with his Sotheby superiors in Bond Street, London. He was not his own person, so maybe he never *was* in the right place at the right time. Just now, he was furious. Together, he and Menten had agreed to make Menten's auction at the end of the month *anonymous*—no name anywhere on the catalogue, no mention in the press. And now the whole life's story was splashed across the page of *De Telegraaf.* Deep down, Glerum feared that the Menten collection contained "tainted" art. Sure, some of the pedigrees, the provenances, were known. Rare was the auctioneer who wanted to sell stolen art, *knowingly.* So the trick was not to know, to artfully

215

play the ostrich. Sotheby–Mak van Waay thought of Menten as an "unpopular man with a disagreeable aura—unsavory."

Nobody in the world of art knew how unsavory better than the Glerums, father and son. Menten had been their "most difficult" client since the war—maybe the most difficult ever. At the Rokin main office of Sotheby–Mak van Waay, Menten was notorious among pretty social-register secretaries for his temper tantrums and bullying behavior. Once, he was barred from the auction house for a year. For one thing, he paid late, if at all. And he always questioned routine charges—freight costs, for instance— for which he had contracted in advance, on the assumption that Sotheby–Mak van Waay had cheated him. Time and again in fits of pique he threatened never to deal with Sotheby–Mak van Waay, but after a while he again was seen inspecting works on preview. Once, after he had successfully bid on a nineteenth-century painting of a landlord whipping his cossack serfs, the secretaries laughed, remembering how Menten had recently turned off the heat and electricity to penalize his tenants.

Some critics complained that Menten was nothing but "a decorator" who filled his house with "flashy," "pretty" nineteenth-century pictures of cows, windmills, pastures, and rivers. The subjects of his paintings had to please the eye—nothing difficult, nothing too artistic. To that simple rule, the critics said, he owned three exceptions, portraits by Jan Sluijters of two nudes in rich violets and reds and a beautiful 1920s portrait by Isaac Israels. Connoisseurs ran down the collection by claiming that it contained nothing marvelous, nothing exciting. There were no Vermeers, for example, and no Rembrandts. (The Raphael was neither for sale nor on public view.) But the truth was, by any standard, the collection of Pieter Menten was truly exceptional, a fact that no amount of carping changed.

Pieter Glerum had first visited De Horn in 1973 at the time of the Yom Kippur War. He remembered how his host had popped open a bottle of champagne to celebrate the defeat of what he called "Russia's clients," the Egyptians and Syrians. Glerum had noticed then Menten's unnatural fear of the Russians. As Lammers, the butler, had followed them carrying a tray of smoked

Scotch salmon, Menten had given Glerum a grand tour of the house, insisting that he appreciate nearly everything, again and again encouraging compliments. He boasted about the expensive wood in the door panelings, its price per pound, how much it weighed, how many gallons of water (153,000) filled his swimming pool, at 118 feet in length the largest owned privately in all Holland, how many hours artisans had worked to carve the ornate teak staircase banisters, and on and on. It must be tedious to be a frequent visitor, thought Glerum, who viewed Menten as a *nouveau riche*.

Then, two years later, Glerum had visited Menten's house again, this time to discuss the details of the auction. That evening Menten had expressed his fears openly. To be honest, he no longer felt safe in Holland. The Russians were threatening Western Europe, he said, and they would occupy countries like Holland in only a short matter of time. While he rambled on, Glerum listened distractedly, not really interested in why Menten planned to leave either for Ireland or the United States once his collection had been sold. Despite his anxieties, Menten drove a hard bargain. He knew what the sale meant in commissions to Sotheby–Mak van Waay, and he negotiated a reduced 7.5 percent seller's commission. Glerum agreed but only if Menten's name would not appear in the catalogue. He would be described as "a millionaire collector."

Once the terms were set, Glerum had planned four "balanced" sales of more than 2,000 objects estimated in value by the experts at Sotheby–Mak van Waay at 15 million guilders (roughly $7 million). This, Glerum had thought, would be the second largest sale in the history of Sotheby–Mak van Waay. He had been delighted to get things under way, and the owners in Bond Street had praised his entrepreneurship.

And now this! Glerum thought as he read that Saturday's *De Telegraaf*. Sotheby–Mak van Waay had already printed all 160 pages of Catalogue #263 at a cost of around 60,000 guilders (roughly $30,000). Glerum could not distribute the catalogue of an anonymous collection when the so-called millionaire collector had declared himself by name—with his whole life's story—in the

217

biggest Dutch daily newspaper. Not only was it a threat to the sale, but it also made Glerum look foolish.

The week before, Wim van Geffen, the art and antiques editor of *De Telegraaf,* had been listening to the forced cheerfulness of a caller. He recognized this as the Voice of Something for Free. Familiarity and bonhomie from a stranger, like this person on the phone, usually foreshadowed The Touch in service journalism. Van Geffen needed the museums, galleries, auction houses, and collectors as grist for stories. In turn, they needed him and the newspaper he represented for free publicity. Yet, there was an unspoken understanding between them. No one cared to call the quid pro quo by its true name, which was why this person on the telephone, Pieter Menten, offended him with a straight-out pitch. A scowl formed on van Geffen's face.

"Well, you know me, of course, because . . ." Menten said.

Van Geffen thought, then said, "I met you at an auction some time ago."

"Do you know there's an auction of my collection at Mak van Waay?"

"No, I don't."

"Well, I don't understand. Didn't they tell you? Are you interested?" Menten asked. For days he had fought the temptation to call the newspaper. He had never really wanted to agree to Glerum's demand for anonymity. Of course he was proud of his art collection; it reflected his view of himself as a man. But there was a reason beyond pride, a dollars-and-cents reason for breaking the anonymity agreement. The more advance publicity an art sale received, the higher the prices people were willing to pay. And by that reasoning, if a newspaper article increased his percentage of profit from the sale by even one point, the heightened visibility of publicity—and the risk—seemed worth it.

"All right, I'll come by," van Geffen said finally, once Menten promised him the story exclusively.

As a journalist and particularly as the art and antiques editor, van Geffen, a tall, spare man in his fifties with snowy hair and chiseled features, had seen how the other half of society lived. The important collectors whom he had interviewed enjoyed good food, aged liquors, and luxury beyond description. Van Geffen shared their expensive tastes, if only by association, and he felt comfortable in their company, discussing sculpture and paintings, business and politics, as if he were one of them. He was not unhappy when the "millionaire collector" named De Horn in Blaricum as the venue for the interview. Menten had suggested they make a day of it, starting at four in the afternoon. First they would get the business out of the way, then have dinner. Naturally, van Geffen's pretty wife would join them—Meta was anxious to meet her.

Meta Pauw–Menten had become Pieter's second wife in 1952, soon after Elizabeth had died suddenly of a heart attack. An attractive Dutchwoman with a sharp mind and an astonishing capacity for loyalty, Meta had met Pieter even before Elizabeth had passed away, when she had been the secretary to the journalist Henry Lunshof, who had written so disapprovingly of the Resistance's postwar behavior. Naturally, Meta had heard gossip about Pieter's collaboration in the war, but she believed the truth as told by her former employer. All these years later, those painful questions of collaboration or resistance just did not arise as they had done at the end of the war. Pieter at seventy-seven had a remarkable vitality and drive, swimming nearly every summer day, despite his diabetes. His health and attitude, Meta was proud to say, were those of a much, much younger man. Most of the time they attended auctions and sales throughout Europe as a team, and by now, Meta knew nearly as much about art as Pieter. They traveled annually to Ireland, where they owned a castle in Waterford County, and sometimes in summers they drove south toward Spain with Lammers the butler along. When back at De Horn, Meta organized frequent dinner parties for a wide variety of guests. Generally, Meta could say that life had treated them with kindness.

If art was Pieter's forte, Meta knew the press. The media had made an "event" of the van den Heuvel auction at Sotheby–Mak van Waay earlier that year; the prices had far exceeded estimates.

219

In a market where prices were subjective, the media had the power to whip the buying public into a frenzy or, if it chose, to ignore the sale altogether. Meta and Pieter had bid and bought at that sale, and they wondered how much media hype accounted for the 200,000 guilders (roughly $80,000) they had spent on paintings. Meta had noticed that van Geffen of *De Telegraaf* had written several articles in anticipation of the van den Heuvel sale, including a portrait of the deceased collector. Everybody agreed that the articles made a big difference.

The visit started out well enough. While giving a running commentary, Pieter showed the house to van Geffen, who felt that the ambiance was oppressive. Everything was overdone. Art was on the walls from attic to basement, from ceiling to waist level. In the cellar, sliding racks held even more pictures. Menten solicited van Geffen's opinion often. As a guest van Geffen felt that he had to flatter his host, and although he wondered why Menten had insisted initially on making the sale anonymous, he did not ask. Once, years ago, as a crime reporter, van Geffen had learned how art collectors and dealers often cavorted with theft and fraud. Not that he had any suspicions about Menten, not that he even cared one way or another how collectors acquired their art. If anything, he thought, Menten was seeking to avoid taxes through anonymity. Anyway, the question was none of his business and simply not germane.

Later, when the women joined them, Meta was formal, almost cool, constantly deferring to Pieter. Van Geffen's wife could not shake the feeling that the art represented money, wealth, power, and status—and nothing else. Upstairs, where the van Geffens were overwhelmed by more paintings crowding even the bathroom walls, they passed a table in the hall with the silver-framed photograph of a beautiful dark-haired woman. Pieter stopped and pointed to her. "My first wife, Elizabeth," he said.

"She was beautiful," van Geffen's wife remarked.

"Yes, she was," Menten agreed.

Van Geffen's wife had the feeling, though, that he was merely pointing out another beautiful possession.

Dinner was a princely, groaning affair that began with poached salmon with dill sauce and ended with a soufflé. As different, superb decanted wines were poured, the conversation turned inevitably to money, which provided Menten with the opportunity to boast of his personal assets—more than $100 *million,* he told his guests. Van Geffen estimated that his host that night was one of the ten richest men in Holland—indeed, a contender in any "richest" category anywhere in the world. But with a sobering wistfulness, Menten said to van Geffen, "I would give everything I have, you know—all of this—if only I could be young again."

The next day, as an expression of his gratitude, van Geffen invited the Mentens to come by and read the article he had just finished writing about the auction for *De Telegraaf.* The ethics of journalism required him, at the most, to read Menten direct quotes. Menten *had* asked if he could see the story before publication to check its accuracy.

After coffee was served in the small, comfortable living room of the van Geffens' apartment, the article was brought out, like a talented child, to entertain. Delicately insisting that *he* read the piece aloud, van Geffen began, "Great Dutch Collectors are a Dying Breed." He looked up, and Menten nodded his approval. Van Geffen continued reading until he reached the first of several quotes attributed to "Pieter N. Menten."

"Oh, no! No! You mentioned my name," Menten said, surprised.

Van Geffen said, "Of course." And he laughed.

"But . . . I want to have it all anonymous."

Van Geffen did not care one way or another, but his editors were sure to complain when they read a long article about a collector that failed to mention the collector's name. Again, van Geffen assumed that Menten wanted to hide from the tax man. "What do you suggest?" he asked.

This problem needed thought. Years ago, when Prince Bernhard had started to call himself "PB," Menten had encouraged friends to address him as "PNM." "Why don't you just use my initials?"

"Initials?" van Geffen asked, throwing back his head in laughter. In Holland, Dutch newspapers referred only to convicted criminals by their initials. "You're not a *criminal,* are you?"

"Of *course* I'm not," PNM replied. But from then on, he made no further comment about the article. And he did not bring up the question of the use of his name again.

Days later in Tel Aviv, Bibi looked like an anxious lover as he waited in front of the Café Stern on Dizengoff Street, checking his wristwatch every so often. The van Geffen newspaper article had finally arrived from Holland, and he had arranged to meet the Dutch husband of *Ha'aretz*'s librarian, named Benjamin, who had promised to translate for him. At the sound of every motorcycle and scooter, he turned his head. Mr. Benjamin had told him to expect a man on a Vespa with a broken muffler. As he waited, Bibi thought again about his plan. He had cleared everything out of the way so that he could devote the evening to writing at home. Once he had finished, he thought, he would present the article— the *third* he had written about Menten since 1945—as a *fait accompli* to a new generation that Gideon Samet represented at *Ha'aretz*. Samet had been chosen as managing editor by Gustav Schocken five years before. He had come from the obscurity of the Israel Army Radio, and his appointment had surprised the older professionals. The choice had pleased Bibi, who could not forgive Kotler, whose term as managing editor had been short, for spiking the story in 1969. Besides, he liked Gideon, probably because Gideon's father, Simon, was one of Bibi's oldest colleagues on the newspaper and Gideon's mother came from Lwów, too.

At a loud popping noise, Bibi looked around to see Mr. Benjamin parking the Vespa near the curb. He wore a Bell helmet with a leather strap, as if he flew. When he saw Bibi's strained expression he immediately took the folded newspaper article from the envelope and translated slowly. Listening intently, Bibi was more convinced than ever that Menten had made the mistake that now would hang him.

The following morning, weary but satisfied with his night's work, Bibi entered the managing editor's office. "Gideon, I have a sensation," he said, holding up the pages of written copy.

Despite the gap in their ages—and the freckles and fair skin that made him seem younger still—Gideon knew what constituted good journalism. And now, as he read, he thought, This is a significant story, even one with international repercussions. Bibi's

222

personal involvement did not disqualify it. That he had hunted Menten for so many years even gave the story more appeal, Samet thought. By his record at *Ha'aretz* alone, Bibi satisfied Gideon's requirements for balance and substantiation of fact, and he foresaw no legal obstacles to the article's publication, since effectively the same accusations had appeared years ago in a Dutch daily. He made the decision to run the story in the weekend edition of June 11, 1976, on page one with plenty of pre-publication publicity. He chose the headline "THE SECRET OF AN ART COLLECTOR," beneath which, in a subheadline, he decided on, "The correspondent of *Ha'aretz* reveals the past of Pieter Menten, who hopes to auction valuable art in Amsterdam."

Now Bibi waited—and after so many years what were another few weeks?—for the response of a new, young generation that wanted to discover the truth.

Hans Knoop normally would have refused Henrietta Boas's call. As far as he was concerned, she was a pain in the neck, a gadfly. In a former incarnation, when Knoop had briefly edited *The Jewish Weekly,* a day hardly passed without either a letter or a call from Henrietta complaining about some minor error in the recent issue, or this or that. She was honest, and she had courage and integrity. In more generous moods Knoop described her as "remarkable," but when she had telephoned his office at *Accent* magazine, a dark cloud of obligation had descended on him. If he were less ambitious as a person and less alert as a journalist, Knoop would have told his secretary to field the call. But now, he was desperate for a "hot story." He needed to blow new life into his moribund magazine that the directors of the parent company, De Telegraaf, had hired him to edit two years ago. If circulation did not pick up, they had told him, within a year or less he would be back on the beat reporting for *De Telegraaf*—a violent, whiplash career change at thirty-three, especially now that he had tasted the power and prestige of running his own show. He sought "to go for the sensational, high-profile story," and if he could not afford to buy those stories from expensive German, American, or British publications—his annual editorial budget was only $100,000—his own staff had to somehow find an *original* sensation in Holland.

But stories on the scale of sensationalism that he required were indeed rare, especially on the exclusive basis Knoop demanded. He had tried nearly everything, and nothing had seemed to improve the flagging circulation. Well, maybe the interview with Itzhak Rabin in Israel. But nothing was working quite the way he needed. His handpicked reporters on *Accent*'s editorial staff had tapped their sources, too, but there was only so much they could do without sinking to the level of the Hitler-Spotted-in-Bolivia story.

Knoop had targeted an unrealistic circulation projection, and that was the bind. *Accent* had been the gift to *De Telegraaf* of Fritz Phillips, scion of the huge Dutch multinational electronics corporation who had started the magazine in the mid-sixties to stem the tide in Holland of anti-Americanism caused by the unpopular war in Vietnam. Right from the start, *Accent* had plodded along with a steady circulation of around 25,000 readers. The finances did not matter much to Phillips, as long as an image of family decency and tradition shone in *Accent*'s pages. When the Vietnam War ended, Phillips lost his reason to finance the loss, but he did not want to close *Accent* down either. In 1974 friends of Phillips at *De Telegraaf* wanted to acquire a vehicle with which to compete with the prestigious and highly profitable *Elseviers* magazine. Phillips sold them *Accent* for a token sum.

At the time, Hans Knoop was *De Telegraaf*'s correspondent in Brussels, covering the Common Market and NATO, the Lotusland of European journalism. Knoop saw himself as *De Telegraaf*'s "star" reporter, the war correspondent and interlocutor of great men on grave issues. Indeed, he had covered the two wars in Israel since 1967 and interviewed Richard Nixon at San Clemente. But there had been no getting past the fact: he had been in danger of hitting the long slide, the leveling out of a career. When Henrik Bokhazius, the rumpled, chain-smoking editor in chief of *De Telegraaf*, offered him the editorship of *Accent*—based on Knoop's brief tenure as editor of *The Jewish Weekly*—Knoop had pledged to *triple* the circulation in three years or quit, conceding defeat. Such had been Knoop's confidence and enthusiasm that nobody at the parent company saw the obvious. Knoop was a reporter, a resourceful investigator, an action man. Nobody ever claimed that he had the talent to edit. Now, with less than a year to hit his circulation target, he had clicked the telephone off hold and listened.

Rather secretive, too secretive, thought Knoop, who tried in the next few minutes to bully the story out of Henrietta with that staccato, tough-guy delivery that he had cultivated to seem busier, under more pressure, more the On-Deadline-Johnny. Henrietta refused to say a single word about what she knew, except that it was "sensational"—and that whetted Knoop's appetite.

Henrietta had promised a "very exciting story," and bless her, Knoop thought a few days later as he left the tearoom of the Apollo Restaurant, she had delivered. As they parted, she had said, "It's in your hands now." And he had assured her that his hands were steady. But for all his interest in what she had told him, he did not know where to begin either. He had not read the Saturday newspaper with van Geffen's article. Menten's name and his art collection meant nothing to him. He had promised Henrietta to give the story of the real Menten to *De Telegraaf* to report and write, and that made sense since the parent newspaper, and not *Accent,* had run the van Geffen story in the first place. Henrietta had described the "bare bones" of Bibi's murder charges and given him his telephone number in Tel Aviv. The next morning Knoop passed along the information to Bokhazius.

Bokhazius acknowledged the merits of the story, but he sensed danger. Knoop was a very good journalist, but he often formulated his own ideas about stories, contrary to facts. The editor in chief believed that the story would be very emotional for Knoop as the only Jew working for the De Telegraaf Company. Besides, Bokhazius vaguely recalled Lunshof's journalistic defense of Menten. All these years later, what profit was there in badgering the man? Indeed, he had been *cleared* of some charges, although he doubted if the charges ever included murder. Bokhazius decided, at least, to go through the motions of checking out the murder charges. He told a social friend and an experienced newspaper reporter to see what he could uncover, and several days later when Henk DiMari made his report, Bokhazius was not disappointed. DiMari had read the material on Menten at the Rijks Institute, and just as Bokhazius had suspected, it was old news. Frankly, DiMari did not see a story, and Bokhazius, satisfied with the effort, agreed.

Knoop was surprised. "But it's such a good story," he said to Bokhazius.

"DiMari doesn't think so."

"All right, then *I'll* do it."

"Fine, it's all yours, just so long as the facts pass the lawyers." He said, "I won't fan any flames in *De Telegraaf,* but in *Accent,* I don't care." And with that, he drew the lines.

The same day—Friday, June 11, 1976—Knoop followed the tracks of Henrietta and Henk DiMari to the Rijks Institute. A reading of the 1949 press clippings intrigued him, but he did not yet comprehend the whole story. Joseph Stieglitz had traveled from Tel Aviv to Amsterdam in those days, even when his grandfather was deathly ill in Tel Aviv. If Menten had indeed possessed the influence with the Nazis to save Stieglitz's life *three* times, as the press reports indicated Stieglitz had testified in court, how had Menten acquired such influence, and at what price? Murder, maybe? Knoop smelled something wrong.

He went away from the Rijks Institute thinking to run one story in *Accent* expressing two points of view: Krumholz's accusations on one page and Menten's defense on the other. He assigned the *De Telegraaf* reporter based in Israel to interview Bibi, and he called Pieter Glerum at Sotheby–Mak van Waay for an interview with his client, Menten. After the *De Telegraaf* story Glerum was no longer shy of publicity, and Knoop had said falsely that he planned to write up the forthcoming auction in *Accent.*

Helpful and pleasant as usual, Meta Menten readily agreed to receive Knoop. She and her husband, she said, were only too pleased to answer any of his questions about the collection and the upcoming sale. Saturday, tomorrow morning, was fine, at De Horn. As she was giving Knoop directions to the house, the telex near his desk in the *Accent* offices began to clatter. After thirty-one years of effort, Bibi's story in *Ha'aretz* finally had gone to press that same day, and he was sending a copy for Knoop's edification. After he hung up with Meta, Knoop read the charges made by Bibi as they came out of the machine. Essentially, Henrietta had already told him what Krumholz had written, he thought, but he had no accurate means to assess the judgment of the author, Bibi Krumholz. He would feel more confident confronting Menten with the charges if he knew the accuser only a little, but unfortunately there was no time for that now.

The next morning, seated across from Pieter Menten in the second-floor study of De Horn overlooking the back garden, Knoop asked politely, "Do you know why I'm here?"

"Of course I do," Menten replied. "My wife told me. And naturally, I'm pleased to have you as my guest."

The man looked every inch the aristocrat, Knoop thought. Earlier that sunny morning Menten had greeted him at the bottom of the ornate staircase, dismissing the uniformed maid at the door with a wave of his hand and a look. Beyond his dress—the pale yellow shirt with wide French cuffs and scrolled monogram over the breast—the seventy-seven-year-old man surprised Knoop for his youthful vitality. Smoothly, he had extended his arm and grasped Knoop's hand and, with a pleasantry to fill up the silence, showed him to the study.

As they ascended the stairs, here he was, Knoop thought, an editor of a moribund magazine, about to accuse a multimillionaire aristocrat of mass murder; he felt the discomfort of acute embarrassment, all the more so because he was a guest in the man's house. If the charges were correct, he was staring into the face of a true monster; if they were not true, then what was *he*, Hans Knoop, but a purveyor of the most malicious, secondhand gossip? Until this very instant, when he either had to present the accusations or get out, he had not actually organized his thoughts, and suddenly he felt very, very foolish. "I apologize for a misunderstanding because it's my fault," he said, thinking now he could get up and leave. But he stayed. "I'm here to ask about some very serious charges that you should have the right to answer." There, it was finally out, he thought. Menten would surely ask him to leave.

Menten's pleasant expression did not fade. "What charges?" he asked.

Knoop described the essence of Bibi's article in *Ha'aretz,* ending

227

with, "He claims to have known you quite well from your time in Poland."

Menten stared at Knoop with a look of deepest incredulity. "I never heard of him," he said.

Knoop now knew that a gross error had been made. A guilty man confronted with his crimes does not react in such a diffident, calm manner. As a crime reporter he knew how guilty criminals responded, but Menten had not so much as blinked his blue eyes. "Krumholz . . . as a small boy he went fishing and hunting with you, and you treated him like a son, he says."

"What's the name again?" He cocked his ear to hear better.

"Krumholz."

Menten shook his head. "No, I've never heard it before. Perhaps we met. I was well known in Poland, but in any case the name means nothing to me."

"What about the name Pistiner?" By now Knoop was feeling desperate.

"I did indeed know Isaac Pistiner, but not socially. We did a few things together, business things, but I lost track of him during the war."

That Menten had not *denied* the relationship gave great credence to his other statements, Knoop thought. Only the guilty issued blanket denials. "You had a series of lawsuits with Pistiner, and you were angry with him, I am told," he said, thinking that perhaps this would trip up Menten.

"No. Never any trials," Menten said. Then he asked, "Have you his story with you, what he wrote? What is the name of his newspaper?"

Now thrown off balance, Knoop knew that Menten had caught him "flying blind." He had no supporting evidence of his own origin. He had not met Bibi, nor even talked on the telephone with him. He had only the credibility of *Ha'aretz* and reassurances of Bibi's honesty—hell, what about his *sanity?*—from Henrietta, who was herself no stranger to flakiness. If he heard right, Menten was now actually making apologies.

Menten said, "I'm sure he means well," and he thanked Knoop for bringing the charges directly to him first.

Slowly Knoop started to feel relaxed again. Meta walked into the study. Looking fresh, she offered Knoop a cool, gracious hand. Menten told her what Knoop had just said, and she responded easily, lighting the first of many cigarettes. They *chatted* about the charges, and every time Knoop tried to drop the subject, Menten kept it alive, as if it somehow amused him. He said, "If this man claims to know me, let him come here, and we'll clear up how the story got started."

Menten was searching for a fair, reasoned solution, Knoop thought, as if *they* should roll up their sleeves to help this demented man in Tel Aviv. Getting in the spirit, Meta told the maid to prepare a pot of coffee and lay out a plate of Danish, a sort of working breakfast, Knoop thought, by now more bewildered than before.

Menten asked Knoop, "Would you be kind enough to call that man and tell him I'd like to clear up this misunderstanding. I'll even invite him to fly here first class, and we'll put him up here in the house." He asked, "Doesn't good journalism have a duty to right the wrongs of bad journalism?" Barring that, maybe Knoop would act as his emissary—thinking out loud, of course? Or should they write an irate letter to the editor of *Ha'aretz?* Was that better than going to Israel or sending Knoop there? Meta and Pieter searched Knoop's face for an answer, once the options had been laid out. Naturally, whatever was decided, Menten would pay for any expenses.

Knoop wanted desperately to leave, but Menten continued. "Not only is this untrue," he said, "but the opposite is true. I *saved* many Jews during the war."

Knoop said, "I know about Stieglitz."

For the first time, Menten's eyes flickered. *"How* do you know?"

"The Rijks Institute," Knoop said.

Menten leaned forward in his desk chair, as though to impart a confidence. "And many more Jews than him," he said, then opened a drawer. He took out sworn statements of Jews and the written findings of the West German court stating that in Poland during the war he had been "treated like a Jew." Knoop read, now convinced of Menten's innocence. He accepted a glass of sherry as a token of understanding, as an apology for his rudeness. When he was leaving De Horn and shaking hands with Pieter, Knoop felt they shared an unfathomable secret.

By the time he reached the *Accent* offices, Knoop began to be bothered by the encounter. Boas and Krumholz had ruined a pleasant, sunny Saturday by raising his expectations for a much-needed sensational story and then disappointing those expectations. He had been duped. They had made him look like a moron in front of an important man like Menten. Now he wanted to vent his anger down a telephone line at Krumholz, to return the "favor" by making Krumholz feel like just as much of a fool. And he did just that a few minutes later as the telephone connection to Tel Aviv went through. At first Knoop tersely explained who he was and what he had just come from doing. He wanted answers, he said. Knoop told Bibi how Menten had replied to the charges, and to Knoop's utter surprise, Bibi lost *his* self-control, as if the new proximity—actually hearing secondhand Menten's rebuttals to the age-old murder charges—had triggered his temper.

"The bloody monster, how *dare* he?" Bibi shouted across the thousands of miles. "Accept a ticket from the man who killed my family? I'm not prepared to meet with him anywhere but in a courtroom at his own trial for murder!"

Soon, Bibi calmed down enough to hear Knoop's points one by one. He strongly advised Bibi to make the trip to Amsterdam, but Bibi asked what such a trip would prove. Menten had bluffed Knoop. "What am I to do," Bibi explained, "go to his front door and say 'Mr. Menten, I know you are a murderer'? He will show me to one of those twenty rooms in that mansion, and he will say, 'Bibi, remember how we used to walk in Podhorodse? You remember how I taught you German?' I would say, 'Yes, I remember. I remember also that you killed my family.' But I am not a police officer or a judge. So, there are two possibilities, because I know him. He says to me, 'Well, you know the war was bad. Jews were killed. I was in Lwów. I was a Nazi. Now, how much do you want?' I am sure he will say that. He would even arrange for part of the money to be paid, and then he would say, 'He's an honest man? This man is a thief! And he is calling me a thief, a murderer? Nonsense!' And then he would ask, 'Why don't you stay with me?' After a day I would be found dead, and Menten would say, 'Dead? Really, he was found dead? I was trying to tell him that I didn't do anything to his parents.' He would come to my funeral. No, no, no—never!"

The intensity of his emotion dissolved Knoop's anger. Clearly, the man *thought* he knew the truth about Pieter Menten. After what he had said, lying made very little sense unless Krumholz were a lunatic. Henrietta had vouched that Krumholz enjoyed the reputation of a veteran, hardworking journalist employed by the most respected newspaper in Israel. As a Jew himself and a journalist, too, Knoop knew that "emotions and journalism do not mix," and he said this to Krumholz, who agreed, saying, "except when journalism disciplines emotion, then they can work side by side."

After both men had begun to reach an understanding, Bibi asked Knoop, "Tell me, who is Pieter Menten, really? I mean, what do you know about him?"

Knoop recalled the newspaper clippings at the Rijks Institute and answered, "A convicted war collaborator with an unsavory past."

"Will you at least admit the possibility," Bibi asked, "that he might have also killed?"

"I suppose so," Knoop replied. "If you work for a murdering enemy, then you might murder, too?" And he thought again about Stieglitz. How had Menten managed to save him three times from the Nazis, unless Menten had cooperated to a degree that had gone well beyond mere "collaboration"? He asked himself, as well, who was more credible, Menten or Bibi, considering what he knew right now?

"This could be the biggest story of your career," Bibi said.

"Yes, it could," Knoop admitted.

Knoop then decided to run the story with both points of view in the June 19, 1976, issue of *Accent*. He planned to "peg" the story to the auction, which was scheduled to start two days after the magazine article hit the stands. In the meantime, he had work to do.

That same Saturday, after he had talked with Bibi and returned home from the office, Knoop's wife, Betty, said that Menten had called to invite them for lunch the next day and, weather permitting, a splash in the pool. Knoop thought, even if it were not true

231

that his countrymen had such a meager reputation for hospitality to strangers, it was a little odd for the man he had accused of mass murder to invite him and his family poolside. The invitation did not set off alarm bells, but it made him wonder about just what Menten wanted from him. And, oh, Betty suddenly remembered, Menten had also asked for the number of their bank account because he wanted to reimburse Knoop for the long-distance calls to Israel. Never overly sensitive to such nuance, Knoop indignantly went to the telephone. Indeed, as he dialed Menten's home number, he wondered who this guy was, anyway. Maybe other journalists accepted "emoluments" from their sources; after all, Menten had told Knoop he had paid van Geffen to write an introduction to the revised Sotheby–Mak van Waay catalogue. But Knoop was not for sale, especially for the price of expense money. When Menten came to the phone, he seized the initiative and asked if Knoop had talked with Krumholz.

"He said he isn't interested in your invitation," Knoop said. "He'll only come here to testify against you in court." He realized now, the swimming pool invitation had been to grill Knoop, as he was doing now, about Krumholz. Menten was worried.

Menten said, "Then he is a coward."

"I'm not convinced of that," Knoop said. "I find his reaction legitimate."

"Well, what he says is questionable, and I hope this clears up everything."

"No, it doesn't. I'm going ahead with the story."

In so many words Knoop had just declined the swimming pool invitation, he realized.

"How?" Menten asked. "I mean, how can you do that?"

"I'll give you both the opportunity to tell your own versions."

"Stieglitz will tell you *exactly* who I am or Simon Wiesenthal in Vienna." If anybody did, Wiesenthal knew the identity of fugitive war criminals, Menten said.

With acrimony thickening the air, they broke the connection, and Knoop immediately called the Vienna office of Simon Wiesenthal, whom he had met years before on a visit to Holland. They talked for some time, and once they had hung up, Menten was again on the phone. "I have good news for you," Knoop told

232

Menten. "Wiesenthal doesn't know you, and I'm prepared to mention that in the story."

"What's the sense of writing it if Wiesenthal, expert number one, doesn't know me and can't back up the charges of this man in Tel Aviv? What more proof do you need of my innocence?"

Knoop thought, Why should Wiesenthal be expected to know the identity of every soldier who killed Jews in the Third Reich? There were so many massacres, so many criminals, how would he know this one Dutchman? Wiesenthal had heard only that a few Dutchmen in eastern Poland during the war "had really gone at it."

Knoop saw no reason to speak further with Menten. Their conversations were leading nowhere, and as far as he was concerned, nothing Menten said was going to stop him from completing a balanced article, printing it, and watching the fallout. All the same he listened to Menten, who called him repeatedly that evening, first to reason with him, then implore, then harangue, and later still, threaten, as if each successive call were a stage toward final abusive drunkenness. Late that night Menten arrayed the threat of "powerful friends."

Knoop replied, "Go ahead and try. Nobody can tell *me* what to print."

Starting the next week, Knoop experienced a "conversion" bordering on fanaticism. It had begun a few hours after a source he had uncovered had agreed to meet him at the Jan Tabak restaurant in Blaricum, midway between their houses. The day before he had visited Frans Rohling, retired now and even more prone to lengthy silences, at his home in Wassenaar. From his search at the Rijks Institute, Knoop had discovered Rohling's name in the news reports from the Menten trials in the postwar era, and he had thought that a visit might shed light on Bibi's allegations. Knoop essentially wanted some encouragement. "Do you think it'll be worthwhile if I proceed?" he asked. "Do you recommend that I do?"

Rohling replied impatiently, "Go on, go *on*. You are digging into something that needs revealing."

The force of the answer impressed Knoop, who knew the reti-

233

cence of police, prosecutors, and judges with the press. When he mentioned the name Menten, he was discovering, people changed from reticence to avid support. As Rohling had told him, "You will find people who insist on being quoted on the record, who refuse to obscure their involvement in this Menten affair. That's how much they hate this man."

Not long after the appointed time, the door to the Jan Tabak opened, and Knoop instantly identified the man from the description he had given of himself over the telephone. He was tall and still trim despite his more than sixty years. He had white hair and a gentle, friendly face. Knoop waved, and he smiled, coming over shyly to hold out a big hand. "I'm Pete van Izendorn," he said.

The whole night before, once he had ended his brief telephone conversation with Knoop, van Izendorn had pondered the irony of how, after all these years, the Menten case had surfaced once again, this time for examination by a generation that had barely been born when the crimes were committed. He wondered if there wasn't an imperative to justice for crimes against humanity, almost as though justice were some implacable, totally indifferent force of nature. If this were true, van Izendorn had thought, he could not resist involvement, though something in him said to leave it alone. He was still wary of the subject, and for good reason. Rohling's wrecked career was not something van Izendorn had easily forgotten; but now the threat was not nearly so direct, at least to van Izendorn, who had retired recently as the commissioner of police in the Amsterdam suburb of Hilversum. His pension was guaranteed and secure from Menten's interference, but he still had wondered if he should get involved. Sitting through the night in the living room of his comfortable house, accompanied in his vigil by his two Weimaraners and a bottle of *jenever*, he had asked himself, Would Menten accuse him once again of stealing and worse in that postwar period of anarchy, when emotion dominated the law? Did he really hate Menten for what he had said about him? Did he believe in justice to that extent? It will all come back, he thought, and the hornet's nest will be stirred up again. Although he might be stung, a further confrontation was now or never. "I must step in," he had said to himself.

Now in the Jan Tabak, as he listened to Knoop talk, van Izendorn realized that Knoop h d stepped over an imaginary line into advocacy journalism, and that was good if he were to challenge Menten and survive. He asked if Knoop had hard evidence against Menten. Knoop shrugged—only the testimonies of witnesses in Israel, probably witnesses in Poland, if they were still alive, and bits and pieces in Holland.

"Then you need more," van Izendorn said, thinking of his decision the night before, "Now or never." The Justice Ministry in The Hague would not give Knoop the records of Menten's previous trials. Dutch law forbids public access to trial records. But without that material, Knoop had nothing with which to substantiate his charges but hearsay. If he were to build a concrete case of murder, he needed a lot more than he now had. But first things first. Van Izendorn pounded the bartop with his fist and said, "We hid a box." Quickly he corrected himself. "At least, there *was* a box."

Two nights later, they were driving Knoop's Ford southwest from Amsterdam toward the town of Gouderak on the North Sea coast of Holland. Rain lashed the windshield, and the farther south they drove, the worse the storm grew. By midnight, they reached a dike and, beyond, an isolated farmhouse with windows that glowed a warm and inviting amber. The owner of the house, a former colleague of van Izendorn's in the Resistance and later the Forces of the Interior, had recently moved there. Finding his new address had taken the extra day and the cooperation of van Izendorn's old friends in the police. There was no telephone, so all during the drive they had speculated nervously whether the man had dug up the box and brought it along to this new address. Maybe he had just thrown it out as a relic that was better forgotten. They knocked on the door and were greeted immediately. With only a cursory exchange of salutations, van Izendorn asked the man, "Do you still have it?"

"I don't know," he said. "Maybe my wife threw it out." He had dug it up, though, and brought it with the furniture and other household objects.

Van Izendorn asked, "If it *is* still here, can you find it?"

The next half hour stretched in Knoop's imagination as he waited while van Izendorn and their hosts searched the house from

235

top to bottom, reminiscing along the way of Resistance days and "Rolls-Royce." Knoop remarked to himself how their host had known automatically what "it" was. Finally, van Izendorn came out from a back room holding a box in front of him in both hands, as if it were a Magi's gift. He set it on the table and jimmied the lock with a knife blade. The photocopies were still recognizable after a quarter century, neither damaged by the decades nor the elements. Just as they had placed them there so many years before, van Izendorn recognized the photographs of Menten in uniform, the letters from Poland, the testimonies, police investigation reports, their speculations, the interrogation reports of General Schoengarth. . . .

This was, thought Knoop, a discovery such as was only supposed to happen in movies. Add this documentation to the testimonies of the witnesses in Israel and time collapsed. No longer could the Dutch ignore what Menten thought the world had forgotten. Yet, to awaken those slumbering memories presented real dangers that van Izendorn expressed in the gray dawn of their return, when he said, "You can't win without bearing the mark. Even if you win, you *lose*."

Knoop dismissed the warning in his excitement to study the documents again, as if they revealed the lies and half truths of a whole generation of Dutchmen in the war. Reading those pages, he reached an important decision. Against such an adversary— Menten *and* that older generation with its thirty-year investment in obfuscations—Knoop needed an equally powerful ally. And he called Bibi in Tel Aviv to see what he thought.

In all their future consultations, Bibi spoke with the voice of experience, which he gladly shared. He told Knoop to save time and otherwise frustrated energy, and skirt official institutions. Their stated purposes were to help people like Knoop, but Bibi knew the reality. In all his experience, he had never received one bit of assistance from anything except, finally, *Ha'aretz,* and even then, the newspaper had not helped him so much as the managing editor, Gideon Samet. Bibi added that he had always trusted journalism as the weapon with which to defeat Menten, and there was no reason to doubt journalism now. *Accent* magazine, however, did not have the power to make a difference in Holland; there was really only one mass medium, and that was television. Bibi asked if Knoop trusted any of his television colleagues. Knoop replied that there was one man, Wibo van de Linde, of the influential and popular television program *TROS-AKTUA.* "Then call him," Bibi said.

Wibo van de Linde compensated for his enormous height and the massive breadth of his shoulders with his voice, his manners, and a character of almost arresting gentleness. At the studios of his weekly magazine-format show, *TROS-AKTUA,* Wibo seemed constantly on the move, with secretaries and production assistants mincing behind his giant strides like a gang of coolies.

As a television journalist who ranked among the best in the world Wibo loathed the recent rampancy in Holland of shoddy, left-wing ideological journalism. He avoided choosing sides as a journalist for the simple reason that the choice halved the challenges. He *insisted* on objective reporting and editing, not just because he genuinely believed in balanced journalism but also because objectivity made for lively television. More than most other television journalists, Wibo actually respected the viewers' intelligence. And he thought, if given the facts, viewers would be able to distinguish the truth for themselves. He marshaled and dispatched his "troops," the reporters under his "command," with imagination and daring, demanding that they get as close to the truth as humanly possible, no matter if that truth ruined the preconceived tension, drama, or sensationalism of a particular story. The executives of TROS, one of several state-run Dutch networks, rarely questioned Wibo's judgment. He was so often right, and, they knew, "right" meant ratings that constantly beat the competition. Some 2.5 million viewers now watched the hour-long show every Monday night, ranking *TROS-AKTUA* the top news program in Holland.

In the *TROS-AKTUA* editing room that Monday afternoon, June 21, 1976, Wibo worked the Steenbeck, a film–editing table, with speed and concentration. He chopped and fit the hundreds of splices from the film footage that his team members had shot in the last six hectic days, ever since Hans Knoop had tipped him off to the Menten story. And now, with only hours remaining before the show aired before millions of viewers—it was to be the longest in *TROS-AKTUA*'s history—Wibo would not leave the Steenbeck until he had "got the balance right."

Video: Pieter Menten in yellow shirtsleeves walking in the garden of De Horn past a sculpture of a nude standing woman.

Audio: "We'll walk to the swimming pool. I have four of them [sculptures]. They're Italian, 1720, by a great Italian sculptor, and these are museum pieces."

Video: The dachshund Menten is holding squirms in his arms to be set free.

Audio: "Oh, gosh, you're also on tape; I'll let you run, there, I'll let you run. It's 580,000 liters of water in the swimming pool, and it's thirty-six meters long. . . ."

When Wibo had read the pre-publication proofs of Knoop's article in *Accent,* boldly headlined "IS MILLIONAIRE MENTEN A MASS MURDERER?" he had at first glance called Knoop's version of the Menten story "an amazing thing," by which he meant that he questioned its veracity. But he saw no reason why *TROS-AKTUA* should not make its own objective examination of the facts. After Wibo had set up an appointment to interview Menten at De Horn, he had ordered his toughest reporter at *TROS-AKTUA,* Ard Horvis, to fly to Tel Aviv and *grill* Bibi, he had said, on the assumption that the Israeli was a pathological liar. Once the reporter had broken Bibi down, if he did not believe Krumholz's story in every minute detail, *TROS-AKTUA* would not broadcast the accusations against Menten. Meanwhile, Wibo had wanted to hear Menten's rebuttal to the charges in Knoop's *Accent* article. To prepare for the taped interview that he was now editing for that night's program, expanded from its normal fifty to eighty-seven minutes, Wibo had visited Menten alone. At the end of the evening, Menten had asked confidentially for advice about the upcoming issue of *Accent.* "Do you think it's advisable to buy them all up so people can't read them?"

Wibo had replied, "I'm not in a position to advise you, but if you ask me, I'd find it incriminating to buy up the magazines."

Yet, when Wibo had returned to De Horn the next afternoon to continue his interview, Lammers, the butler, had showed Wibo a cellar filled with copies of the *Accent* issue. All that morning, the butler had driven the station wagon from newsstand to newsstand buying copies at the cover price, thousands of them. Ten minutes later, alone with Menten, Wibo had asked offhandedly, "By the way, what did you finally decide?"

"I took your advice and didn't," Menten replied. And Wibo had his first hint that beneath the smooth surface was a liar. From then on, Wibo had not trusted Menten, but he had needed the rest of the afternoon with Menten for mistrust to turn into distaste. On the inevitable grand tour of the house and grounds, Menten had speculated how the world was populated by somebodys and nobodys. (For that moment, Wibo was a somebody.) Then he had sat fingering documentation of his defense, with the sheer bulk of which he had tried to imply his innocence.

Video: Pieter Glerum in his office at Sotheby–Mak van Waay.
Audio: "Mr. Menten has given us orders to postpone tomorrow's auction until further notice, until he in the meanwhile can clear certain things up. . . ."

Pieter Glerum had called *TROS-AKTUA* earlier in the day to ask Wibo if "something was wrong with Menten." When Wibo had told him what the television program planned to show that night, on the eve of the auction, Glerum had decided to cancel the sale. Already, the Sotheby–Mak van Waay auction house was under great pressure. The Jewish Art Dealers Association in Holland planned to boycott the sale, and the BBK, a left-wing organization of Dutch artists, had picketed Sotheby–Mak van Waay on the Rokin since Saturday, making all sorts of trouble with their chanting and placards, which suggested that Sotheby was in collusion with a mass murderer. When the television news teams from nearly every Dutch station had filmed those placards and interviewed the protesters, Glerum had panicked. None of his training as an auction house director had prepared him for this volatility of human emotion. Wondering what to do, he had telephoned Bond Street, London, to Graham Llewellyn, the director of Sotheby, who quite honestly had not understood all the fuss and instructed Glerum to field the problem. On Sunday, only after Glerum had told Wibo about the cancellation had he advised Menten that "the climate was not conducive to the sale at all."

Menten had said, "That's a very wise decision." And he had opened a bottle of champagne that Glerum really was not in a mood to drink. After all, this was only the second time in the history of the venerable auction house that a sale had had to be canceled. The first and only other time, the Italian government had stepped in to buy up all the items in advance of a Rome auction. So in a manner of speaking that Glerum hoped Bond Street did not catch, this was the first time ever that Sotheby itself had told buyers to take their money home. In the circumstances, the cancellation took guts.

Video: Menten seated beside his wife in their living room.
Audio: "Yes, I've read it [Knoop's article]."
Switch back to Wibo: "He has a lot to say, doesn't he?"
Switch back to Menten: "Yes . . . in fact it's nothing and it's based on nothing and the Mr. Knoop who wrote this is only out to get a sensational story, in the first place to commit extortion and to blackmail me because his whole behavior shows it's a matter of money here and nothing else."
Video: Hans Knoop in the garden of his house.
Audio: "I would have seen it as an insult if he had complimented me on my article; the truth is just the opposite of what he says. Menten offered me money if I were to go to Israel to plead his case there. . . ."

The finding that Menten was "treated like a Jew" in Poland during the war had impressed Wibo, who thought the court judgment unique under the circumstances, until the correspondent whom he had assigned to the story reported that the addresses and names that Menten had given in Germany to confirm that he was nowhere near Poland at the time of the massacre in the village did not exist. All the same, he allowed Menten his side of the complete story, with equal time for filmed rebuttals, despite his personal feeling that Menten could lie without even being aware of it.

Video: Menten seated beside his wife in their living room.
Audio: "Knoop is nothing more than a character assassin. That's the right word. . . . And above all, he's attempted to blackmail me."
Video: Knoop in the garden of his house.
Audio: ". . . I've heard the craziest stories coming from his mouth, but so far he's been barking a lot. He's not bitten yet."
Video: Bibi in the living room of his apartment in Yad Eliahu.
Audio: "He wished me all the best."
Switch back to Menten: "Well, that's all made up. I know nobody by that name. . . . There are so many psychopaths walking around all over this world, do you have to take everyone's story seriously, and do you have to go into his story? In our country the institutions are full of psychopaths. . . ."

Wibo leaned back and stretched, remembering how he had told Menten in advance that he planned to present both points of view, more or less as Knoop had done but with his own original reporting. Yet until only a couple of days ago he had felt uneasy about the material without an accurate reading—other than the assurances of Knoop—of Menten's prime accuser in Tel Aviv, Lieber Krumholz. All along in the reporting *TROS-AKTUA* had a backup program on "the two-thousandth new Italian government" in case the Menten program bombed because the principal accuser, Krumholz, in Israel was discovered to be perpetrating a serious, if unintentional, lie.

The reporter in Israel, Ard Horvis, had telephoned finally, to Wibo's total relief, saying, "He can be trusted." And from then on *TROS-AKTUA* had shifted into high gear. As the pace accelerated, the story expanded in nearly a geometric pattern. Rohling led to van Izendorn, who suggested filming Menten's former house at Westerlaan Street, the house with the myriad hiding places. More problematical, because Wibo had insisted on filming them, witnesses to Menten's crimes told of other witnesses who

241

had to be interviewed—in Holland and abroad in Sweden, the United States, Poland, and Israel. By Saturday, two days before the broadcast, Wibo thought he had uncapped a volcano.

Video: A head shot of Wibo.
Audio: "You mean the whole trial [in 1949] was a farce?"
Switch back to Menten: "A farce, just a farce. It has been ascertained that I never collaborated with the Germans, that I was never an interpreter, that has all been ascertained. . . ."

Wibo advanced the film on the Steenbeck.

Video: Menten seated in his living room.
Audio: "I have trunks full of witnesses' statements. Because many, many Jews were terribly indignant about what happened to me, they heard about it and they wrote me letters and asked, 'How is it possible?'"
Switch back to Wibo: "So you did it to help people?"
Switch back to Menten: "Only to help them. Stieglitz didn't even want to accept the twenty thousand dollars from me; he said, 'Ah, I'll get them [the paintings] sometime, we'll see how that goes.'"
Video: Joseph Stieglitz in his small antiquities shop in an alleyway off Allenby in Tel Aviv. Almost unbelievably, confronted by the camera and the *TROS-AKTUA* reporter, Ard Horvis, Stieglitz radiated the old fear in his eyes.
Audio: "By his protection he helped me and he helped secure my release."
Ard Horvis: "How?"
Switch back to Stieglitz: "That was the way he was. He had contacts with very high officers and so on, and it was through them that he helped me. . . ."

Wibo tried to take care not to incriminate Menten on film. In every instance, in the running narration and the reporters' questions, he had qualified statements with such phrases as "is alleged," "might have been," "looks like," "is accused of." Yet each *TROS-AKTUA* team reporter–editor, almost all of them old enough to remember the war, had worked on the Menten program with the prejudice of experience. Wibo remembered the German occupation, his father in hiding, the V-2 bomb landing in the churchyard, sitting fearfully in the cellar of his grandfather's house until it was exploded. Because they lived outside the city, his family had never gone so hungry that they ate tulip bulbs in the 1944–45 winter, like other members of the *TROS-AKTUA* team had done, but he remembered his mother making jelly from sugar beets. Most vividly he recalled his father one day trying to find the BBC wavelength on their clandestine shortwave radio set. Wibo had shouted from the garden, "Does it work yet?" and his father had come down and spanked him hard because a German transport unit was garrisoned within earshot of their house. Wibo, even now, harbored a certain latent hatred of the Nazis. That hate found a specific release in the Menten story.

Despite Wibo's demand for evenhandedness and his dislike of half measures, the seamless, uninterrupted *TROS-AKTUA* program that the Dutch nation watched that Monday night was a full dress trial by television.

Video: Rohling seated in a chair.

Audio: ". . . Schoengarth was friendly with Menten both in Poland and Holland, and he visited Menten in Aerdenhout and also stayed there."

Switch back to Menten: "Rohling is a specialized expert in forging documents, especially reports and interrogations. That's the most lugubrious figure ever to serve justice. . . . He had only one goal in mind, that was to do harm to me in the interest of people who owed me money."

Video: In the living room of the Menten house, Wibo shows Menten a photograph of himself in an SD uniform.

Audio: "What do you think of this?"

Switch back to Menten: ". . . Well, these pictures . . . anyone can see that right away, bear no resemblance to me. It's only presented as if I was the person in the picture, but that, of course, is a pure forgery."

Switch back to Wibo: "So you think it's falsified?"

243

Switch back to Menten: "A falsification, a pure falsification. . . ."

TROS-AKTUA's reporter in Tel Aviv, Ard Horvis, had worked feverishly to meet the deadlines of the program, to film and tape his interview subjects—Bibi, Mara, Stieglitz, and others. Before the cameras were even switched on, Horvis had questioned Bibi for twelve hours—reaching for the relentlessness of a courtroom prosecutor. In fact, Ard, the "fireman" on the *TROS-AKTUA* team, loved nothing better than to break down witnesses; his devil's advocacy had the reputation for brutality.

Video: Bibi wearing an open-necked shirt, seated at the desk in the small living room of his apartment in Yad Eliahu.
Audio: "Menten appeared like a tempest."
Video: Mara Pistiner-Cygelstreich, looking dignified in a gray suit.
Audio: "He was in our village, and he gathered all Jews, all families, I can't say how many. There were quite a few in any case, and it was there that they dug a big common grave."
Switch back to Bibi: ". . . The name of the man is Samuel Schiff. Schiff wrote, 'I remember exactly that when I approached the terrace. . . .'"
Switch back to Mara: "I ran into him [Schiff] . . . and he told me everything."
Switch back to Bibi: "Schiff remembered, 'Immediately I saw the Jewish women returning, crying, together with their children, and shouting, and from them I learned that Pieter Menten together with the other officer took the Jewish males, told them to pass on a board that was placed there, and while the Jews passed over the board two of them [Menten and the officer] shot them and killed them.'"
Switch back to Menten: "What can I say about such contrived, false accusations? They have nothing to go on. Hearsay, that's just ridiculous, but the lowest of all this—the meanest—is that they didn't tell me . . . when that supposedly happened, what day, what month, what year, where?"

244

Video: Gershone Lengsfelder, section chief for Nazi crimes, Israeli Police, in his office.

Audio: "We had no government approaches. We work only when asked by a government. No government approached us and therefore we did not act."

The link between Schoengarth and Menten was crucial enough for Wibo to ask the Rijks Institute's director what he knew. The director had said, "Well, if Menten calls Schoengarth one of his best friends, there must be something very wrong with him, because Schoengarth was not exactly a nice guy."

Video: The director of the Rijks Institute under the *TROS-AKTUA* studio lights.

Audio: "As for Mr. Rohling . . . I consider him one of the more noble and accurate people I've met in my life. As for Schoengarth, that 'good man' Schoengarth, if I may repeat Mr. Menten's words, let me say this: He was involved in the planning of the greatest mass murder that history has ever known. So in other words this 'virtuous' Mr. Schoengarth, who helped such a 'great' number of Jews, we here see him involved according to a completely authentic document with the most important organizational talk that took place in the Third Reich concerning the mass murder of the Jewish people [the Wannsee conference protocol of January 20, 1942]. Many Germans attempted to save individual Jews during what we call the Final Solution. So when people claim that saving Jews was in the Germans' favor, I'd like to say just the opposite: I believe that the horrible organizational task that this man [Schoengarth] had to carry out was a lot easier for him psychologically when he was able to put his conscience at peace by saying, 'Yes, but there were a couple of Jews that I've helped out of the country and whose lives I've saved.'"

Switch back to Wibo: "But what about the testimonies of Jews who said they were saved by Menten?"

Switch back to the director: "I have to stress that I can't pass judgment about what you call the Menten Case."

Video: Knoop in the garden of his house.

Audio: "This [written] statement [by Menten] tells quite a lot. . . . 'Dutchmen are German and as much German as the Germans are. Dutch are a Germanic tribe. . . . I am an outspoken and enthusiastic follower of the *Führer* and of his ideas and plans.'"

Switch back to Menten: "Yeah, well . . . what you just read to me right now could also have been written yesterday. . . . I'll tell you something, because everything was forged, that's why it was buried. . . ."

To serve the interests of fairness, once Wibo had completed the initial film editing at the *TROS-AKTUA* studios, he had invited Menten to sit beside him at the Steenbeck and watch the interviews of his accusers. A camera crew recorded his responses, starting with questions about Simon Wiesenthal, the celebrated Nazi hunter.

Video: Menten in the *TROS-AKTUA* editing room.
Audio: "There are claims that this Mr. Krumholz . . . or whatever his name is . . . was on good terms with Mr. Wiesenthal. Well, all right, and he's mad at me. If he could drink my blood and he's so friendly with Wiesenthal, why didn't he hand this case over to Wiesenthal twenty or thirty years ago? Everybody knows [Wiesenthal has] committed his whole existence to tracking down war criminals, that would have been easy for him. Why did he [Bibi] keep his mouth shut? Why, why? As if Pieter Menten hid all those years. And if Wiesenthal couldn't find me, then that's really something, and judging by that, you don't have to go any farther in this case."
Video: Knoop again in his garden.
Audio: "When does someone go to Wiesenthal? Someone goes to Wiesenthal if someone wants to track down a war criminal. [Mr. Krumholz] had all the evidence. The Wiesenthal in this case is Mr. [Krumholz] himself."
Switch back to Bibi: ". . . They were not able to open the file against Menten for murdering Jews, so I left the whole thing. I was waiting for *destiny* to punish this murderer."
Switch back to Menten: "I will break Hans Knoop."
Switch back to Knoop: "Yes, he has broken a lot of people, but

he should not be mistaken about one thing. . . . It is now 1976, and the people who protected him then, most of them are dead now. There are, however, younger people who are still alive, and he will hear a lot from them in the future."

Switch back to Menten: "I am a fighter. I've always won, I've always been right, I've never lost, and I won't lose this time either. . . ."

CHAPTER X

✗

"Don't let them break you."

NEARLY FIVE MONTHS had passed (it was now November 1976) since *TROS-AKTUA*'s first broadcast on Menten, and Knoop could only imagine that the fix was in. What else could explain the monumental silence that had resulted? The most sensational story he had ever handled had wilted, like a delicate plant in glare, as if, as Knoop suspected, powerful friends in high places whose names Menten had invoked had ordered the inquiry laid aside; officially and otherwise, it was not to be dug up, period. The *TROS-AKTUA* program had stirred a tremendous controversy that inspired "an avalanche of calls—the most powerful avalanche the show ever had," Wibo had boasted to Knoop. *Accent* had followed up the show with a rapid-fire succession of well-researched and damning stories, week after week. But once the initial wave of reaction had broken, as Wibo had said to Knoop, "The story fell in a void."

They had tried to analyze this rejection of their efforts. Knoop had raged, taking the indifference of the public and the government as a personal affront. The day after the *TROS-AKTUA* broadcast, two members of parliament had asked the Prime Minister questions on the floor of parliament in The Hague, but the tone was very low key. A day later, the Ministry of Justice had reported rather offhandedly that it didn't "feel much about the opening of the Menten File," explaining, "We have a *passive* policy towards people who were 'wrong' during the war. It is not the case that we track them down at all costs."

248

With every new suggestion that there "wasn't any meat on the bone," Wibo sank deeper in gloom, taking Knoop along. To the official reaction of stony silence, an old friend had told Wibo, "Don't think you are tilting at windmills, my boy. This guy has a lot of powerful friends." That had embarrassed Wibo, who was beginning to think that they had only skimmed the surface. Hindsight would show Wibo and Knoop just how accurate but poorly timed their suspicions were.

After the *TROS-AKTUA* show, far from reacting to defend Menten, Prince Bernhard was fighting the battle of his life, too, by adjusting to a new world in which old princes were being held to account.

Right after the war, based on his position in Queen Wilhelmina's London government in exile, the Prince had every reason to anticipate a heightened role, finally taking the reigns of monarchy from the hands of women, but in an abrupt turnaround, the Queen had spurned him bitterly, leaving no doubt about what she thought. Soon, everybody started to treat him like a court eunuch. He had the trappings of power and influence as the Consort, but the reality was quite different: he was living off the generosity of the Dutch people, with access to the monarchy's vast fortunes strictly curbed. "Quite apart from the economic difficulties of our countries," he had complained, "we princes have financial problems of our own."

Faced with such a future, he had rebelled first to free himself from the matriarchal bind by entering into celebrated liaisons with beauties who possessed a sexiness that Juliana so painfully lacked. When the paparazzi caught him in the arms of Eva Perón, he said that anything more than friendship was malicious gossip. "The stories will amuse the children," he said to Juliana, "and at the same time prepare them for the barbs they will one day have to endure." But what, then, of the Paris "Poupette," his mistress, and their child who lived on the Avenue Foch—were they stories to amuse the children, too?

The philandering was merely a prelude to a more serious rebellion from the females' cosseting. Loyalties and old friendships died hard in Europe, as elsewhere. I. G. Farben had been broken up after the war by the Allies, but with a certain few exceptions, its former executives were not held legally accountable for the atrocious crimes to which the company had contributed during the war, as though Farben had been a mindless entity without leadership and direction. After the war the former Farben executives supported West Germany's *Wirtschaftwunder* ("economic miracle"). Two of them, Max Ilgner and Gunther Frank-Fahle, formerly of I. G. Farben's NW7 Intelligence section, asked their friend and old colleague to help them out. Prince Bernhard eagerly agreed to represent what they now represented, for a price.

The new postwar employer could not have suited the old Farben gang better. The Lockheed Aircraft Corporation was run like a satrapy with its own rules and laws.

As Inspector General of the Netherlands Armed Forces and a member of the National Council of Defense, the Prince's opinions counted among career procurement officers. At his urging not just Holland but NATO bought the F-104 Starfighters from Lockheed. (Called "The Widowmaker," more than 230 Starfighters crashed in peacetime maneuvers because of poor design, killing at least a hundred pilots.) The Prince sat on the board of directors of KLM, the Royal Dutch Airline, to which he represented Lockheed's line of products, the Elektras and the Tri-Stars. And his influence went well beyond the boundaries of his country through the Bilderberg Conference, the "1001 Club," and of course the World Wildlife Foundation. What nobody except his old Farben colleagues knew, the Businessman Prince, as he was called, was taking bribes as fast as he could pocket them "to improve the climate" for the sale of Lockheed's products in Holland and beyond. From 1961 to 1971 he received $1.1 million in three installments paid through a Zurich lawyer into an account in the name of Colonel Alexis von Pantschulidzew, who had died in the late sixties.

That Bernhard had misjudged the times dawned slowly. In December 1975, a full six months before the announcement of Pieter Menten's auction appeared in the pages of *De Telegraaf,* the first warnings came from Washington, D.C. Carl Kotchian, the vice-chairman of Lockheed, had testified before a U.S. Senate subcommittee that "a high Dutch official" had received a million dollars "to establish a climate" for the sale of Lockheed's products in

Europe. Specifically, Bernhard had introduced Lockheed's "Widowmaker" to his confreres in the Dutch military. Later, a colleague at Lockheed named Bernhard as the contact who had
demanded payment of $4 million if Lockheed was ever again to
"do business in the Netherlands."

As much as some staunch Dutch republicans detested him, nobody wanted to hurt the Queen. The Dutch press had always applied different rules to the Queen and Prince, and editors did not
want to embarrass them now with documented tales of bribery.
But the Prime Minister had no choice, with the American revelations threatening the Dutch government before an increasingly
leftist electorate. He appointed a commission of inquiry that reported soon and very privately. The evidence against the Prince
was "overwhelming."

In reality, Queen Juliana had been estranged from Bernhard for
years, but she possessed abundant loyalty. If the evidence was
plain and sordid against Bernhard, he was still her husband, de-
serving of her protection. She told the Prime Minister that either
he clear Bernhard totally of the charges or she would abdicate,
bringing the government down with her. If she abdicated, the
Prime Minister countered, the government would prosecute
Bernhard as a private citizen. So they compromised. She did not
abdicate, not right away. Bernhard, hardly chastened, issued a
tepid disclaimer ("I admit and sincerely regret this"). For its part,
the Dutch commission of inquiry fuzzed its report to the public.
"H.R.H. the Prince, in the conviction that his position was unas-
sailable and his judgment was not to be influenced, originally entered much too lightly into *transactions which were bound to create the
impression that he was susceptible to favors."* [Italics added.]

Long-established defense mechanisms died hard; they were
even now being moved into play, as Wibo and Knoop had suspected, but now, at last, with the Prince disgraced and the monarchy never more vulnerable, if it came to that, nobody was
prepared to go to the wall for Pieter Menten, unless the threat of
the letter to Hitler was made more real than it was right now.

Still wondering weeks later why their revelations had not
caught fire, Knoop and Wibo were momentarily heartened when

251

Elseviers magazine produced a cover story that was both original and thorough. Naturally because of *Elseviers'* postwar association with Emile Menten, Knoop anticipated a whitewash, but the magazine chose instead to give the case a fair and balanced hearing. It rehashed Menten's defense of the murder charges (that the Russian KGB, as the NKVD "had done before" in the late 1940s, had trumped up the charges. "Jews could not be murdered where there were no Jews," Menten said. "In Podhorodse . . . there were no Jews. They wouldn't have dared to live there"). The cover story quoted his humor ("A Russian goes to play bridge, but his partner is not there. 'What happened?' he asked. 'He was sentenced to fifteen years in jail.' 'What did he do?' 'Nothing.' 'That's impossible—you get *eighteen* years in Russia for doing nothing'"), and expressed his outrage ("They want to see me hanged," Menten screamed, with Meta interjecting, "Don't let them break you. This is food for these dogs who haven't done a damn thing all their lives. I told Knoop, 'You're nailing Christ to the cross a second time'"). The story also gave expression to his none-too-veiled threats ("I'm warning you. Whoever turns against me, I'll follow even to the ends of the earth").

The *Elseviers* editor concluded after hearing Menten and reading his file of defense documents, "This goes to the monarchy. Menten said so too. He said, 'It will be easy for me to get Prince Bernhard to help . . . well, I have a letter to prove Bernhard's involvement with Germany in World War II.'" The *Elseviers* editor said, "The things he said about Bernhard's job with I. G. Farben, facts and details—he either had read personal documents from the Queen and Bernhard or he was there and he knew firsthand." What Menten had not assessed correctly, however, was the public's reaction to Prince Bernhard's disgrace. The country pitied him, and they circled around to protect the Queen through their protection of the Prince. The public now was less prepared to believe damning facts—let alone incriminating letters—about the Prince's wartime life, especially if Menten brought the blackmail forward.

The magazine also revealed a curious story from the 1950s: Menten had failed to pay his lawyer–political fixer, Mr. Kortenhorst, 10,000 guilders for legal services rendered. Kortenhorst died without receiving the fee, but his relatives had tried to collect. *Elseviers* wrote, "When they knocked at his door, Menten told them he had no cash in his house. 'Just pick out a painting,' he told them. The family chose a Goya. They were rather surprised when this masterwork went at a London auction for 150 guilders. It was a poor copy. When asked about this Menten said, 'Yeah, well, that's their fault. They should have picked a different painting.'"

The magazine article gave Bibi the last word: "Everything he's doing is a delay of execution." The magazine agreed, lending its weight in a rare editorialized conclusion. "In the twilight of Pieter Menten's life there now appear vague contours of a gallows. The file of incriminating testimonies against the screaming and cursing Menten grows higher and higher. . . . One would think there are grounds for a new trial. . . ."

This seemed logical to Knoop, too. Yet, except for *Elseviers* and Menten himself, the silence continued. Menten wrote a letter to *Accent* accusing Knoop of acting "like a madman . . . this man only sees ghosts . . . the man is a hangman. Murder stories seem to be 'in' these days . . . Knoop is an anti-Christ . . . KGB mentality . . . HOLLAND MUST BE AWARE!"

If Bibi had not constantly shored up Knoop's confidence in long telephone conversations with his own tales of frustration and official indifference, Knoop probably would have despaired. The greater Knoop's anxiety, the more readily he ignored long-held and basic principles of journalism. Because of indifference or, worse, a conspiracy to protect Menten, Knoop needed to find a way to force the Dutch Ministry of Justice to arrest Menten. So far, the Minister of Justice, Andreas van Agt, an ambitious Catholic politician, had done no more than instruct the Federal Police to conduct an "orientating" investigation of the allegations against Menten, specifically the ones uncovered by Knoop and Wibo van de Linde. Through July and August 1976, two intrepid and honest detectives had followed the tracks of Knoop and van de Linde across West Germany, Israel, the United States, and Sweden to interview the same witnesses. They found incriminating material, but even so, by their more rigid definitions and rules of evidence, they did not think they had enough of a case to arrest Menten yet. Soon after, the "orientating" investigation turned into a "criminal" investigation, but still, no arrest. It went so maddeningly slowly that Knoop wondered if the Ministry of Justice was thwarting the will to go beyond the bare requirements of mere public relations. When Knoop tried to direct the minister's attention to the facts of the Menten case, someone in the ministry, clearly annoyed by his meddling, had told him, "We would rather run a 99 percent risk of his escaping than risk a possible judicial defeat."

Knoop knew this was plain nonsense. "But if you adopted that same rule for everyone, you would never arrest *anyone*," he answered.

The man replied, "Yes, but Menten is very dangerous, and we have to make sure we can get him forever. If we take him, we keep him."

That was not good enough for Knoop, who was told in no uncertain terms to butt out. "It's not your business anymore," they said insultingly. "With all our respect, as a Jew you are too involved emotionally to judge this correctly. If you really want to serve the investigation, lay off." Furious, Knoop now played with the truth. He urgently told the ministry that a group of angered ex–Resistance fighters planned to drag Menten out of his bedroom in the middle of the night and drown him in his swimming pool. Knoop used this fiction to pressure the police to arrest Menten. But when Knoop refused to reveal the conspirators' names, the police guessed at his charade. Not surprisingly, the "conspirators" finally abandoned the "plot" to throttle Menten, when Knoop "awakened" the would-be killers to reason—that by killing Menten they risked making him a martyr.

The reluctance of the officials to take them seriously drove Knoop and Bibi to extremes of inventiveness. They talked nearly constantly on the telephone and followed up with long advisories on the telex machine in Knoop's office in Amsterdam and at *Ha'aretz* in Tel Aviv. When they discussed what they might do next, they tried to examine what would be the most alarming new fact, as yet uncovered, to shake the public apathy and force the police from the official position of indifference. Bibi hit on the idea first, although he withdrew it immediately. For him, with so little money for travel, the idea seemed mad, but it made Knoop think hard over a period of a week. Then he agreed that, yes, he would try. Gritting his teeth, he decided to search for a garden of cadavers.

Several weeks after he had discussed his problem in Amsterdam with the press attaché, Knoop received his visa to enter the Soviet Union. Only later, weighing his anti-Communism, his militant Jewishness, and his active paranoia, did he wonder what had impelled him to volunteer to slog ankle-deep in mud with his pants rolled up on a cold, rainy October day toward the realization of an image that Bibi Krumholz had implanted in his mind. But he had come this far—from Amsterdam to Moscow, Moscow to Lwów in an Ilyushin of questionable airworthiness, and from Lwów to Podhorodse over spine-cracking roads, past "Fiddler-on-the-Roof" countryside in a Russian-built sedan. A few more steps up the muddy hill were nothing.

He had applied for the visa at the Soviet Embassy in The Hague. Despite the understanding and cooperation of the Russian press attaché to whom he had told the Menten story, Knoop had expected the Russians to respond to his application in their usual silent manner. Lwów, in eastern Galicia, was now the military headquarters of the Warsaw Pact Forces and therefore strictly out of bounds to a Western journalist, to say nothing of a conservative Zionist reporter. But against all odds, and all logic, the Kremlin had chosen him to represent the Dutch press—indeed, to represent the whole Dutch nation—at the exhumation of the grave in Podhorodse.

The original request submitted weeks earlier by an official delegation of the Dutch Ministry of Justice to witness the exhumation had seemingly been ignored by the Russians, or perhaps the Soviet ministries involved in approving such an official request worked more slowly than the press channels. The Russians had agreed to exhume the graves, but they had not yet sent approval for visas to the Dutch police. Knoop did not question his amazing luck; he decided early, even as the consular attaché stamped his passport,

255

that it didn't matter what the Russians got out of it, just as long as he got the bodies.

He was walking toward Isaac Pistiner's house on the hill, up the gravel road sheltered by the fluted cypresses that whispered in the wind. As he broke the crest of the hill, he saw Russian Army soldiers in rain ponchos. Near where they worked in silence, they had built a bonfire of kindling and boards from what now remained of Isaac Pistiner's "villa." A hundred or so feet from the front porch, other men, in white coats, were classifying items lined end to end on wooden tables, sheltered from the incessant rain by an army mess tent. A few more steps and Knoop saw a whole area littered with children's shoes, braids, human skulls, vertebrae, everything chaotically mixed together, and the grave staring at the gray sky like a great open eye. If he had not been so frightened of the Russians, he might have been sick—all those skulls, all those skeletons.

He ducked under the shelter of the tent. A pathologist seated cross-legged on a ground cloth scraped striations of ligament from shards of human bone, then carefully marked the section before joining it to another, finally to complete one human puzzle. To Knoop the skulls seemed unreal. Later, after he had introduced himself, the chief pathologist, a Russian, gave him a tour, narrating as they walked. He picked up a shoulder blade and showed Knoop the bullet hole. It was fortunate, he said, scooping up a long hank of hair that was still intact and braided, how well preserved these corpses were: the clayish composition of the soil was making their work easier. As if to prove his point further, they walked from the tent to the Pistiner house. On the floor of what had once been the living room, off the door to the porch, lay the shriveled corpse of a woman whom the soldiers had exhumed from her burial place in the cellar, her yellowish skin still stretched over her bones like a mummy's. Knoop gave his photographer instructions about what he wanted to take back as photographic proof.

Before he went into the village itself in search of witnesses, with names Bibi had supplied him in a telephone conversation the day he had left, Knoop went over to warm his hands by the bonfire. He looked out over the Stryj to the beautiful foothills and beyond, and he felt a nearly overwhelming sadness, as if this one small plot of land and the people buried here somehow represented *all* Europe and *all* Jews who had vanished in the Holocaust. He felt through Bibi, for whom he had a growing admiration and the deepest respect, and through his brief acquaintance with Pieter Menten, that the people buried in that grave were not just heaps of bones and artifacts. This experience had somehow touched Knoop's deepest feelings, and standing there, he pledged to do what needed to be done to bring Pieter Menten to justice, as though Menten embodied all the hatred and viciousness, all the criminality, all the bestiality of that period. It seemed to him that if he and Bibi prosecuted Pieter Menten, they would have symbolically prosecuted all the crimes of that war, and once prosecuted, the living victims like Bibi could forget the past for the first time since 1945. Knoop knew that he had finally found the ultimate weapon with which to destroy Menten, here on this plot of land, and the irony of it nearly overwhelmed him. He had his corpses, and it was as if these victims were returning from the dead after thirty-five years to eloquently confront their killer with his crimes.

Knoop returned to where the Russian pathologist was working on another human puzzle. Knoop asked him about a heap of forty or fifty muddied coins that the soldiers had placed on a nearby table. They seemed somehow out of place here, and Knoop wondered about them. The pathologist shrugged. "We found them in the graves, but we don't know how they got there," he said.

"What do you mean, 'How they got there'?"

"They weren't in the victims' pockets. It doesn't make any sense to us."

A few days later, once he had returned to Amsterdam from the Soviet Union, Knoop skidded prints of the photographs across the tabletop. In spite of themselves, the Federal Police detectives and Franz Habermehl, the prosecuting attorney, leaned forward, lingering over the ghastly images of the corpses, as if they were pornography. One to another, they passed the enlarged photographs in silence, occasionally nodding, often looking up into Knoop's face with expressions of resignation. They even continued to examine the photographs while Knoop played back the tapes of his interviews with the villagers of Podhorodse, of whom fully twenty had identified photographs of Menten in the SD uniform as "The Dutchman" and "The Landowner from Sopot."

Prosecuting Attorney Habermehl spoke first. "What do you plan to do with these?" he asked. With these photographs and taped interviews, they had enough evidence to arrest and indict Menten, but there was a catch. The prosecutor had to duplicate this evidence. By himself and with the police under his command, he had to retrace Knoop's steps, as they had damnably done all along. He did not doubt that these pictures were genuine, but no court of law on earth would prosecute a defendant on the basis of a reporter's evidence alone. The prosecutor had to travel to Podhorodse, and the Russians had still not responded to the visa request from the Ministry of Justice.

Knoop replied, "I'm going to publish them."

"When?" Habermehl asked, knowing the answer in advance. Knoop was gloating; of course he would publish and soon.

"This week," Knoop said.

"Do you fully understand what you'll be doing?" Habermehl asked. He knew how this made him look. His superior in The Hague, Andreas van Agt, the Minister of Justice, was going to be furious. He bluffed—at least he *hoped*. "Menten will run, you know," he said.

Knoop said, "That's *your* responsibility. Mine is to publish." Not even the minister had the power to stop him now. He had the whip hand, and he planned to use it, hard.

"I admire what you've done," Franz Habermehl said. "All the same, will you hold off for two weeks?" He thought to himself that Knoop would have been less impetuous if he were not so young, and, perhaps, if he had survived the Japanese prison camp at Changi as Habermehl had done, he would have realized that cooperation was the best way to get results. Habermehl had a loathing for war criminals that Knoop could not begin to imagine. At the end of the war in the Pacific, prosecuting Japanese war criminals, he had demanded and received the death penalty ten times as public prosecutor. What he had learned in those trials, he thought now, glaring at Knoop, was caution. He had learned the hard way that few witnesses ever survived to testify in war crimes

258

trials. Anyway, he thought, those witnesses back then had to remember four or five years back in time. These accusations against
Menten were thirty-five years old. The thought made him doubly
cautious, no matter how Knoop pushed him to move with alacrity. He said, "I wonder if you understand what we're dealing
with here." He looked at Knoop, who nodded but said nothing.
Habermehl went on, "The problem facing us is memory over
thirty or so years, and the accused in this has denied everything.
More than that, he has been convicted in a similar case—not of
war crimes but of collaboration."

After a pause Knoop said, "If you don't go [to Podhorodse] to
see for yourselves in two weeks it's not my business." He was
aware that the Soviet Embassy would probably not issue the visas
in so short a time, especially in view of the already lengthy delay.
However, he wanted to present the illusion of cooperation while
forcing the prosecutors to do what he wanted, like puppets. They
were not going to like doing business this way, but they had no
choice—not with the national elections of 1977 four months
away, not if the Minister of Justice was to realize his ambition to
be elected Prime Minister. Knoop would give them two weeks as
a token of his cooperation, but then, once he published the grisly
photos and the testimonies from Podhorodse, either the minister
arrested Menten or Menten ran, incriminating himself as certainly
as if he had proclaimed his own guilt. Either way meant the same
to Knoop.

Less than two weeks later, on November 15, 1976, as he drove
his Ford toward Blaricum and the house of Pieter Menten, Knoop
did not imagine there might be a third possibility, something
that fell somewhere between escape and seizure. Just as he had
thought, the Russians had done nothing to expedite the visa ap-
plications. When they knew that they would miss Knoop's deadline, the prosecuting attorney had no other choice. The *Accent*
story with the photographs of the exhumed bodies would appear
in days, and Habermehl could not risk the public outcry that
would be heard if Menten fled the country, although that seemed
unlikely considering his age.

As he neared Vlieweg, the shady street in this ultrarich suburb where Menten lived, Knoop was unaware that the prosecuting attorney, along with his police officers, had coordinated their tactics two days before. They had chosen this day, Monday, to arrest Menten in the sincere belief, after years of experience, that the specific day was irrelevant. Whether the arrest occurred on a Monday or a Friday did not matter. Let the guy enjoy his last free weekend. And just as importantly, let the police enjoy their weekends. If he escaped, they would pick him up on another Monday or another Friday. The point was that eventually he would be caught, so the exact timing did not matter. They had experienced more trouble agreeing on a time. Detective Richard Pasterkamp had argued for 6 A.M.—the normal time for arrests, he had told Habermehl, who voiced no objection until The Hague started to meddle. The Prime Minister wanted to make political capital out of the arrest, so he had scheduled a press conference for that Monday at eleven o'clock at which he planned to announce triumphantly Menten's "capture." Finally, they had compromised. The time of the arrest would be ten o'clock, an hour before the press conference in The Hague. Over the weekend, to ensure that Menten did not run, Habermehl ordered Federal Police from the barracks in Blaricum to cruise past the driveway a couple of times a day—strictly nothing more than that, definitely nothing on the level of telephone taps and surveillance.

Knoop had known nothing about these arrest plans until the night before. His home telephone had rung after dinner, and the minute he heard the voice of the police detective, he knew that he had finally succeeded. The detective had not identified himself. He said only, "Tomorrow morning at ten o'clock," then hung up. For the rest of the night, Knoop had not slept. It had all come down to this, and he worried. For an instant he had thought to call Bibi with the news. But he decided against raising his expectations in case something went wrong. Bibi had sought this moment for thirty-one years, and he had infused Knoop with the same desire to see Menten brought to justice for the crime of murder. Now, after all that time and the intensity with which both Knoop and Bibi had pursued this case, they had only hours to wait before achieving their goal.

Now, as Knoop turned his Ford off the main road leading out of

Blaricum and left into Vlieweg, his heart started to beat faster. Already, white Volkswagen police Golfs were swarming in the neighborhood. Knoop stationed his Ford in the street at the bottom of Menten's U-shaped driveway, turned off the motor, and watched. Minutes later, the Volkswagens fanned out to cover the streets behind De Horn and to block the front access to Vlieweg.

The policemen in charge of the arrests, Detective Richard Pasterkamp and Comissioner G. G. J. ("Joss") Peters, walked up to the heavy, oaken front door. Peters then lifted and released the iron knocker. Under his jacket he carried a standard-issue 9mm automatic. A few seconds later, the door opened a crack, and Peters took a step backward.

The maid in her uniform and little linen cap smiled at them as if they were milkmen. "Good morning, gentlemen," she said.

Peters cleared his throat. "We've come for Mr. Menten."

The maid looked confused. "Why, they are not here."

Peters glanced back at Pasterkamp, who was standing behind him. "Where did they go?" he asked her.

"To the lakes in Friesland, to sail."

"A little cold for that, isn't it?" Pasterkamp said gruffly, as they rushed inside.

Annoyed by their suggestion that she was lying, the maid snapped, "Well, that's what they *said.*"

In the next few minutes, they searched every closet and beneath every bed in all the twenty-odd rooms of the mansion. There was an unreal feeling about what they saw. Pieter and Meta were indeed not there, but by the looks of the house, they had not left in a hurry, either. There were no signs of panic. Pasterkamp thought too many people had known about the time and day of the arrest. Normally that information was confined to a few officers with a need to know. But now, because of the Prime Minister's press conference and his desire to make the Menten capture a triumph, too many people had been told, and obviously, one of them had tipped off Menten. If it had been left to Peters and him, Pasterkamp thought, there would have been no problem. Surely the situation was now completely out of hand.

Peters was furious. He had to make the telephone call telling Habermehl of their failure. And then Habermehl would tell the

Prime Minister. In other words, Peters, who was near the bottom of the pecking order, would get the blame. If this debacle did not destroy his career, it promised at the least to slow his advancement, and Peters was as ambitious as the next officer. The public was going to want answers, and the Minister of Justice was surely going to point an accusing finger at the police. It was a disaster, Peters thought, as he climbed behind the wheel of the Golf and sped down the driveway. As he turned left into Vlieweg, he saw Knoop's Ford. Catching his eye, he angrily shook his head no.

Minister of Justice van Agt, the man who would be Prime Minister, actually had thought little about the case until Menten's escape threatened to wreck his ambition of being elected Prime Minister. The fate of war criminals had never interested him, except in law as legal precedents. Van Agt was first and foremost a lawyer, and a good one, though as bloodless as a turnip in his approach. He even looked ascetic, with an angular, tall physique and jet black hair that he slicked down at an angle across his brow. In his first meeting with the Dutch press, six years before when he had been tapped by the Prime Minister to represent Justice in the cabinet, he had summarized his plans for the so–called Breda Three, the remaining life–term Nazi war criminals in Dutch jails. For years one liberal group after another in West Germany and Holland had championed their release. After all, they were old men by now, and few people alive in Holland could still remember their specific crimes. Van Agt said if he received a request for clemency the decision of whether or not to release them from prison would be more difficult for him than for his predecessor at the Ministry of Justice. He told the reporter who thought to ask why, "First of all I'm an Aryan, which my predecessor was not, and second . . ." Later he apologized in parliament with an equally awkward turn of phrase. He said, "I used the word 'Aryan' without realizing . . . that it has a loaded meaning for a lot of people."

And now, on this Thursday evening, November 18, 1976, three days after the failed arrest, only a green baize-topped desk separated him from a howling mob in parliament who were demanding to know why Menten had been allowed to flee when the images of the corpses of innocent victims in Podhorodse printed in that week's *Accent* were fresh before everyone's eyes. What made their questions all the more insistent was that they were each playing before a larger audience, and their individual futures depended on their performances, with the general election only a few months away. The debate that night was being televised live before an angry nation. The greater their perceived indignation, the higher their ratings in the polls, they thought.

For the same reasons, the Minister of Justice saw his ambitions crumbling. He denied knowing anything about the plans to arrest Menten, but he had been "extremely shocked when he heard" that Menten had escaped. "This is not related to me personally in any way," he said. When some member asked why he had not seized Menten's passport, van Agt replied, "The Public Ministry told me at the time that there were insufficient grounds for that." He fended off attack after attack, until at one peculiar moment in the exhausting, fourteen-hour marathon debate, he started an oratorical technique known as "stem winding," a big, dramatic, verbal buildup leading, everybody guessed, to a final statement of great moment. He was playing them, some members thought, like fish on a line. He knew something they didn't that he was soon going to spring on them, saving himself, embarrassing them, and winning the admiration of the viewing nation. But the stem winding went on and on. Members began to think that the Minister of Justice had turned to plain old filibustering. By now his performance, not the content of the debate, fascinated them.

At roughly the same time, forty-two Federal policemen and a half-dozen police dogs in twelve cars were converging on the Sanctuary of Maria Toevlucht, a Trappist monastery near Zundert in the south of Holland, less than ten miles from the Belgian border. Set back almost half a mile from the two-lane country road, across a rutted pasture for grazing a herd of Friesian cattle, the monastery gate was shut as usual to shelter the refugees inside—men on the run from the law, misfits, petty thieves, dope addicts, wanderers, and orphans. By tradition, as long as the fugitives remained behind the gate, the police did not harass them. For as long as monks inside remembered, nobody from the outside world had ever violated the prayer paths that spread like veins through a gentle copse of oaks, or invaded the private chambers where monks slept.

263

The police convoy stopped in formation, the headlights of their twelve cars shining accusingly on the gate. One policeman rang the bell, and a monk on "watch" peered through a small window, sleepily asking what they wanted at this unseemly hour. The head monk, in his off-white surplice and black bib, was summoned and answered their questions, but the police did not believe a word he said. Over his protests, all forty-two of them swept across the oval-shaped grass lawn toward the main dormitory, while the head monk sheared off at a run to the left, taking the path to the chapel, where he prayed. The Federal Police sealed off the grounds, then searched everywhere, even the cow barns, silos, and chicken coops. The monks, roused from their beds, stood on an identity parade. Frightened—and that was what disturbed the head monk—the refugees were good men with bad pasts who did not deserve this jackboot treatment. For more than two hours the police searched, as if in frustration and fear of what failure would bring, through the same rooms again and again, until finally they gave up. They had been wrong, and now they had to report their failure.

At the same time Prosecuting Attorney Habermehl was settled in front of his television set, watching the parliamentary debate at home. He realized that the Minister of Justice was suggesting something about an imminent arrest—something with reference to Knoop's badgering interference in police business—when a parliamentary aide in a black swallowtail coat passed the minister a piece of folded notepaper. As Habermehl watched, the minister's face filled with a mixture of humiliation and embarrassment. He even gulped perceptibly. God, he knew he looked like a fool in front of the whole nation. They had *promised* him that Menten was hiding at the monastery! And now that promise of a swift, triumphant conclusion to this Menten affair was as dead as his political fortunes. That was, unless he found Menten before the general election.

Starting the next day, people thought they had sighted Menten in a hundred unlikely places. His capture now became a new national pastime. Captain Reinier Bordewijk, a blond, clean-jawed, green-eyed young officer of the Federal Police, had to check out nearly every lead, no matter how absurd. In all, from the Search

Command Center on the second floor of the Federal Police headquarters at Sarphatistraat #110 near the Amstel Hotel, twenty-five detectives coded and classified 350 "sightings" and tips, from Apeldoorn to Zundert, in the biggest manhunt in Holland's history.

A Dutch underworld figure claimed that he had captured Menten. For only 10,000 guilders (roughly $4,000) he would hand him over. As proof, he would give the police Menten's photograph, his car keys, and his driver's license (Menten did not drive). Former members of the Resistance submitted a hundred theories from secret underground bunkers to disguises. Simon Wiesenthal offered his opinion. As a matter of procedure, Bordewijk put Menten's description on the INTERPOL network. An anonymous caller reported that Menten had crossed the Dutch-Belgian border, where he affixed Belgian license plates to his car before crossing into France. Menten then had abandoned his gray Simca at the Port Neuilly Metro station, taken a train to Le Bourget, and from there flown to Lisbon using the name of DeVerug—within forty-eight hours he was due to transit to Basel, where doctors were standing by to perform plastic surgery. Last and most bothersome for Bordewijk, all the political and police bosses got involved, telling him to look here, look there.

Bordewijk felt that he was a circus high flyer without a net. The circus needed an illusion, and a week or so after the parliamentary debate, the will to find Menten started to run out, as if the nation had discovered that once he was gone, he couldn't embarrass them or, worse, confront them with their past. The political imperative diminished, too, as it does sometimes, in direct proportion to the public's interest. But as a policeman, Bordewijk followed his orders as closely as humanly possible. He had been told in no uncertain terms to find Menten, but in reality, Bordewijk had been asked to create the "illusion" of finding him. He knew that, in a sense, to succeed now meant to fail. But Bordewijk was incapable of a pose, no matter how much his career was in jeopardy. At one point, he decided to pay lip service to the illusion by following orders *slowly*.

From interviews with Menten's household staff, Bordewijk learned where the trail of his escape began. Menten had been tipped off, probably by someone in the Ministry of Justice. But

265

understandably the tipster had been uncertain of the exact day and time of the arrest, because the Federal Police had changed their minds so often. At first, the Mentens had been warned by telephone to expect the arrest late that week, probably on a Friday, because one of the police officers liked to keep his weekends free to work in his tulip garden or watch soccer on TV. Menten had packed five suitcases on the Wednesday and loaded up the silver-gray Simca station wagon, then, with Meta behind the wheel, drove to a motel in Wolfheze, where they had registered in the name of van Heeckeren, presumably with the plan to cross the border the next day.

During the night, Meta and Pieter had again heard from the tipster, who now apologized for making a terrible mistake. The next morning the Mentens again packed the Simca, this time for the road journey back home to De Horn, where they unpacked again. During the next two days, Menten used the time profitably, by paying bills and writing letters. On Saturday night, they had dinner with friends at the Dorrius, a traditional Dutch restaurant in downtown Amsterdam. The next morning, Sunday, the telephone rang again, this time with the tipster giving them the new time of arrest, around ten o'clock Monday, tomorrow morning. Yet again Meta packed the suitcases, while Pieter mixed a cocktail in the upstairs bar. Around six that evening, telling the maid that they were off for a few days of sailing on the Friesian Lakes, they loaded the Simca one last time.

Late in November, a few days after Menten's flight into hiding, Prosecuting Attorney Habermehl issued a report to an anxious public. Its conclusion was notable for its candor: "How Menten was able to escape arrest is up until now completely unexplainable."

With recriminations thickening the air, the question of why Menten had escaped, and not just how, seemed to avoid the public's scrutiny. Of course there were many reasons, but the most immediate was Knoop. Issue Number 47 of *Accent,* with photos of the exhumation in Podhorodse and the witnesses' testimonies, had only opened his campaign to frighten Menten into running. One day before Menten's escape, placards had appeared on the telephone poles of Blaricum with the photograph of Menten in the

SD uniform and the question "Did you know a mass murderer lives in your neighborhood?" On shifts, Menten's antagonists drove past his house, hurling abuse and, sometimes, balloons filled with red paint to simulate blood. For several days a freelance photographer working for *Accent*, Guus de Jong, buzzed De Horn in a low-flying airplane, from which he took aerial photographs. One afternoon the police stopped de Jong in a mechanical "cherry picker" from which he was peering with his cameras into the Mentens' windows.

Like a field general, Bibi directed the campaign by telephone from "headquarters" in Tel Aviv. He knew the enemy well, and he had a more comprehensive notion than Knoop of the forces they could marshal. Of course, he encouraged interviews with the foreign press that were somehow more poignant for being in Israel, a land in which symbols of the Holocaust are ubiquitous. But his real contribution was his optimism. Despite everything that had occurred to frustrate his efforts, Bibi did not know what wasn't possible. He constantly reminded Knoop to question assumptions. Sometimes, too, Bibi dug deep into the well of his journalistic experience. From an older, shoe-leather school of reporting, he knew better the value of ingenuity.

The week after Menten had fled, Knoop called him to explain the terrible news. To his astonishment, Bibi had not seemed in the least bit surprised. There wasn't time for recrimination right now. "Look at it this way," he told Knoop. "His escape confirms his guilt. That works for us. Now, finding him should be simple."

"Finding him?" Knoop thought that was insane. How could two journalists do what INTERPOL and every police agency in Holland were failing to do? Without much enthusiasm, Knoop asked, "How?"

The resources of journalism alone—often reluctantly—had brought Bibi this far. He would return now to that strength. Everyone knew from looking at a masthead, the list of editors and reporters, that newspapers and magazines had extensive networks of correspondents and part-time reporters called stringers spread around the world. "Why not use them?" he asked.

If the thought struck Knoop as unusual, he had few alternatives to offer the old man in Tel Aviv. More to placate him than anything else, he agreed. Earlier, he had negotiated the sale of the original Menten story in *Accent* to *Der Stern,* the highly successful weekly German magazine, which employed a large corps of talented correspondents and stringers. Knoop called *Stern*'s national affairs editor in Munich, who readily agreed to flag his network to stay on the lookout.

Two weeks went by, and again Bibi and Knoop put their heads together in a telephone conference. The police were searching in Ireland, Paraguay, Argentina, and South Africa, the traditional Nazi sanctuaries. But Bibi had ruled out these places from the start. Bibi knew Menten would not abandon a mansion, a fortune in paintings, and stocks and securities—an estate valued at more than $100 million. No, he guessed, Menten was not far away, trying to liquidate his holdings in preparation for an eventual, *permanent* disappearance, probably to South America or Africa, someplace that had no extradition treaties with Holland.

In a gloomy mood that night, Knoop was returning home from what had failed to be a revitalizing sauna, when the mobile telephone in his car alerted him. His secretary at *Accent* said she had tried to reach him for the last couple of hours. She had been worried. He never remained out of contact for more than minutes. "What is it?" he asked.

Stern had called.

Knoop depressed the car accelerator and raced home. As he entered the driveway he could hear the telephone ringing inside the house. Without turning off the motor, he ran to answer it.

Stern's national affairs editor said, "Knoop, I have Menten for you."

Knoop laughed into the telephone. *"What?"*

"One of our stringers found him—in Switzerland."

"Oh, God," Knoop said, suddenly realizing the importance of the information. "Does anybody else know?"

"The three of us, that's all."

"What's his name?"

"Walser—Martin Walser. He lives in Uster, a suburb of Zurich."

"Is he certain?"

"I don't know. You'll have to ask him." He read out Walser's number. "He expects you to call in a half hour." Then he wished Knoop good luck.

The next thirty minutes were among the longest in Knoop's life. Finally, on the appointed minute, he dialed the country and city code for Switzerland and Zurich. Walser answered, and after a few preliminary comments, he said, almost matter-of-factly, "Yes, he's here."

Knoop became suspicious when Walser demanded the promise of 5,000 German Marks (roughly $2,500) before he would say anything more. Knoop asked, "How can I be certain you have the right person?"

"I saw them just an hour or so ago," he said.

"Describe her," Knoop said, knowing that Meta's photograph had not appeared in any publication that he knew of. Without hesitating the twenty-four-year-old Swiss described her in a detail that convinced Knoop that he had seen them. "I'll come there tonight," Knoop said before hanging up. He immediately dialed his secretary to reserve a seat for himself and Guus de Jong, the magazine's photographer, on a Qantas 747 outbound from Schiphol Airport for Sydney with a stop in Zurich.

Knoop certainly did not intend to frighten Menten into a deeper, darker hole than the one he had already found. Nor was he interested in embarrassing the authorities. He needed help, which he sought from Commissioner Joss Peters, who had been helping Bordewijk review the hundreds of "tips" at the search headquarters. When Knoop called him, Peters saw no reason to handle this tip any differently. Even if Knoop had not caused the police no end of trouble already, Peters was suspicious because of Walser's demand for money; the state was already offering 10,000 guilders (roughly $4,000) as a reward. Peters advised Knoop to check it out first. If Menten was where Walser said, the Dutch police would come to Zurich as fast as protocols allowed.

"You're playing with fire," Knoop told Peters. If Menten fled a second time, the public reaction in Holland would be overwhelming. Knoop did not need to remind Peters that the election was now only weeks away.

Peters complained, "We're not journalists, you know."

And that was certainly true. Police sometimes seem awkward

and slow in their reactions, and by comparison, journalists move faster. But journalists do not have the same exacting legal requirements. Peters was upset to see Knoop again with the advantage. If Menten were found by him as a result of a journalist's tip, the police were going to look like bunglers. "It's too good to be true," he told Knoop. "I'll suspend judgment until we meet your journalist," Peters said without enthusiasm, agreeing to send Captain Bordewijk with Knoop to check out his tip.

Less than five hours later, Knoop left the Qantas plane in Zurich, followed by Bordewijk and two other officers of the Dutch Federal Police. Just beyond the barrier at passport control, he saw a younger man in a herringbone suit, Walser, who waved when Knoop held up a copy of *Accent* magazine, as they had arranged beforehand. After they had cleared customs and were waiting at the baggage carousel, Walser wrote on a notepad and handed the paper to Knoop. Written there was the license plate number (63-OR-73) of Menten's Simca. That number, Knoop knew, had certainly not been published. When Knoop showed the paper to Bordewijk, he remarked, "You must have given it to him."

Back in Holland, Commissioner Peters had feverishly contacted the Swiss authorities, explaining why his police were poaching on jealously guarded Swiss territory. The Swiss understood the urgency and agreed to meet Peters's men at the airport. Of course there was to be no question of taking Menten back to Holland. The two countries did not have treaties of extradition for war crimes. The Swiss would handle the arrest. Four plainclothes police were assigned to the job, but that night Uster, the Zurich suburb, had only two detectives on duty. Two other policemen, in charge of directing traffic, were ordered to change their uniforms and meet the posse in civilian clothes. Before they set out for Uster, Bordewijk took an enlargement of a photograph from his briefcase and put it quickly in front of Walser's eyes. "That's it, that's them," he said. Now, Bordewijk assumed a more positive attitude.

Less than an hour later, they were standing at the registration desk of the Hotel Illuster, a second-rate hotel in the undistinguished Uster neighborhood, now dark and silent. The desk clerk eyed the contingent—it is not in the constitution of a Swiss just to volunteer information, yet respect for authority is unquestioned, so the man's momentary confusion was understandable. When they asked, he told them that no one by the name of Pieter N. Menten was registered. The description . . . well, it fit several guests; many elderly people stayed there. Then the clerk thought about the name again. *Minton,* yes. A Minton had registered. Was that the same person? Bordewijk showed him the photograph, and the clerk pulled the card: Herr N. Minton, occupation landlord, nationality Irish, home Leamybrlen, Ireland.

Herr and Frau Minton, the clerk said, were staying in room 703 and were, by now, probably asleep.

The police told Knoop and his photographer to stay downstairs by the elevator. If Menten were indeed in room 703, he would be brought down, and they could record the arrest then with their cameras and in their notepads. Knoop did not like the plan at all. It excluded him. He was not going to see the look on Menten's face, the fear and hatred and, perhaps, the confusion. Knoop wanted more than anything to witness that moment of Menten's downfall. But he was so happy with how things were working out that he did not complain.

Bordewijk, as translator, took the elevator up with the Swiss. They walked quietly down the seventh-floor corridor to the room and briefly, they listened at the door, then knocked softly. One of the Swiss police had thought to ask the clerk for the master room key, which he inserted in the lock, then turned the door handle and pushed. Once inside the room, for an instant they saw nothing. The drapes were drawn tightly across the window and the room was lighted dimly from a light in the bathroom. They heard a confused rustling on the bed, and one of the Swiss policemen threw on the overhead light. There, struggling and disoriented, was an old man trying to remove himself from the bed, while a completely nude younger woman tried to cover herself with the blanket. She yelled, "What are you doing here? Who are you?"

Just then Bordewijk stepped forward and in what he hoped was a soothing voice said, "Take it easy, I'm a Dutch policeman."

"But you have no jurisdiction here."

271

"I know," said Bordewijk, looking to his side. "That's why I have these men with me. They are Swiss police."

By now, the woman was fighting mad. To her husband she yelled, *"Kampfen, Pieter, kampfen, kampfen"* ("Fight, Pieter, fight, fight").

Turning to the man, Bordewijk asked him if he were indeed Pieter N. Menten from Blaricum. The man sat back on the bed, nodding. "We'll have to ask you to get dressed," Bordewijk told him gently, then watched as he pulled on his pants. He wondered what all the fuss was about. This was a flabby old man, a helpless man, unshaven, disoriented, homeless. Then Bordewijk forced himself to remember: this man had murdered people as innocent as he himself seemed just now. The attempt to fill his mind with an image of evil notwithstanding, the sympathy remained. Whatever Menten had done, he was now just a pathetic old man. While Menten packed a small suitcase, Meta covered herself with the blanket. Menten went into the bathroom and came out with medicine bottles, for his diabetes he said.

When the elevator door opened, Menten was blinded by the camera flash, and he tried to shade his eyes, tilting back on his head the woolen knit hat he had bought the summer before in Ireland. When his eyes adjusted, he saw Knoop, who was yelling with all his strength, "Murderer, *Nazi* murderer!"

Menten strained against the grip of the police, and with icy contempt in his voice he replied, "You Jew, you *filthy* little Jew!"

Stung by the ferocity, Bordewijk stepped between the two men, warning them to take it easy. He realized suddenly how misplaced his sympathy toward the old man in the room had been. His body might be old and slow, Bordewijk thought, but his mind was filled with the same hatred he had just aimed at Knoop. This was not a man of ordinary anger, he thought, or ordinary hatred. Without any further delay, the police steered Menten across the hard-packed snow to the Uster precinct station, in which the plan called for Menten to spend the night. Knoop was too shaken to feel elated by the capture. When he finally reached the station, he sat down alone on the steps, and he started to cry. When Bordewijk came out, he said to Knoop, "Congratulations. Now let's get a drink."

Later, as they were celebrating with cans of warm beer in the Hilton Hotel near the airport, Menten asked the guard in the Uster precinct cell if he could use the bathroom. There was nothing odd about the request. The individual cells were not equipped with toilets and sinks. The cells had been designed to hold prisoners for only a few hours, until they were transferred to the main holding center in Zurich. Menten went into the bathroom and closed the door behind him. The guard walked away, and nearly thirty minutes went by before he remembered Menten and returned to the bathroom. When he opened the door, he gasped and went down on a knee. The old man had passed out and was in an extremely distressed state, nearing death. The guard left him to telephone for an ambulance. When he returned to the bathroom and tried to raise Menten up, he saw on the floor an empty medicine bottle that had contained sleeping pills.

As Menten was being wheeled on a stretcher into the emergency room of the Uster hospital, Knoop and Bordewijk were en route home to Amsterdam and a greeting at Schiphol Airport of such enthusiasm that it made Knoop think that he had won the Europa Soccer Cup for Holland. With a word of thanks for Bibi, he accepted the laurels as Holland's hero of the day. Thousands of congratulatory telegrams confirmed his status. While most members of parliament sang his praises, Minister van Agt was embarrassed by the discovery of Menten by a journalist; his hopes for the national election eroded further. The polls reflected the minister's decline, with two-thirds of the nation now firm in their belief that he had done a rotten job. Indeed, the polls showed he should "do the honorable thing" and resign from the cabinet. Almost a fifth of the respondents pledged to switch their votes because of his pathetic showing in the Menten affair.

More than anything now the minister gave the Menten case his undivided attention. Menten (regrettably, thought the minister and the police) had survived a serious suicide attempt—sixty sleeping pills together with alcohol already in his system had nearly killed him. But now the Swiss adamantly refused to extradite Menten. They did not want to set a precedent, although they did not exactly welcome inevitable questions about their refusal during World War II to admit refugee Jews, condemning them to certain deaths in Nazi Germany. Minister van Agt promised that if the Swiss cooperated with him now, he would provide Menten with an "honorable" trial. An agreement was negotiated, but after the deal was set, the Swiss backed out.

The reason was Meta. Through the press, she had nearly convinced the Swiss public that Pieter was persecuted for his wealth by a pack of envious Dutch journalists. She manipulated the Swiss press brilliantly, telling reporters how her twenty-first wedding anniversary to Pieter was that Friday, but sadly, she said, he probably would kill himself before then, such was his anguish. "Pieter is a broken man," she told them. "He has been dealt a tremendous blow, and I wonder if he will survive it. When we left Holland, he pretended that we were going to Ireland on vacation. All the documents connected with the case he left behind, and I, stupid woman that I am, closed the safe in our house without activating the digital lock, so that it has probably been broken into by the authorities by now. When I told Pieter, he said, 'Oh, my God.'"

The safe had indeed been rifled for the incriminating letter to Hitler, which the authorities carefully removed, then delivered into the hands of the palace authorities, eliminating perhaps the largest impediment to Menten's prosecution.

But for that moment, Meta was more interested in describing how they had planned on Ireland that Sunday afternoon, but when they had reached Belgium, Menten had telephoned a lawyer there who told him to stay away. Because Menten was one of the ten richest men in Holland, the Irish Republican Army might try to kidnap him. The two of them had only then chosen Switzerland, she said appealingly, as if it had been picked from a travel brochure. "It is neutral and we have faith in its laws. It was safest to let the storm pass here. Everything went so quickly my husband could not check out if we are in danger of extradition. We just drove down here, but we took precautions in that we didn't tell anybody where we were. We didn't want to burden anyone with that knowledge. We were not hiding though."

Alarmed by this drift and her success beyond all reason with the Swiss public, Knoop telephoned Bibi in Tel Aviv to discuss how to pressure the Swiss to extradite Menten back to Holland. Bibi saw only one rebuttal to Meta's emotional public appeals. If

Knoop's magazine paid for his airplane ticket, he personally would show the Swiss press photographs, read out to them the testimonies of witnesses, and tell his own story. The Swiss newspapers had not covered the Menten affair before this. If they had only Meta's side without sufficient background, the case did have a ring of persecution.

Knoop scheduled a press conference in Zurich on a Tuesday, three days before a special session of the Swiss cabinet was to decide whether to extradite Menten. Bibi landed on the same day, but he directed the taxi driver to the wrong hotel in Zurich, so he arrived late at the Hilton. When he walked into the banquet room that Knoop had rented, Bibi could barely believe his eyes. There, facing a dais, were scores of print and television reporters from several European countries assembled to hear a story that editors now thought was hot. He asked someone to point out Hans Knoop, who walked to the back of the room and embraced Bibi warmly.

The next morning and in the days that followed, Bibi's story filled the front pages of the Swiss press, with not a word from Meta or a rebuttal from Pieter. As Knoop leafed through a stack of publications, he thought how this had changed from a legal problem decided by government officials to a moral dilemma. In the end, he knew they had to win.

Days later, after the Swiss cabinet had announced Menten's fate, Bordewijk landed at the Zurich airport in a Cessna Citation on loan to the police from the Dutch Civil Aviation Authority. A private car took him to the terminal, where his Swiss counterparts were guarding Menten in handcuffs. As Bordewijk led him out Menten hid his face from news cameras with an enlarged photograph of Meta that she had given him to keep in his cell. On the nearly two-hour flight home, his handcuffs off, Menten seemed subdued, neither up nor down, although he confessed to Bordewijk that he looked forward to the trial. He told Bordewijk a joke. "There were two rabbits fleeing from Russia to the West, and one of them called out to the other, 'Why are you running so fast? I can't keep up.' The other said, 'Didn't you hear? They're out to shoot all the elephants here.' 'Yes, but you're not an elephant.' 'No, I'm not, but before I've proven that to them . . .'"

Later that day, the Citation landed at a small airfield in Beek. Dutch police then drove Menten to Amsterdam in a speeding Mercedes flanked by police motorcycles with Golfs in front and rear. Inspector Richard Pasterkamp booked him, reading out the charges, the dates, names, and places.

"Mr. Pasterkamp, I didn't do it," Menten said. "I had nothing to do with these charges. Anyway, I'm not a Dutch citizen."

Pasterkamp laughed. "If you're not Dutch, then you're Polish."

"That's right," Menten said, encouraged.

"If you're Polish, fine. Maybe you'd like us to send you *there* for trial."

CHAPTER XI

∞

"... Maybe ... there was no victory."

IN THE EARLY MORNING of April 4, 1977, Bibi paced his hotel room, alone with the old demons of memory. The drapes were opened to let in the light that filtered up from the street lamps. He did not want to turn on the room light for fear that people might notice, and think that he was afraid. Earlier that sleepless night, he felt like a walk by the peaceful Amsterdam canals, but he did not want the doorman of the hotel, the Jan Luyken, to think that he was "nervous" on the eve of the most celebrated trial in Holland's history.

After dinner, while lying on his bed, he had drifted into sleep only to dream that everybody was dead, and this was his house. Then came the image of his parents in the Lwów apartment. He saw Menten enter the room and say, "Come with me." And Marek told his father, "I'm going with you." Malvina took off her apron, as if to symbolize a vulnerability, a resignation to Fate. . . . A voice in the dream had said, "Why do they do this to the Jews?" And he heard shots, then more and more shots, people moaning in a pit, wives shouting, children crying, and someone saying coolly, "No one will remain alive."

Bibi awoke, sweating. He thought he was going mad. He flipped on the wall switch, not caring what people might think. He asked himself, When will the light come? Placing his hands over his ears, he started to pace the room—anything, he thought, to stop the images and the voices in his head.

Later, he wondered what he would say that morning at the

opening session of the trial. He went to his briefcase for the sheaf of foolscap and read, as if the words confirmed that he was a completely sane man about to testify to a completely *in*sane crime. The official indictment read: "That the suspect in or around the months of July up until September 1941 was a member of a foreign army, of Eberhardt Schoengarth's staff, and that he possibly committed war crimes and/or crimes against humanity. (1) That on July 7, 1941, in Podhorodse, alone or together with other persons, the accused purposefully and with clarity of mind killed approximately 20–30 people, including the Poles Alexander Nowicki, his wife Bronislawa, Albert Stephan. . . . That he killed them by shooting them or crushing their skulls, and possibly by shooting them and then wounding them, had buried them alive, thus killing them. Even if he himself had not committed these executions, he was in any case present, and he made them possible by supplying the opportunity, the means, and the information."

What Bibi would say in court, he decided, was the truth as it had been told to him. He wrote it down, then and there. "This is the man who came to Poland, fascist Poland, and he became rich and entered the highest society. . . . This is the man who murdered the Poles and Jews he had known for seventeen years. . . . This is the man who robbed art treasures from the houses of the friends he had murdered. . . . *This is the man.*"

Later that morning, Bibi walked up the shallow steps and across the Hessian carpet in the Kantongorecht court, a modern building on the edge of Amsterdam, chosen for its enhanced security. The court, a cold, antiseptic room of blond polished wood, bare modern lights, and straight-backed chairs, was dominated in the front, behind the desklike bench set aside for the tribunal's three judges, by a photograph of Queen Juliana, resplendent in an ermine-fringed red robe over a floor-length blue satin dress.

From his seat on the front bench, which he shared with Mara, Bibi acknowledged Knoop with a nod; in the back of the room with the other reporters, Knoop seemed for the moment to enjoy the status of "star," a role he sometimes wore awkwardly but always with enthusiasm. Bibi had seen how Knoop had changed in the year since Henrietta had telephoned him. By now Knoop thought of himself as more pivotal in the prosecution of Menten than anyone else, including Bibi and Henrietta, who was covering the trial for *Ha'aretz*. Henrietta seemed to be everywhere in the courtroom at once, asking questions and taking notes of conversations; she was reluctant to admit her role in Menten's discovery and arrest. The policeman, Inspector Pasterkamp, to one side of the room, was thinking how trials can sometimes turn out to be circuses.

Sudden quiet in the back of the room signaled the arrival of Lodewijk van Heijningen, a persistent civil lawyer of spare distinction who had been chosen to defend Menten when nobody had volunteered. Tall, angular, and bony, with a lantern jaw, a ready smile, and an easy laugh, he arranged his materials from his briefcase on the desk set aside for the defense. Looking up, he noticed Bibi and forced a smile, exposing teeth that smoking had stained yellow. Van Heijningen believed in his client's innocence, and there was every reason in his mind to hope for an acquittal. The case of the prosecution was not strong, and besides, he had a surprise or two up his sleeve.

Once he had organized his agenda, he went over to Franz Habermehl, the prosecuting attorney, white-haired and movie-star handsome, in his early sixties. With a trump card or two of his own, Habermehl felt confident in his case. He had even debated with himself what to demand for a prison sentence. Generally, he thought it was more humane to shoot a man than to keep him in prison for more than, say, thirty years. His black-and-white views on capital punishment, however, were out of step with modern Dutch law, which abolished the death penalty. Habermehl supposed that since capital punishment had been law in Holland when Menten committed his crimes, hanging could be reinstated, but that would come later. First he had to get the conviction.

Suddenly, the door beside the tribunal's bench admitted a duo of uniformed, sober-looking police. Journalists and spectators lowered their voices in anticipation, then quieted down altogether when Menten came through the door. He wore a dark-gray, pinstriped double-breasted suit, a silk shirt, a new necktie, and shined shoes. Despite his seventy-eight years, there was a spring in his step, as if he were indeed anxious to prove an innocence in which he truly believed. He had lost weight since his arrest and extradition, and he looked younger. His shaved cheeks were ruddy from a lamp tan, and he smiled all around with flashing blue eyes, as the male nurse, who had accompanied him from the maximum security prison in Scheveningen, where he had been transferred from Amsterdam to await trial, showed him to his seat beside van Heijningen. An instant later, aware of his status in the room, he was again on his feet. Spying Meta, he blew her three kisses off his hand. He turned completely around, and one by one looked into the faces of those present. For a time it seemed as if he were searching for one face in particular. Indeed, when his eyes lowered on Bibi and Mara, his expression changed, distorting and spreading anger through the room like a foul odor. Bibi thought his face contained the hatred of a thousand people. The blue of his eyes had intensified with that anger, Bibi told himself. Menten stared at him, and then a smile crossed his face, and he whispered something to his lawyer.

Mara tugged at Bibi's jacket sleeve. "Look!" she said. "Look there—the murderer!"

Bibi said, "He knows. He knows, Mara, who we are."

"Of course he knows."

"He's asking himself, 'How can it be that these two people are still alive?'" Mara started to say something and Bibi hushed her. He thought his heart would stop. He knew Menten wished that he would die right there in his seat. He said to himself, So this was our friend. Bibi was reminded of another trial, the one in Jerusalem that he had covered for *Ha'aretz* in which the defendant had sat inside a glass booth, isolated from humanity like a contagion, and he thought of a difference. That war criminal had not killed with his own hand as Menten had done. That one by comparison had been resigned to his fate.

Bibi's thoughts were interrupted by the arrival of the three judges in white jabots and flowing black gowns. Versed in the peculiarities of laws and procedures pertaining to the trial of war criminals, they called the court to order and read out the charges. The defendant, like a fighter at the sound of the bell, rose from his chair and, ignoring decorum and the rules of the court, started his defense with a harangue.

"I'm afraid the judges won't be able to judge me objectively," he said. "I have no faith in the prosecution, the police, and certainly the witnesses because behind the whole trial stands the KGB of the Soviets—the whole trial is nothing more than a theater, a circus of the KGB."

By his side, van Heijningen shook his head, as if to say, Don't believe what he says, Your Honors; he'll cooperate, just you wait and see. Not for the last time, van Heijningen reminded himself that this was an old man fighting for his life. He hoped the court would consider the evidence, not what his client said in constant outbursts that could only prejudice the court. Van Heijningen remarked again and again, "What my client said, he said without my consent. I never heard such a thing before."

Fittingly, Bibi was the first witness to take the stand. His testimony was devastating. "As a boy, he was our image of the civilized West," he told the court, repeating the story that by now he had rehearsed, written, and rewritten scores of times since the day he had met Jacob Leubel. But now, *this* repetition of the story was not over cups of coffee with Henrietta Boas, or in the office of Schocken or Finkelstein. Almost unbelievably, he thought, this was for real—this was the moment he had dreamed of, that in a sense he had dedicated his life to, and yet, as he stood on the witness stand, he thought, This was also the most tragic moment of his whole life. To stand here, so close to Menten, to answer these questions—this was no victory. Maybe . . . there was no victory. The night before, especially, he had wanted vengeance, but now, in this setting, before Pieter Menten, after all these years, things just seemed to change, and he was afraid of losing control. He had not realized before this moment that Menten had been his connection with his dead family. In a sense, Menten had kept them alive, because as long as Menten was free, Bibi had not forgotten, and now, that strange, twisted, blackened connection was being severed, and Bibi felt as if he were falling through the air. He stumbled over his words, apologizing to the court. He looked uncomfortable in the tweed jacket and the new necktie, and at times during questioning, he seemed confused, as if this setting had somehow shifted his narrative. The ad-libbed badgering of the defense did nothing to help. Bibi was telling the tribunal how the lawsuits against his Uncle Isaac were "the real reason for the vengeance." He claimed to have had once in his possession letters supporting the assumption that Menten had wanted to kill all the Pistiners, starting with Isaac, because of the land dispute.

"You lost those important testimonies?" van Heijningen asked. "Come, come now. Nobody will believe that certainly."

Menten rose from his chair. "I have *never* seen this man . . . I didn't hang around with his sort . . . besides, what would I have been doing, a grown man, with a boy of sixteen?"

Bibi turned a quarter turn, as if struck. "Of course you knew me," he said with indignation.

"Lies! All lies!" Menten shouted, then described a region of Poland that his lawyer, in his defense summation, would claim Menten had never visited. "Jews could not be murdered where there were no Jews," Menten said. "In Podhorodse . . . there were no Jews. They wouldn't dare live there. They lived in larger towns, like Cracow or Warsaw. In those villages there were hardly any shops. The people couldn't afford to buy anything there. People in the countryside often had to buy things from me. Being the industrialist and businessman I was, I often supplied the people with foodstuffs. The Ukrainians would never want to buy from a Jew, anyway. You have to be able to prove these people ever lived, that they aren't just made up. The Russians murdered everybody in that area, and the Mongolians [*sic*] moved in after the original population was murdered."

As if dumbstruck, the court watched and listened without interfering. How this man distorted the truth, Bibi thought: He wasn't there, he wasn't a Nazi, he didn't know these people. . . .

"All lies," Menten continued, waving what he said were the verdicts of the Polish courts from the civil trials against Isaac Pistiner, dating to the 1930s. "Read them yourself, Mr. President. I won those lawsuits even on appeal to the highest court."

At this point, the president of the court, Judge Johannes Schroeder, said, "I don't read Polish, Mr. Menten, do you?"

That flustered Menten, who had denied working for Schoengarth as a translator. To change the subject, he returned to the village. "What would I have to do there?" he asked. "Those people were of a very low cultural level. If you saw the houses of those people, it was a pigsty, a couple of chairs and a table, that was all. I didn't go around with that kind of people."

"But if you had never been to Podhorodse, how could you have known these people?" asked Judge Schroeder.

Flustered once more, Menten replied, "You are confusing me, Mr. President."

"And you, Mr. Menten, are telling fibs."

Menten slumped into his chair, then watched Meta leave the courtroom for a cigarette, and turned to hear his lawyer, who was saying, "The witness [Bibi Krumholz] has all his information from hearsay. He wasn't even there in the years between 1940 and 1941. These are all lies from people who want to take revenge because my client won all the lawsuits against Pistiner."

Meta returned to the courtroom, and, sensing her husband's need for support, she took a seat in the first row, then, as she would do throughout the forty-six court sessions of the trial, she handed him a note. *"Courage, mon cher,"* she wrote him at one point. "I wish you courage and I hope you wish it to me, too."

Against the prosecution, the defendant alleged that the charges and evidence were "precooked KGB material," a case of "mistaken identity," and an instance of *ne bis in idem* (that no one can be tried twice for the same crimes). Menten had created his own strategy, which he forced his lawyer, whom he bullied without relief, to execute. Ultimately, he hoped to exhaust Habermehl's resolve and then find a route to freedom. At the start, he charged that, historically, only soldiers in the Wehrmacht could have been near Podhorodse on the day of the massacre, as battles were being waged all around. Military and supply vehicles choked the roads. The SS could not possibly have gone through.

Hans van der Leeuw, the researcher from the Rijks Institute for War Documentation who had helped Henrietta Boas, presented the Nazi Order of Battle from archives in Berlin, proving that Menten, as part of an SS *Einsatzgruppe,* could easily have driven to Podhorodse on that day. Van der Leeuw wondered as he listened to Menten's lawyer on cross-examination, why, according to Menten, *every* document was a forgery, *every* witness a liar, *every* judge on the payroll of the KGB. If he admitted to only certain

283

facts, van der Leeuw thought, denied others, agreed with some evidence, rejected some other, his defense might have succeeded to throw the prosecution off balance.

Soon after, Mara was called to the stand. She, too, made a strong impression on the court with the facts as she knew them directly: her father "was an industrialist and a landowner who was highly respected," and "Menten visited us often, due to the business relations between the two men." She continued, "We considered him a gentleman. We hunted together, danced, and walked together in the areas of Urych and Podhorodse. Before they got into a fight over business, one could even call it a friendship. Menten's wife at the time stayed at our house."

"Nonsense," Menten railed. "I don't know this woman!"

She gave him an icy stare, then as the court listened, she recounted stories of a child thrown from a window, of three young men shot in a cemetery, and the death of an old man in a ghetto, and the lives of another family snuffed out on the edge of an execution pit. As she recited these stories, her voice bore no emotion, as if she were too exhausted to convey anything more than the unvarnished facts.

On the second day of the trial, when the defense tried to prevent Knoop from covering the trial on the grounds that he was scheduled to appear later as a witness, Judge Schroeder changed the order of the witnesses' appearances, putting Knoop first. Knoop, wearing a yarmulke—an ornament so obvious for its symbolism, that no matter what its personal meaning it seemed overdone— answered defense questions that had little to do with anything. "Did you punch witnesses when you showed them the photographs of Menten?" "Is everything you wrote . . . the truth and nothing but the truth?" "Did you discuss kidnapping Menten to Israel?" Knoop called the questions "insinuating."

On that day, too, three old women in black, sisters, appeared from Poland.

"Yes," said Carolina Selner Tuzimek, who had watched Menten from the garden of Pistiner's house that day. "That is Pieter Menten."

"Yes," said Paulina Selner Tyczynska, the sister who had seen Menten at the executions. "That is Pieter Menten."

"Yes," said Sabina Selner Jaworska, who had covered her eyes soon after the first shots were fired. "That is Pieter Menten."

Menten yelled, "This is a sham trial. This is false justice. All the questions are prearranged. How is it possible for people to remember everything so exactly after thirty-six years?"

"Mr. Menten," President Schroeder said, and all the courtroom listened, "a mass execution is *not* something that most people tend to forget."

On the third day, a surprise witness appeared for the prosecution. A simple lampshade maker from Arnsberg, West Germany, Hans Geisler had read about the trial in his local newspaper. It was his duty, he told the court, to clear up a misunderstanding. Menten testified that he had never been a member of Schoengarth's *Einsatzgruppe*. But Geisler had been a member, and he knew. He even brought along a couple of interesting old photographs. One showed a group of military officers surrounding one civilian, like students around a teacher in a graduation pose. At the time, before he sent the photograph home to his parents, Geisler had written on the back, "The man with the glass in his hand, that's me, because war makes one thirsty." The civilian, he had written, was "van Menten, a Dutchman who has a great deal of possessions."

"Yes, that is Menten sitting there," he said.

"That's *not* me," Menten said, examining the photograph through a loupe.

Ignoring him, Geisler said, "I had a lot of contact with him. I used to sit next to him at the table. One day I went for a drive with him and a few others to see his possessions around Lwów. In those days, executions of Jews were beginning on the edge of Lwów, near the electricity plant. No, I am not aware of the Professor Murders [of the Ostrowskis, Greks, and others on the night of July 3, 1941], but Menten did seem enthusiastic about the executions. He said to the ambitious Holz Apfel, who killed a lot of Jews, that he [Apfel] deserved the Iron Cross."

"If I said that, I meant it ironically," Menten said.

Timidly, Geisler replied, "Yes, maybe you meant it ironically." He turned to the judge, "But he considered Holz Apfel a hero. He also had a friend from the *Einsatzgruppen* named Kipka. Kipka was a bad person. He had a girlfriend who played the piano. When he didn't like it any longer he shot the piano to pieces."

Soon after, Menten asked permission of the court to visit Podhorodse and himself question the villagers. "The people there won't say anything bad about me," he said.

Prosecutor Habermehl took the opening, saying, "That would be rather difficult because the village was nearly completely slaughtered, as *you* know."

When the trial resumed after a summer break, the defense tried to prove that the damning photograph of Menten in SD uniform was a forgery. Van Heijningen called Dr. Maria Sickesz, a physician specializing in something she called "manual therapy," who was very precise when she said, "That man in the SS [*sic*] uniform could never have been Pieter Menten. The witch hunt must end!" She pointed to enormous blowup photographs of Menten in the SD uniform and then to a recent photograph. She had measured the noses in the two photographs, she said, and found a remarkable difference. "The nose does not change in a lifetime," she said, "even when a person drinks a great deal." Then she shot a pointer at the Menten-in-uniform photograph. "Look at that cap," she said. "It's slightly askew, completely out of keeping with the German sense of strict discipline."

Van Heijningen, who by now was well out of his depth, boasted that "the false document stunt has really backfired on them with these pictures." But nothing had backfired, and the whole issue of forgery was put to rest when the prosecution heard from the nun who had attended the physician those many years ago in the reshaping of Menten's nose. Anyway, another physician told the tribunal, certain features do indeed change, even when they are not altered by surgery. There were "very strong indications" that the man in the SD uniform was Pieter Menten.

Now, the proceeding started to resemble a sideshow. But Prosecutor Habermehl did not seem to mind. No matter what the defense proposed, he had his trump, which he played near the end. He had discovered this "card" quite by accident during his preparation for the trial when he had requested the Interior and Foreign ministries to search their archives for Menten's passports from the thirties and forties. After a period of time without a reply, he had called the Foreign Ministry in The Hague, and he had eventually been passed on to a young woman who apologized for not being able to help him. "We don't have the passports—at least I haven't found any yet," she had reported, then paused. "But you know we still have those old documents here."

"What documents?"

"Ones from Poland. They're *very* old."

Soon after, Habermehl had returned from The Hague with what from then on were called the Cellar Documents, a series of letters signed "Pieter N. Menten" and written in longhand to Reichsführer-SS Heinrich Himmler, among other Nazi supremos, begging their indulgence and generally boasting of supporting Nazism while a member of Schoengarth's zbV *Einsatzgruppe*. Habermehl knew these were not forged. They had been discovered in the cellar of the Dutch Consulate in Cracow after the war and sent to the Dutch Foreign Ministry, where they had remained ever since. Handwriting experts had substantiated Menten's authorship.

On the last day of the trial, Habermehl referred repeatedly to the Cellar Documents. "It's hard to believe," he told the court, "that anyone would have forged this incriminating correspondence, which showed how Menten could not have been where he said on the day of the massacre in Podhorodse." On June 26, 1941, when Menten alleged he was in a Polish resort town many, many miles from the village, he wrote, "I take this chance to tell you that in the coming days I will leave for the already occupied territories as a *Sonderführer* together with the people from Sipo [Sicherheitspolizei]. My task will take ten to twenty-four days. Since these activities will take me to the area of my estate, I request that you permit me to immediately appoint a Ukrainian [overseer on] my property, a Ukrainian who has a reputation for competence."

Habermehl then summarized the testimonies. "What do all these statements boil down to?" he asked. "In broad lines, on July 7, 1941, a date everyone has remembered since it was the holiday of John the Baptist, around twelve in the afternoon there arrived in the village of Podhorodse a car with a number of military officers in German uniform. Orders were given to the Ukrainian militia, led by Philip Müller, to bring the Jews to the house of the

287

Pistiner family. The witnesses made it absolutely certain that Menten was present there. They knew him as 'The Landlord of Sopot' and 'The Dutchman.' Some of them had worked for him. As for what happened after that, there is no consensus of opinion, no unanimity. . . . A minority of witnesses state that Menten did the shooting. What clearly has been proven is that Menten . . . had a leading role at the execution. . . . I say a 'leading role' and not an 'executive role,' Mr. President. His intention was to kill the victims and he took part in the execution of that intention, working closely with fellow criminals. . . ."

Since Menten was insisting that the Soviets had framed him, Prosecutor Habermehl asked, "Has a gigantic conspiracy been fabricated to ruin an innocent man—or, did Menten indeed commit the monstrous crimes for which he is now standing trial?" He paused for dramatic effect, then asked, "Mr. President, what could possibly have caused Lieber Krumholz, Mara Pistiner-Cygelstreich, and others to have made false statements and confirm these statements under oath?" For the life of him, he said, he could find no reason why. "We are dealing with a man for whom money played a dominating role during his whole life, a man who was also unafraid of tricky maneuvers. That attitude can explain that when he saw everything taken away . . . he mercilessly began hunting anyone who had been responsible for that. When he felt the need of the Germans' help, he was not even reluctant to commit mass murder to achieve his goal. . . ." Finally, Habermehl asked for a life sentence, adding, though, that the "atrocities committed by him deserved the death penalty."

Aware of the defendant's daring, Habermehl expected surprises—and he was not to be disappointed. He had reasonably expected to hear the name Joseph Stieglitz called again in Menten's defense, but Stieglitz wanted nothing to do with Menten this time around. He said in Tel Aviv that he had not known of Menten's crimes of murder. If he had known in the late 1940s, he would not have testified on his behalf, despite the debt he owed Menten for saving his life.

The rejection had not seemed to upset Menten. He had a more reliable defensive weapon, which he had instructed his attorney to wait for the last moment to introduce. Van Heijningen said in his summation that the Federal Police, whom he called "creatures of a fairy tale," had made a mockery of the criminal investigation. Hans Knoop and Bibi "just wanted fame and money and for that reason and just for the sake of publicity and sensation have stigmatized Pieter Menten, making him a war criminal without any evidence." The witnesses "after thirty-six years could not possibly remember every event or detail and thus the witnesses must be considered unreliable." There was no reason for Menten to have participated in the massacres and killings because "there was no reason for revenge" since Menten had been successful in his legal proceedings against Isaac Pistiner. Indeed, "There is more reason now for the Pistiner clan to be resentful." Not only that, but his client could not have been in Podhorodse that day. "These massacres could well be done by normal Wehrmacht commandos." The USSR had accused Menten "to distract the attention from itself of crimes in that area." The Cellar Documents had originated with the notorious Polish "Falsification Council," and no matter what the experts said, they were indeed forgeries.

Now, the main points dealt with, Menten pulled his trump. Certainly, his case was lost in this court, this "Shakespearean drama," as he called it. A court could not convict "on the basis of hate and slander campaigns, on the grounds of surmises and mass blindness," van Heijningen said. In his words, his client "was already guilty before he was tried in the eyes of many." Therefore, he set up an appeal: Menten claimed that the Minister of Justice between 1951 and 1953, Leen Donker, had offered him immunity from prosecution for the war crime of murder—the crime he was now being tried for—in return for his silence. He knew too much that threatened to compromise Prince Bernhard and therefore the monarchy. If he were ever tried for murder, Menten said that he had warned Donker, he would make public the letter to Hitler. Van Heijningen told the court, "I want an investigation into the matter because there still must be a lot of notes, made by civil servants in charge of the case then, that may clarify the situation. . . ."

The court ignored the request and soon after regretted the oversight.

For now, on December 14, 1977, the tribunal declared, ". . . we find you guilty of the crimes committed in Podhorodse." The sentence, in consideration of Menten's advanced age, was reduced considerably from what Habermehl had demanded. Menten received fifteen years in jail.

When Knoop asked what he felt about the sentence, Bibi repeated what he had said to Schiff many years ago, that he wanted justice, not vengeance. He felt neither jubilant nor smug, but satisfied that Holland had recognized the existence of a murderer in its midst. Menten was soon going to be in prison. The length of time did not matter. It was enough. Menten's life would end in jail—that was enough.

However, the sentence enraged one particular man who became his own court of law.

It happened one night soon after the conclusion of the trial, while Meta Menten was entertaining—a rare occasion at that time. All but a few former friends had abandoned her, but she had her family, particularly a brother, who was dining with her that evening. They were eating dinner and she, drinking a bit too much these days, had begun to recite again the litany of her woes, as if by repetition they could be worn away.

Since the trial, she had been treated by her Dutch countrymen with shameful prejudice. Innocent of any crime, disbelieving the charges for what they necessarily said about her own judgment as a woman, Meta bore the brunt of Dutch anger as the available, and mostly helpless, symbol of her husband's crimes. It was not a proud moment when on Liberation Day, whole parades of cars filled with holiday gawkers had passed the house, hurling obscenities at De Horn. Or when they had painted swastikas on the rock wall, or had written "Gestapo" and "SS," or smashed the windows with rocks and thrown poisoned waterfowl and rancid garbage in the swimming pool, or threatened by letter and telephone to do her physical harm. The abuse had been incessant. If only she were not so loyal to him—she drove once a week on visitors' day to The Hague just to be with him in prison—Meta would have fled *anywhere*. She planned to stay until he died or was freed; and in the meantime, she truly lived in fear. More than once—*eighty* times, Meta estimated—she had asked the Prosecuting Attorney's office and the police to provide her some small measure of protection, but they had shrugged. So she had fended for herself.

At first only her unconscious registered the thought of an acrid, unfamiliar smell at the dinner table that night, and then she thought, Fire! She threw back the chair and started upstairs, but she had gone no more than halfway, when the choking smoke turned her around. Back downstairs, she telephoned the fire brigade and yelled for her brother to help her salvage some of the paintings on the walls. She had wanted to reach the attic. It had been so stupid to put Raphael's "Portrait of a Young Man" there, she thought. And now, unless a miracle happened, the only picture that Pieter had been adamant against selling at the auction, perhaps the only object of art for which he had ever *felt* anything, was lost. Without the painting and without the house, she feared, Pieter would lose the will to live, and for that she would feel like his executioner.

The orange glow of flames reflected on the faces of hundreds of people who had come to watch, like pagans at a ritualistic cleansing. Word had spread faster than the flames, and soon the police had enough to do just to control the crowds. The fire had been started when a man who now melted into the crowd of gawkers threw a Molotov cocktail on De Horn's thatch roof. The firebomb wick had touched the tinder-dry twigs and straw and then fell, without exploding, to the ground. As the fire licked and spread, rising from the roof in a ragged orange column, the arsonist stared at the flames in slack-jawed wonder.

The trucks of the Blaricum Volunteer Fire Department arrived first. Hoses thrown into the swimming pool sucked out nearly 53,000 gallons of water between 10:30 and 12:30, while the fire was brought under control. Despite their efforts, the cinders flew from one dry thatch to another, always ahead of the hoses. The roof soon caved in, as the flames ate through the heavy wooden beams. By the end, the house was gutted. The walls that remained were charred black. Meta had watched the fire from across the street in the coach house. She had thought, angrily, how the authorities had left her alone, and this was what had happened. Fi-

291

nally they had got what they wanted—not just one sad lunatic, but all the persecutors of her husband everywhere.

Five months later, the whole affair had receded into the folds of memory—even Meta by now was enjoying a modicum of normalcy—when the Supreme Court in The Hague, deliberating the appeal, did an inconceivable thing: it declared a mistrial. Indeed, the court said, the Amsterdam judges had failed to consider the "expectations" of the defendant based on the alleged promise of immunity for murder granted back in the early 1950s. To settle the question it ordered a new court to decide whether the immunity was real.

How a new court could decide the question, the Supreme Court did not say. The former Minister of Justice, Leen Donker, was dead. However, a new tribunal did what it could to form an opinion, first by hearing from the widow of Menten's attorney from that period, Kortenhorst. Mrs. Kortenhorst testified that Donker, while still the Minister of Justice, had promised immunity to Menten. Donker's wife, Georgina, on the other hand, remembered nothing of the sort. "Leen was not that kind of man," she said. "He waited for the moment when he could deal harshly with Menten. He wanted it to rest for a bit. He knew more things would surface. But I know this, my husband could have drunk Menten's blood he hated him so much."

"Why then didn't he persist in the Menten case?" Georgina Donker was asked by the court.

"He wanted political calm in the country. His motto was, 'If you want to find something you have to look slowly and thoroughly.'"

"Wouldn't he have made a deal?"

"Leen wasn't that kind of man."

"He wasn't willing to throw out the case for the good of the country?"

"He said that justice did not make distinctions between friend or foe."

"Did your husband send Menten a letter confirming his decision to drop the case in return for silence?"

"I have serious doubts."

"Then you probably know if he had doubts about Prince Bernhard's role before and during the war?"

"Yes, that was one of his greatest worries."

No written proof existed, but Mrs. Kortenhorst's statements under oath "made up for that." The Justice Ministry, she said, in 1952 had built a case against Menten for murder with the testimonies from the witnesses in Tel Aviv, including Bibi and Mara. The evidence had pointed to a cut-and-dried case, but Donker had said no to a murder trial because he feared Menten.

When he heard the verdict of The Hague Court, Prosecutor Habermehl thought he had misunderstood. None of it made any sense to him, except for one thing. Unless he sorted it out fast, Menten was going to go free, and by now Habermehl had too great an investment in the case to allow that to happen. He said, "There was no trial [against Menten in 1952] . . . in which a person named Menten was accused of committing war crimes or crimes against humanity. There was no suspect Menten and thus no possibility of a deal."

Van Heijningen, delighted by the mistrial, wanted to make certain that no one misunderstood. "If people had said in 1952, 'We throw out the case, but we'll reconvene it twenty-five years from now,' then my client would have insisted on a preliminary legal investigation, because at that time he was still able to reach people in Poland. In the meantime, evidence has been destroyed or lost and witnesses have died."

The effect was a stalemate—nobody could answer what was unanswerable, nobody could revive the dead, nobody could prove anything, either way. The Hague Court ruled that there had been a violation of the European Treaty on Human Rights, that prosecution should have led to a verdict within a reasonable period of time. In so many words, the state had shown an inhuman side by prosecuting Menten after such a long period in which, because of the supposed deal with Donker, he was immune from further prosecution, especially for murder. Therefore, the court in 1977 had no right to try Menten.

Released from maximum security prison after ten days less than one year, on December 4, 1978, Menten was a free man.

293

★ ★ ★

"Free?" Bibi said when Knoop called. Bibi did not understand what Knoop was saying. Because of a loophole in the law, Menten, convicted of crimes against humanity, had rejoined society? The victory in Amsterdam had compensated for all the disappointments, Bibi had thought. But now, this was an insult. "What loophole?" he asked. Knoop tried to explain. "A long time ago when you and Mara and the others went to the District Court in Tel Aviv to testify. . . ."

"Yes, and in Holland they did nothing."

"The Minister of Justice, Donker, prepared a case then against Menten for the murders, but he didn't do anything about it. Menten blackmailed people with information. . . ."

"What information?"

"I don't know, but it involved important people here, and Donker made a deal. If Menten kept quiet about what he knew, Donker promised never to prosecute him for these war crimes."

Bibi remembered. He, Mara, and Schiff had told what they knew in the Tel Aviv District Court. Then their evidence had fallen into a void. Knoop was saying that the Dutch had actually planned to prosecute. "Why didn't they?" he asked.

"Like I said, only Minister Donker knew that, plus Menten and probably a few others. The blackmail presumably frightened Donker, though, into a deal."

And now, Bibi thought, all his efforts had finally come to nothing. He expected some emotional reaction—anger, outrage, *something,* but instead he felt nothing.

In the year since the Amsterdam trial Bibi had changed. He had succeeded in large measure in finally putting Menten behind him. After more than half his life the obsession had ended, and he had started to forget all about it. What had worried and briefly angered him was the realization of how Menten had dominated his thoughts, if not his actions entirely, for those many years. Angered, because Menten had filled up such a large space and demanded so much from him, he had the feeling that if Menten had not been there, his life would have been much happier and somehow fuller. Menten had come to represent the Holocaust, and

294

now, so many years later, now that he had hunted his personal villain of the Holocaust, Bibi wanted to start life anew.

Besides, what did this new development matter? Menten had been judged and found guilty of murder. Justice had prevailed. Trickery did not change the verdict of guilty. In that sense, Bibi did not care. Anyway, he asked, what could they do?

They would have to wait and see, Knoop told him. Prosecutor Habermehl had appealed to the Supreme Court, which now would either validate or overturn The Hague Court's decision to release Menten and prevent his retrial. But were some of the same "influences" in Holland still afraid of Menten, just as they had been afraid since 1952, when Donker had allegedly made the deal? Would they again try to influence the court? Or had they already?

They waited more than five months, until May 22, 1979.

When the Supreme Court was about to announce its decision, Knoop and Bibi expected the worst, an upholding of The Hague Court decision, and that would be that, unless they wanted to appeal to the European Court in Strasbourg. After he learned what the Supreme Court decided, Knoop called Bibi with the news. "We're back in business," he said triumphantly.

"Where?" Bibi asked.

"This time it's Rotterdam."

Knoop explained that the Supreme Court had "annulled" The Hague Court's reversal verdict. It did not see how the court could have made its decision on the basis of the evidence presented, the testimony of Mrs. Kortenhorst. Just because Menten held the *opinion* that Donker had given him immunity should not have prevented the prosecutor, as The Hague Court had said, from reopening Menten's case twenty-four years later.

"What about Menten now?" Bibi asked.

"He will go back to prison until there is a new verdict."

"And witnesses?" Bibi supposed that the new trial in the Special Court for War Crimes in Rotterdam would rely on transcripts of statements sworn at the trial in Amsterdam. It did not make sense for the witnesses from Poland, the Soviet Union, the United States, Sweden, Israel, West Germany, and France to come again

295

to Holland, just to repeat the same words that they had spoken in Amsterdam.

"Some will be called, some won't," Knoop said. "You definitely will."

In that summer of 1979, many of the old witnesses were indeed called again, as the second full trial of Pieter Menten convened. The prosecution had wanted to eliminate the witnesses by relying on their Amsterdam testimonies, but Menten had called 120 defense witnesses, from the Prime Minister of Holland to Soviet dissidents living in the United States, ex-SS officers, war historians from West Germany and Holland, members of parliament, lawyers, and journalists. At Menten's insistence, the state interviewed 500 elderly inhabitants of Podhorodse.

Before the trial started, Menten refused the help of an attorney. Alone, he set out to prove a case of mistaken identity. His brother, Dirk, had murdered those people, he claimed when the trial began. "We knew about this for a long time," he told the court. "People finally convinced me to reveal the truth [about his brother, Dirk], and besides it seems to be the only way out now. . . . Now the truth of the matter will have to be brought forward violently."

Soon after, Dirk Menten counterattacked by declaring his intention to clear his name by destroying his brother, once and for all. He had the means, he implied by his willingness to appear, and now he had no other choice. Dutifully the prosecutor added his name, beside that of his French-born wife, Nina Hélène Hobe-Menten, to the list of witnesses. Pieter had hoped by his ploy for an acquittal and, later, for the court to demand Dirk's extradition from France, where he lived north of Cannes. But when Dirk agreed so readily to appear in court, Pieter's tactic collapsed.

Now, with few remaining offensive resources, Menten became incoherent in court and seemingly mad. Strangely, he could not seem to carry on a sensible conversation, or follow an argument, or understand the meaning of witnesses' statements. He refused to answer questions. He appeared listless, and he jumped at sudden sounds and movement in the courtroom. This unusual behavior continued for several days, worrying the court, until finally, a motion was filed to suspend the trial. The court had no choice but to agree so that Menten, at some later date, could not use their refusal as a basis for an appeal. The judges asked the psychiatrists in the Pieter Baan Clinic in Utrecht to examine Menten for three weeks to determine if he was indeed mentally fit to continue.

The clinic director, Dr. F. H. L. Beyart, felt competent to determine a man's relative sanity but not his fitness to stand trial—that was a legal opinion, he believed. But he realized what was happening. The court wanted to shirk its responsibility by ordering the psychiatric profession to make its decision for them. This was more than unfair, thought Beyart, it was dangerous. Only the year before he had examined a suspected war criminal, a man who had appeared at the clinic completely normal, with a healthy psychiatric history. Psychiatrists probed, forcing the man to explore a past in which murder had been a central component. The man became psychotic, and Dr. Beyart nervously wondered why. Then he realized, the clinic had *forced* the man to recognize a past that he had repressed totally for more than thirty years. Dr. Beyart had stopped the examination. In the pursuit of justice the law did not have the right to condemn a suspect to a life term of mental illness. Had that same pattern occurred in Menten? he asked.

After a few days, Dr. Beyart recognized yet another ethical dilemma in what the court was asking him to do. An old man with slight deterioration, Menten suffered from diabetes and arteriosclerosis, all natural processes of aging. Otherwise, Beyart thought, he was fit to stand trial. But, Beyart wanted to know, if a person is eighty years old and incompetent to stand trial, is he incompetent because he is eighty? Therefore, *all* people eighty years of age are incompetent and should not stand trial? Wasn't that a precedent for the courts, not the medical profession, to decide? And so Beyart alone dissented among the three voting psychiatrists, who agreed that because Menten was "mentally and physically a wreck," he should not be made to continue with the trial. On their advice, the Rotterdam court suspended the proceedings indefinitely, until Menten's health improved, which everybody knew meant never. Again, Menten went free, living with Meta in the carriage house across from the ruins of De Horn.

For all concerned, this was a final, exhausted standoff in which there were only victims—of the war; of blackmail; of political ambition; of journalistic, legal, and judicial probity. Menten had left behind him a trail of victims that included judges (Rohling and Schroeder), policemen (Pete van Izendorn, Pasterkamp, and Peters), journalists (Knoop and others), an auction house director (Glerum), a politician (van Agt), a businessman (Debrouin), art collectors (Czartoryski, Zagayski, and Stieglitz, among a score of others), wives and lovers (Elizabeth, Meta, Irena, Steengracht von Moyland, Miss Poland) . . . and a warmhearted man in Israel.

But the Supreme Court, in an extraordinary decision, said no, the process had to continue, no matter what the sanity of the defendant. The court wanted justice, not medicine, to decide who should stand trial, almost as if to say, beyond guilt or innocence, justice was responsible to *society,* which was not going to permit Menten's crimes to go unpunished.

In the spring of 1980, thirty-nine years after his crimes, Menten, now eighty-one years old, for the second time entered the Rotterdam court. He showed all the old fire—the lassitude and rambling now absent, almost miraculously, from his appearance and speech. The old witnesses reappeared, again to be tested by the old man's fury. "I put my hands in front of my eyes and cried," said Sabina Selner Jaworska. "I heard a lot of screaming and crying, Menten had a pistol. . . ."

"What kind of pistol did I have?" Menten yelled then. "Why don't you shut your mouth? It's nonsense what you say."

"He arrived in the morning in a car," Carolina Selner Tuzimek told the court. "And I got on my knees and prayed."

"She begged Menten on her knees to save her husband, Philip Wecker, but Menten kicked her," said Mara Pistiner-Cygelstreich.

"This is a dirty intrigue story," Menten shouted out.

And then Dirk Menten answered his brother's central and damning accusations: "The people of Podhorodse knew only one Menten," Pieter had told the court, "and that was Dirk."

Dirk did not acknowledge his brother's presence in the court. They had not seen each other in more than twenty years. With a briefcase beside him, he introduced himself to the court with the words, "Unfortunately, I am Pieter's brother." He looked straight at the judges. "I have known about what happened in Podhorodse for quite a long time. . . . Pieter signed the contracts with Pistiner. The lawsuits concerned themselves with wood from maple trees. There was a lot of chicanery in the contract. But Pieter, an incomprehensible human being, does not know the concept of 'mine' and 'yours'—only 'mine.' We always felt that because of his greed, he was not accountable for his actions. For my own security, we drew up a statement, my wife and I did, and we promised my mother [before she died] that we would only use that statement if our personal honor or good name were ever threatened by him. His accusations have given me good reason to use it now."

He produced a document from his briefcase dated 1953, signed and notarized. It stated that ten years before, in the winter of 1943, Pieter had visited Dirk in Paris. "He was worried about how the war was going to end. It was there that he told us how he had been at an execution in 1941. He said that Jews had dug their own grave, and he had warned two people, Schiff and Altmann. It was the first time he told us of this."

"Forgery!" shouted Pieter.

Now, nobody listened.

EPILOGUE

"... The earth had swallowed him up."

DAYS LATER, AFTER he had testified, Bibi waited for the president
of the Rotterdam court to dismiss him for the last time. As he
turned to leave the court, to one side Menten raised his finger in
the air, indicating to the judge that he had a question. In Dutch, he
asked something to which the judge nodded his assent. "Before
you leave," the judge said to Bibi, "Mr. Menten wants to ask you
something. Do you mind?"

Bibi looked at him. "He doesn't need my permission. What is
it?"

Menten asked, *"Are you sure you will return to your home?"*

The judge shouted angrily at Menten to be silent. Bibi thought
there was something satanic in the question. But he said, "Yes,
I'm sure I will go home." He felt the reassuring hand of Sima, his
dark-haired daughter on leave from Beersheba University to ac-
company him to Holland, who helped him out of the court and
back to the rented apartment in the center of Amsterdam.

Soon after, on a summer day's outing before they returned to
Israel, Bibi and Sima turned into the Dam Rak from the Osterdok,
an inner harbor of sailboats and historical merchantmen. By the
time they reached the Dam, where he wanted to see the National
Monument, Bibi decided to stop long enough to drink a frothy
mug of beer. They crossed the Dam to a Steak & Brew-Burger,
located in the Nieuwen Dijk, a pedestrian mall of tacky shops,
fast-food outlets, porn houses, and discount record-tape stores. As
they entered, Bibi walking ahead of Sima, their eyes adjusted from

the outside glare to the dim interior. Bibi took three steps and disappeared, as if the earth had swallowed him up.

Sima looked down and saw her foot on the edge of a deep cellar. She heard a loud crashing below, an exploding sound, she thought, as her father's head hit the concrete floor. She took her foot back from the edge and shouted, "Please help! My father has fallen down!"

Two Indonesian waitresses and the manager, far in the rear of the restaurant, ran to Sima. "Please help. Help him. He's dead," she shouted.

The manager slapped her hard across the face, then locked the door. "Shut up," he said.

Sima yelled, "Please, please, go into the cellar. Save him!" She tried to drop down, but the depth was more than sixteen feet.

The manager waved a waitress to the rear of the restaurant to confer on this embarrassing and potentially costly mishap. The second Indonesian waitress showed Sima around the back and pointed out a small tunnel that led into the cellar. Sima crawled to avoid scraping her head, the ceiling was so low. Bibi was lying at the far end near the street. Yellow, very pale yellow, he had stopped breathing. When she saw his partly crushed skull, Sima was certain he was dead.

Only a short time before, she had learned mouth-to-mouth resuscitation, which she now applied on her father. Soon, Bibi started to breathe again, but his eyes remained closed and his pallor deepened—dangerously, Sima thought, rushing back into the restaurant. When she did not see a doctor or the police, Sima kicked at the locked door until the manager of the Brew-Burger finally turned the key. She ran into the street and shouted, "Please help me! My father is dying in the cellar and nobody will help him!"

Shopkeepers and shoppers in the Nieuwen Dijk assembled around her, less to help than to stop the public disturbance. A man said something to the waitress, then told Sima, "No, no. Be quiet. He is not dead." A Dutchwoman said, "Be quiet. The police and the ambulance will soon be here." For twenty minutes, all that anybody said to her was "Be quiet," until ambulance attendants finally arrived and awkwardly lifted Bibi from the depths of the cellar. Blood was oozing from his ears and a hematoma colored his spine a deepening blue. At the Wilhelmina Hospital emergency room the doctors said nothing hopeful. He was unconscious and paralyzed, but anything could happen. The night would tell.

The coma lasted three days.

Despite the damage to his brain, which the surgeons could not even estimate, when he opened his eyes for the first time since the fall, he recognized his son, David, whom he thought had lost weight, and Sima, who was looking down on him through tear-filled eyes. A woman whom he vaguely remembered often coming to their house in Tel Aviv stepped close to his bed. She knew the children. Bibi thought she was a nurse and a friend.

The woman now leaned close to him and said, "Bibi, how are you? I am Mala."

"No, you are *not* Mala. You come to our house to *see* Mala." She was a friend, this woman, he thought.

Mala showed him their passport photographs. Bibi said, "Yes, that's my passport."

"And whose is this?" she asked.

Bibi looked, "It's yours."

"What's written on the passport?"

"Mala. You are my wife, Mala."

In that moment, he thought that he might have been dreaming, and he tried to remember his dreams. He remembered the gypsy with her tarot cards as she had appeared out of the evening shadows on the porch of the Pistiner house on the hill, and he understood then that the nightmare had not been a dream from which he finally was awakening. Later, he told a friend, "My life could not be complete until I punished a man who did bad to my people. Now, I am not afraid of death. I have done what I was put here to do."

POSTSCRIPT

—Mara Pistiner-Cygelstreich lives a quiet life in the Ramat Gan district of Tel Aviv. Her husband, Stanislaw, died in December 1982.

—Meta Pauw-Menten lives in the coach house across from the rubble that was De Horn.

—Hans Knoop quit his job at *Accent* magazine. The self-proclaimed "James Bond of the Netherlands" is learning to live with and like a little less celebrity as the director of a two-man public relations firm.

—Prince Bernhard retired to private life on the abdication of Queen Juliana in the morning of April 30, 1980.

—Pieter Menten received a sentence of ten years' imprisonment from the Rotterdam court. With time off for good behavior he will be released in 1986 from the maximum-security prison in Scheveningen, overlooking the dunes on the North Sea coast.

—Bibi Krumholz/Haviv Kanaan was awarded the Sokolov Prize for journalistic excellence in February 1978. He has recovered to a remarkable degree from his fall. His fondest desire is to say *Kaddish* at the graves of the villagers who died in Podhorodse.

AFTERWORD

WHEN I FIRST heard his name, I thought Pieter Menten was "just another old Nazi" with a wartime past that finally had caught up with him, and my assessment at that time was about as accurate as it was unique. Outside Holland, the story of his crimes and the remarkable saga of his discovery sank almost without a trace.

In the spring of 1981, five years after I first heard Menten's name, a close friend who was spending his summer vacation in the south of France read a story in the *New Statesman* by Reuben Ainsztein entitled "The Collector," a delayed but comprehensive account of the Menten affair. My friend called me in New York to ask if I knew anything about it. I told him the story sounded vaguely familiar, but at the time of Menten's trial the story and its complicated background had seemed too confusing to write about. My friend suggested I take a look, at least. When the *New Statesman* piece finally reached me in New York, I read, then re-read it several times, realizing immediately how very wrong I had been. Pieter Menten was anything but "another old Nazi."

The elements of the piece at first left me with a feeling of incredulity—that a man, the owner of a fabulous art collection, had slaughtered Jewish friends whom he had known well for seventeen years, that he had used the chaos of the war not just to line his pockets as a *Treuhänder* for the Nazis, but to settle old emotional debts through mass murder, that this same man, a Dutchman from a powerful merchant family, a millionaire in his own right, had befriended important Nazis in Poland and had lived since

World War II in the open, using his real name with impunity? Those elements just did not seem possible, unless the charges against him in court had been false. The story intrigued me, and I was willing to suspend my disbelief until I could dig into the research, but at that moment of commitment, a further—and to my mind crucial—element had to be found if a book were to work.

Many people in Holland and elsewhere had tried to take credit for bringing Pieter Menten to justice. At first no single protagonist identified himself above any other. The exposure and prosecution of Menten had not been the work of one man alone, or had it been? As it turned out, the editor in chief of The New York Times Book Company, Jonathan Segal, knew the Menten story at that point better than I did; he had tried to get it between book covers since 1976, when he had spotted a small inside item in *The New York Times* about the art auction that had revived the case and finally led to Menten's arrest. Segal was determined, and he was right. Bibi Krumholz had known Pieter Menten as a boy, suffered horrible pain at his expense, and then, for the next thirty-one years, had devoted his life to seeing Pieter Menten punished for his crimes. Bibi Krumholz was one person of millions from the Holocaust experience who had actually identified the killer of his family, tracked him, and finally brought him to justice.

Soon after, I set off to get the facts. Whenever I could in Poland, Holland, and Israel, I spoke at length with principals, and ended with tapes from roughly 125 interviews. Wherever possible, I visited the sites of the events described in the interviews. Unfortunately, the Soviets declined my visa application to visit Lwów and Podhorodse, for reasons known only to them. For a backdrop against which to set the facts, I had to familiarize myself with the histories of Poland from 1912 to 1945; of Holland from the latter part of the nineteenth century to the present; and of Palestine, Israel, and Zionism. I tried to know Bibi Krumholz as well as he would allow me to and then some during two months in Israel. I spent 160 hours hearing about his remarkable life. During our time together I found him to be an unprepossessing hero of great gentleness and an irrepressible warmth.

For most of 1982, I sifted through hundreds of official documents and transcripts with the help of Polish, Dutch, and Israeli translators. Authorities had interviewed more than 500 interested parties in the United States, Sweden, France, Poland, Holland, Israel, and the Soviet Union while preparing their case against Menten, and I benefited greatly from the thoroughness of their work, borrowing freely from witnesses' court testimonies, ballistic and forensic reports, background material on the Nazis in Poland, the structure of *Treuhänder* businesses—facts about which I would have been ignorant had the governments of Holland and Poland not spent so much money and time on this case.

Throughout, there was one blind spot in the research. I did not interview Pieter Menten. The logistical problems aside (the Dutch Ministry of Justice would not facilitate access to him in the Scheveningen Prison near The Hague), I declined for a more important reason. His advisors made the prerequisite that I write the narrative from his point of view, as an apology presumably to encourage Dutch officials to reprieve him after the European Court had spurned his final appeal in the early months of 1982. I could not accept that condition, although I still wish I had laid eyes on him outside the forty hours of videotaped court sessions that I reviewed in The Hague, to get some measure of the man myself.

I should point out, finally, that it was extremely difficult to provide two-source verification for many of the events that had occurred so many years before. Witnesses had died, moved, or forgotten, so, more often than I would have liked, I was forced to rely on unsupported "hearsay" testimonies of prosecution witnesses before the 1977 Special Tribunal for War Crimes in the Netherlands that judged Pieter Menten.

In a project of this duration there are many people and institutions to thank. Without going into elaborate explanations of how they helped smooth the path, I shall name some of them here. In the United States, Knox Burger of K-B Associates contributed enthusiasm and a steadying hand, and he introduced me to Jonathan Segal, who collaborated on the conception of this book and provided the support necessary to plow through the heavier drifts. As for institutions, I am indebted to the New York Public Library and the Modern Military History Unit of the National Archives in Washington, D.C. In Israel, Yekutiel Federmann treated me like family. I made liberal use of the Yad Vashem Museum of the Holocaust and Hebrew University in Jerusalem, and the beautiful Museum of the Diaspora in Tel Aviv. In Holland, Brad Phillips waded carefully through the translation of documents without knowing what I would find useful, Toos Faber of the Ministry of Justice in The Hague helped out where she could with access to police and government officials, and the Rijks Institute for War Documentation in Amsterdam opened its files to me. In Poland, Katarzyna Wandycz translated under difficult conditions and acted as a helpful and enjoyable traveling companion, Andrezj Zakrzewski of P.A. Interpress in Warsaw made it possible for me to move freely in a country that was under martial law, Andrzey Gass of Polskie Radio I gave me tapes of his interviews with witnesses who had passed away, and Professor Czeslaw Pilichowski of the Commission for the Investigation of Nazi Crimes in Poland acted as my "sponsor," without whom foreigners from the West were not being admitted to Poland. In Britain, I made extensive use of the British Library, the Weiner Library, and the Archives of the Ministry of Defense in London, and the Public Records Office in Kew Gardens. Thanks finally to Michael Conroy for 1 Lowndes Square, Stefan Stein, M.D., and Larry and Nadia Collins for pointing out in the early stages the difference between the story of "just another old Nazi" and a good yarn.

Malcolm C. MacPherson
New York
July 1983

SELECT BIBLIOGRAPHY

BOOKS:

Hannah Arendt, *Eichmann in Jerusalem* (Viking, 1963).
John A. Armstrong, *Ukrainian Nationalism 1939–45* (Columbia University Press, 1955).
John M. Blair, *The Control of Oil* (Pantheon, 1977).
Dr. J. C. H. Blom, A. C. 't Hart, and Dr. I. Schoffer, *De Affaire-Menten 1945–1976,* Vols. I and II (Holland: Staatsuitgeverij, 1978).
Norman Davies, *God's Playground, A History of Poland.,* Vols. I and II (Columbia University Press, 1982).
Sefton Delmer, *Trail Sinister* (England: Secker & Warburg, 1961).
M. R. D. Foot, *Resistance* (England: Grenada, 1978).
Hans Frank, *Diary* (Document SSSR-223 of the International Tribunal at Nuremberg, 38 Vols.).
Philip Friedman, *Roads to Extinction: Essays on the Holocaust; The Destruction of the Jews of Lwów, 1941–44* (Israel: Yad Vashem, 1979).
Carel Gerretson, *History of the Royals* (The History of Royal Dutch Shell) (Holland: Joh. Enschede en Zonen, 1936).
Hermann Giskes, *London Calling North Pole* (England: W. Kimber, 1953).
Philippe Granier-Raymond, *The Tangled Web* (England: Arthur Barker, 1968).

308

Hermine van Guldener, *Rijksmuseum Amsterdam* (Holland: Knoor & Herth, 1967).

Gideon Hausner, *Justice in Jerusalem* (Schocken, 1968).

Celia S. Heller, *On the Edge of Destruction* (Schocken, 1980).

Arthur Hertzberg, *The Zionist Idea* (Atheneum, 1975).

Raul Hilberg, *The Destruction of European Jews* (Quadrangle, 1961).

William Hoffman, *Queen Juliana* (Harcourt, 1979).

Heinz Höhne, *The Order of the Death's Head* (England: Secker & Warburg, 1969).

David Kahn, *Hitler's Spies* (Macmillan, 1978).

Hans Knoop, *De Zak Menten* (Holland: H.J.W. Becht, 1978).

Walter Laqueur, *A History of Zionism* (Schocken, 1976).

Nora Levin, *The Holocaust* (Schocken, 1973).

Wibo van de Linde, *TROS Transcripts,* June 21, 1976, four parts.

Anne Lourens, *L'affaire King Kong* (France: Libraire Arthème Fayard, 1967).

Walter B. Maas, *The Netherlands at War: 1940–1945* (England: Abelard-Schuman, 1970).

Curzio Malaparte, *Kaputt* (E. P. Dutton, 1946).

Ministry of Information, Poland, *The Polish Black Book, 1966.*

Ministry of Justice, Trial Transcripts, The Netherlands vs. Pieter N. Menten, 1977–1980.

Werner Rings, *Life with the Enemy* (England: Weidenfeld-Nicholson, 1982).

Howard Morley Sachar, *The Course of Modern Jewish History* (Dell, 1968).

Anthony Sampson, *The Seven Sisters* (Viking, 1975).

William Shirer, *The Rise and Fall of the Third Reich* (England: Secker & Warburg, 1960).

Upton Sinclair, *The Jungle* (Bantam, 1981).

Ida M. Tarbell, *The History of the Standard Oil Company* (Peter Smith, 1963).

ARTICLES AND REPORTS:

Reuben Ainsztein, "The Collector," *New Statesman,* Feb. 11, 1981.

Stephen Aris, "A Right Royal Businessman," *The Sunday Times,* Feb. 29, 1976.

Rene de Bok, "Damning Testimonies Against Menten Pile Up," *Elseviers,* July 13, 1976.

Igor Cornelissen, "Menten, Graaf Tarnowski en prins Bernhard," *Vrij Nederland,* May 14, 1977.

————"Skeletons" (six parts), *Vrij Nederland,* April 12, 1980.

Henk DiMari, "Justice Handled Menten with Kid Gloves," *De Telegraaf,* Nov. 17, 1976.

Wim van Geffen, "Great Dutch Collectors Are a Dying Breed," *De Telegraaf,* May 22, 1976.

Koen van Harten, "Menten's Ex-Secretary Presumed Dead," *Elseviers,* Dec. 18, 1976.

Tom Hendricks, "Lust for Money Was Menten's Motive," *De Telegraaf,* Nov. 8, 1977.

————"Menten Was Rocked to Sleep," *De Telegraaf,* Nov. 16, 1977.

Sarah Honig, "Unmasking an Uncle," Jerusalem *Post,* March 16, 1977.

Office of Strategic Services, "Conditions Within Occupied Netherlands," Mid-March 1945.

————"Hans Frank, Polish War Criminal #1," Military Attaché Report, Sept. 6, 1945.

————"Hubert Menten," Safehaven Report #11535, April 20, 1945.

————"Political Forces in Eastern Galicia and Volhynia Before World War II," Research & Analysis #1979, July 23, 1945.

————"Prince Bernhard. . . ," Research & Analysis #2947, March 30, 1945.

————"Problems of the Netherlands Government in Exile," Research & Analysis #2386, July 28, 1944.

Nico Polak, "The Real Menten" (two parts), *Haagse Post,* Oct. 8, 1977.

————"Pieter Menten's State Secret, a Reconstruction of a Blackmail," *Haagse Post,* Nov. 25, 1978.

————"Ravaged Poland," *De Telegraaf,* Jan. 19, 1940.

Rien Robijns, "Pieter Betrayed and Blackmailed People," *Het Vrije Volk,* Dec. 4, 1976.